WITHDRAWN

Conflicting Worlds

New Dimensions of the American Civil War

T. MICHAEL PARRISH, EDITOR

J. W. Watte, after a drawing by H. W. Herrick,
Reading the Emancipation Proclamation.
Published by Lucius Stebbins,
Hartford, 1864. (Library of Congress)

The Emancipation Proclamation

Three Views

{ Social, Political, Iconographic }

HAROLD HOLZER

EDNA GREENE MEDFORD

FRANK J. WILLIAMS

With a Foreword by John Hope Franklin

LOUISIANA STATE UNIVERSITY PRESS

BATON ROUGE

PORTER MEMORIAL BRANCH LIBRARY
NEWTON COUNTY LIBRARY SYSTEM
6191 HIGHWAY 212
COVINGTON, GA 30016

To John Hope Franklin

Published with the assistance of the V. Ray Cardozier Fund
Published by Louisiana State University Press
Copyright © 2006 by Louisiana State University Press
All rights reserved
Manufactured in the United States of America
First printing

DESIGNER: *Amanda McDonald Scallan*
TYPEFACE: *Whitman with Arcana GMM display*
PRINTER AND BINDER: *Thomson-Shore, Inc.*

Library of Congress Cataloging-in-Publication Data
Holzer, Harold.
   The Emancipation Proclamation : three views / Harold Holzer, Edna Greene
Medford, Frank J. Williams ; with a foreword by John Hope Franklin.
      p. cm. — (Conflicting worlds.)
   Includes bibliographical references and index.
   ISBN 0-8071-3144-X (cloth : alk. paper)
   1. United States. President (1861–1865 : Lincoln). Emancipation
Proclamation. 2. Slaves—Emancipation—United States. I. Medford, Edna
Greene. II. Williams, Frank J. III. Title. IV. Series.
E453.H645 2006
973.7'14—dc22

                                                2005024802

The paper in this book meets the guidelines for permanence and durability of the Committee on Production Guidelines for Book
Longevity of the Council on Library Resources. ∞

BRANCH LIBRARY
LIBRARY SYSTEM

CONTENTS

Just over forty years ago I wrote a brief volume on the Emancipation Proclamation. My principal objective was to call attention to a document that was barely remembered and widely misunderstood. I traced the germination of the idea of emancipation in Abraham Lincoln's mind, his issuance of it at a propitious but dangerous moment in the nation's struggle for survival during the Civil War, and its significance for the four million men, women, and children held in bondage. It was my personal contribution to the nation's observances of the document whose centennial would occur during my absence while serving as Pitt Professor of American History and Institutions at the University of Cambridge.

In anticipation of the approaching sesquicentennial of the Emancipation Proclamation and for other reasons that they make clear, three distinguished Lincoln and Civil War scholars have joined in a major task of examining the proclamation from every possible angle. The universality of the proclamation's appeal is illustrated by what these Lincoln scholars bring to the task. Edna Greene Medford is a veteran university professor with long ties to higher education and to nineteenth-century historical scholarship. Frank Williams is a distinguished jurist whose contributions to Lincoln scholarship vie with his distinguished service as Chief Justice of the Supreme Court of the State of Rhode Island. Harold Holzer is a prolific Civil War scholar well known in New York's artistic and cultural circles, and his books and articles have won for him a special place among Civil War scholars.

While the three authors bring to the table different backgrounds, different training, and different perspectives, the "Three Views" in the subtitle of this book do not represent or even suggest conflicts or critical differences on their views. Indeed, if anything, the "views" they express represent three different, noncontradictory ways of evaluating the Emancipation Proclamation. Medford remarks that with the position he takes in the proclamation, "Lincoln is the embodiment of our national character, either at its best and most hopeful or at its worst and most pessimistic." After looking at the legal and political implications of the proclamation, Williams judges the document as perhaps "the single most significant statement of policy issued by a governing authority in the history of the country." Holzer, after scrutinizing the proclamation in art, iconography, and memory, concludes with Thomas Ball that "no monument of granite or bronze is needed to perpetuate his memory and hold his place in the affections of his countrymen."

The three authors, however different in their approach and in their evaluation of Lincoln's role in the struggle to deliver four million people from slavery to freedom, would surely agree with Lincoln's own appraisal of the role of the proclamation in his presidency. The Great Emancipator, as posterity would designate him, said that the proclamation was "the central act of my Administration, and the great event of the nineteenth century."

These "Three Views" of the Emancipation Proclamation earn for the authors the designation of their work as one of the landmark appraisals in the drama of the Civil War. Indeed, their views serve to renew our interest not only in the problem of slavery and how to exorcise it but also of freedom and how to celebrate it.

John Hope Franklin

ACKNOWLEDGMENTS

A book co-authored by three historians, each living in a different city, each working on other projects simultaneously, inevitably spawns many debts to patient friends, family, and professional colleagues. We can never expect to repay them adequately but do wish to express our heartfelt appreciation for their help and encouragement.

First and foremost we wish to thank Michael Parrish, for including this work in his Civil War series for Louisiana State University Press, and Rand Dotson, History and Southern Studies editor at LSU, for shepherding the project through the sometimes frustrating processes required to approve and speed publication. Special thanks, too, go to Sylvia Frank Rodrigue, formerly at LSU, now at Southern Illinois University Press, who brought the project there in the first place.

We owe an enormous debt of gratitude to the great historian John Hope Franklin, who not only urged this project on but also took time from the writing of his own eagerly awaited autobiography to write a prologue to this volume. Words cannot express how honored we feel to have this giant's words appear in our modest contribution to the literature on which he has had such a long, deep impact.

All three authors meet at least once a year in Gettysburg at the annual Lincoln Forum symposium, where we serve as officers and members of the board of advisors, and often appear on official programs as speakers and moderators. This book was, in a sense, born at the Forum, where the all-important topic of Emancipation has engaged us since the organization was formed in 1994. Over the years, we have discussed the issue publicly and privately, slowly developing the idea for our joint effort at lively lunches and dinners in the Holiday Inn Gettysburg Battlefield, our Forum headquarters. Special thanks must go to all the Forum symposium attendees who have encouraged us along the way and participated as audience members, advisors, fellow historians, and questioners, through almost all of the first decade of the group's life. Special gratitude goes to executive board members Charles D. Platt and John Y. Simon, and administrator Annette Westerby.

Of course, geographical constraints compel us to work separately more often than together, and from our individual headquarters in Washington, Rhode Island, and New York, respectively, we have amassed additional obligations that we are pleased to acknowledge individually.

HAROLD HOLZER

Above all, I am grateful for the opportunity to work so closely with my respected colleague Edna Medford and my old friend Frank Williams. Thanks to them, this project has been a joy from beginning to end.

Special, additional thanks go to my family: Edith, Meg, Remy, and Adam, for their advice and encouragement; and to my executive assistant at the Metropolitan Museum of Art, John Paul Conti, for somehow keeping my busy lives separate and well-organized. Tristanne Walliser helped secure reproduction permissions, and the Met's Julie Zeftel graciously granted the right to publish one of the museum's great works by Thomas Eakins. I am particularly indebted to Mike Parrish for bringing to my attention a hitherto unknown advertising notice for an Emancipation print; John Rumm and Steve Frank of the National Constitution Center in Philadelphia, for steering me to a print celebrating Maryland emancipation; and Cindy VanHorn at the Lincoln Museum in Fort Wayne, Indiana, who again, as always, made gems from that institution's vast collection available for reproduction.

EDNA GREENE MEDFORD

I am indebted to Harold Holzer and Frank Williams for suggesting this joint venture and for bringing it to a successful conclusion. My years of association with these two distinguished Lincoln scholars have led me to rethink (although not entirely alter) once emphatic assumptions. I am appreciative of their respect for my often divergent views.

I thank my husband, Thomas, who allowed me to engage him in endless discussions as I sorted out my views on the meaning of the Emancipation Proclamation; my daughter, Lark, who tolerated many a dinner conversation that led inexorably to discussions of Lincoln and black freedom; and my mother, Agnes Greene Leonard, for her enthusiasm for this and every project with which I am involved.

FRANK J. WILLIAMS

At a Lincoln Forum in Gettysburg four years ago, Edna Greene Medford delivered a powerful paper on the reaction of African Americans to the Emancipation Proclamation. At its conclusion, I asked Edna and Harold Holzer if they would be interested in collaborating on this project. Both were enthusiastic, and this book is the result of that early conference. I thank them for the enthusiasm and hard work in bringing this book to fruition. Also at that Lincoln Forum was Sylvia Frank Rodrigue, then at Louisiana State University Press, who supported the idea and brought the proposal to the publisher, and she and Michael Parrish earn my special thanks. So do Professor William D. Pederson, Director of the International Lincoln Center at Louisiana State University in Shreveport, and Professor Michael Vorenberg of Brown University, who read the manuscript and made important and necessary suggestions.

I am also most appreciative of my administrative assistant Donna M. Petorella, who, on her own time, typed the manuscript, which Thomas F. Puchner, Esq., and Meg Holzer, Esq., generously and effectively proofread. Of course without the loyal support of my wife, Virginia, my chapter would not have been written. She is always there for me.

INTRODUCTION

In 1862, Frederick Douglass greeted the news of Abraham Lincoln's preliminary Emancipation Proclamation by declaring: "We shout for joy that we live to record this righteous decree."

But as Douglass hastened to add with just a touch of bitterness, the president had moved "in his own peculiar, cautious, forbearing and hesitating way" to reach at last the moment of his "righteous decree," even as "the loyal heart was near breaking with despair." Then Douglass changed course again to acknowledge that, however long delayed, Lincoln's order had nonetheless provided genuine "joy and gladness to the friends of freedom and progress."[1]

Few historians question that the Emancipation Proclamation changed the Civil War, and changed America. But Frederick Douglass's first editorial comments on Abraham Lincoln's greatest presidential act presaged the complicated, almost schizophrenic, response it has elicited—now, as then—from even the document's and the president's greatest admirers. In its own time, abolitionists like Douglass reacted to the proclamation with relief, though some complained that it achieved too little too late. Lincoln himself fretted about its political consequences, watching nervously as the stock market plunged and Union troops began deserting in record numbers, unwilling to fight in a war suddenly redefined to embrace not only Union but also black freedom. At the same time, with one eye surely on his place in history, the long-modest president suddenly made himself available to artists, photographers, and sculptors who proposed portraying him as a "great emancipator." Meanwhile, in Europe and the South, editorials savaged both the proclamation and its author, one newspaper in Richmond scorchingly labeling him: "Coward, assassin, savage, murderer of women and babies . . . Lincoln the fiend."[2]

Not surprisingly, the Emancipation Proclamation has traveled—at best—a bumpy historiographical road ever since. Controversial at the time, it has become controversial once again for precisely opposite reasons. A document that originally struck many critics as radical, divisive, and dangerous, has more recently been assailed by skeptics as timid, conservative, and deceptive.

Yet the document that a period artist once called a second Declaration of Independence—"the immaculate conception of Constitutional Liberty"—inspired no full study, remarkably enough, for a hundred years. Not until the document's centennial did historian John Hope Franklin provide the very first full-length book ever devoted exclusively to the most epochal document of the entire nineteenth century. Forty-three years would pass before the second Emancipation book followed. The discussion remains lively in part because it is so new.[3]

More recently, editor Lerone Bennett Jr. issued a volume that in many ways turned Emancipation Proclamation historiography on its ear. *Forced into Glory* (2000) expanded on the author's longstanding charge that Lincoln's proclamation was nothing but "a ploy designed not to emancipate the slaves but to keep as many slaves as possible in slavery." Lincoln himself, Bennett insisted, "was shockingly indifferent and insensitive to the plight of the slaves in particular and African-Americans in general." He was, in short, no emancipator—but a racist.[4]

A significant corrective arrived in 2004 with Allen C. Guelzo's exhaustive and original study *Lincoln's Emancipation Proclamation*. He dismissed Bennett's "acid skepticism," and countered that "one does not have to make the Emancipation Proclamation scripture, or Lincoln a saint, for it to regain the place" it deserves in American history as "Lincoln's greatest document." The following year Michael Lind countered that Lerone Bennett's scholarship was, in fact, "irrefutable," and that Lincoln was above all a white supremacist for whom emancipation was always supposed to be accompanied by the mass deportation of African Americans.[5]

Who, if anyone, is correct? In the search for answers to this complex, vexing, and important historical problem, the authors of this book decided to approach the issue in a new way—or, more accurately, new *ways*. Coming from entirely different training and focus—one of us a professor of American history, another a lawyer-turned-jurist, and the third a specialist in political culture—we thought it might serve Lincoln students well to provide a book that offered insights on the Emancipation Proclamation from each of our distinctly different viewpoints. Thus, each of the three chapters, each by a different author, approaches the proclamation from a unique perspective to analyze as accurately as possible the impact Lincoln's order had on society.

None of us expects to offer the definitive, or final, word on the Emancipation Proclamation. We hope, rather, to add to this important, ongoing discussion a new set of approaches that have yet to be considered in the rejuvenated national dialogue on the document. How, for example, was the proclamation influenced, and later debated, not by other white leaders but by the people it most affected: African Americans? How did the proclamation complicate—or perhaps clarify—the fragile legal and political fabric holding the imperiled Union together during the Civil War? And, finally, how can the document's true period impact be measured by the number and timing of the paintings, prints, and statues it inspired? These areas introduce long-ignored and, we believe, fertile niches well worth combing to add to the discussion.

"We are ready for this service," Frederick Douglass wrote in his exultant editorial on the preliminary Emancipation Proclamation, "in this, we trust the last struggle with the monster slavery." The authors harbor no illusions that the following chapters will constitute the "last struggle" in the historical debate on Emancipation. But we do hope we are ready for this service, which we see as opening new windows onto this once-neglected, now vigorously debated and indisputably decisive moment of American history.

Harold Holzer
Edna Greene Medford
Frank J. Williams

THE EMANCIPATION PROCLAMATION

IMAGINED PROMISES, BITTER REALITIES

African Americans and the Meaning of the Emancipation Proclamation

EDNA GREENE MEDFORD

INTRODUCTION

And Upon this act sincerely believed to be an act of justice, warranted by the Constitution upon military necessity, I invoke the considerate judgment of mankind, and the gracious favor of Almighty God.

—ABRAHAM LINCOLN, January 1, 1863

One month after secessionists bombarded Fort Sumter and plunged the country into a bloody and protracted civil war, three men "held to service" by the Confederate colonel Charles K. Mallory sought asylum at Union-held Fortress Monroe in Virginia.

Believing that they were about to be taken out of Virginia and employed in defense of the purported new nation, Shepard Mallory, Frank Baker, and James Townsend presented themselves to the picket guard. The next morning they stood before the fort's commander, Maj.-Gen. Benjamin F. Butler, who had just arrived from duty in Maryland, where he had pledged his cooperation "in suppressing most promptly and effectively" any slave revolt.[1] Acting on the belief that he was justified in confiscating "property designed, adapted, and about to be used against the United States," General Butler declared the three men "contraband-of-war." Mallory, Baker, and Townsend's bold bid for freedom set in motion forces that had profound and far-reaching consequences, for in the weeks after their arrival, the slave grapevine alerted other bondsmen and women to the potential for sanctuary at the fort. By August, more than 900 fugitives—many of them women, children, and the infirm (property not quite fitting the contraband-of-war designation)—had sought and gained refuge with the Union forces.[2]

This and similar occurrences in the opening weeks of the conflict constituted the first waves in the quest for black freedom and presaged the role enslaved African Americans played in their own liberation during the war. While the rest of the nation debated the efficacy of linking preservation of the Union to the demise of slavery (the institution that stood as the root cause of the conflict), black men and women had immediately recognized the opportunities that the struggle between white men afforded them. Hence, they seized upon every chance to achieve freedom. Their efforts received presidential support when on January 1, 1863, Lincoln issued the Emancipation Proclamation.

In recent years, scholars pondering the meaning and significance of Lincoln's proclamation of freedom have focused essentially on the president's motivations for issuing the document and his actions leading up to that momentous event. As a consequence, a debate has ensued between those who consider the document revolutionary and Lincoln deserving of the title "Great Emancipator," and others who see his policies as unnecessarily conservative and initially deleterious to black freedom.[3]

While this debate is important to understanding the meaning of the Emancipation Proclamation, it fails to fully convey the document's significance to freedom's beneficiaries.

If popular wisdom and scholarly disquisition have largely credited Abraham Lincoln with black freedom, that attribution was shared by many of the freed people themselves and concurred in by their unfettered brothers and sisters in the North and South. The proclamation engendered Lincoln's veneration in the African-American community and encouraged the belief that he was the premier white friend of the race. Children, schools, and businesses bore his name; speeches in his honor found expression in annual Emancipation Day programs; and his martyrdom served as inspiration to a struggling people to press on.

But as freedom's first generation passed away, its children and grandchildren grew less reverent of the president and more skeptical of his proclamation. Ironically, they came to regard Lincoln with the same restraint they felt for the founding fathers, who had sanctioned holding men as property (indeed, many of whom held human chattel themselves). That shift in sentiment reflected the disillusionment that emanated from the dichotomy between black perceptions of the document's promise and the realities they experienced in the postwar years and beyond. Despite its restrained tone and limited scope, African Americans had viewed the proclamation as the instrument by which their lives would be radically transformed. Defining freedom in broad terms, they imagined more from the decree than Lincoln, or even many abolitionists, had intended. They believed that the document, and consequently Lincoln as author, had tacitly promised them equality of opportunity and unrestricted citizenship, the chance to claim their birthright after more than two hundred years of denial in America. The proclamation's significance, hence, must be considered not simply through the lens of its author's intended meaning or motivations but rather in the context of the aspirations and expectations of a heretofore disinherited people.

THE UNIVERSALITY OF THE PECULIAR INSTITUTION

When southern people tell us they are no more responsible for the origin of slavery than we; I acknowledge the fact.

—ABRAHAM LINCOLN, 1854

The conflict that altered the lives of nearly four million African Americans began as a struggle over the issue of slavery but did not reflect either side's desire for black freedom. Despite their avowed love of liberty, white Americans North and South shared complicity in the promulgation of an unfree status for and the degradation of people of African descent. By the eve of the war, slavery had enjoyed more than two centuries of tolerance in America. Beginning early in the colonial period, Americans had codified the practice and tied it to race. Traversing the land until a combination of economic self-interest and revolutionary rhetoric encouraged its overthrow in the North, slavery came to define the southern way of life in the late eighteenth and early-to-mid nineteenth centuries. But even with northern abolition, slavery's influence extended far beyond the tobacco rows of southside Virginia and the cotton fields of the Deep South.

By their very existence, enslaved laborers elevated the status of all white Americans, even those newly arrived and nearly broken by poverty and ignorance in their homelands. However disadvantaged, whites benefited psychologically and materially from the subordinate position occupied by blacks. The least exceptional and unsophisticated white man considered himself superior to the most refined and distinguished person of color. Both law and custom conspired to confirm that belief in white men and women and to reward them solely on the basis of their skin color.[4] Racial ostracism made African Americans aliens in their own land and consigned them to the position of interlopers.

Furthermore, the money made from slavery strengthened the American economy north and south of the Mason-Dixon Line. The cotton picked by shackled black hands fueled the textile mills of New England and kept the factory worker employed just as surely as it enriched the southern planter. Although no more than one-fourth of southern families owned slaves, many more hired the time of such laborers and aspired to have slaves of their own. In addition, the slaveocracy shaped and controlled social, political, and economic institutions in the South and wielded considerable influence in national government as well.

Sanctioned by all three branches of the federal government and protected by the Constitution itself, slavery stood in sharp contrast to America's vaunted democratic institutions and espousal of freedom. Its significance to the newly created United States was reflected in the compromises fashioned by the "founding fathers," which continued the international trade in human beings until 1808, permitted the counting of enslaved people for purposes of taxation and representation, and granted slaveholders the right to retrieve runaways.[5] Subsequently, Congress accepted compromise solutions whenever new territory was secured and even strengthened the prerogatives of the slaveholder in the decade before the war. Presidents signed proslavery measures into law, and the Supreme Court upheld the constitutionality of rights of ownership of enslaved property. Government complicity in the continued enslavement of black people in 1852 prompted Frederick Douglass to ask, "What, to the American slave, is your 4th of July?" His answer would underscore the frustration of black men and women who recognized the hypocrisy of American liberty and justice. Douglass judged the American celebration of independence "a day that reveals to [the slave], more than all other days in the year, the gross injustice and cruelty to which he is the constant victim. To him, your celebration is a sham; your boasted liberty, an unholy license; your national greatness, swelling vanity; your sounds of rejoicing are empty and heartless; your denunciations of tyrants, brass fronted impudence; your shouts of liberty and equality, hollow mockery."[6]

As human chattel, blacks were denied dominion over themselves and their progeny, were housed and sold alongside livestock at public auction, and were relegated to a status that afforded them few, if any, liberties. In the case *Dred Scott v. Sandford*, Supreme Court Justice Roger B. Taney represented the thinking of many white Americans when he delivered the court's majority opinion that confirmed the prevailing notion that African Americans were "beings of an inferior order . . . [with] no rights which white men were bound to respect."[7] By 1860, nearly four million people of African descent lived and labored under varying conditions that ranged from emasculating paternalism to brutal exploitation and physical abuse.

A militant abolitionism had asserted itself in the decades before the war, fueled in part by a general reform impulse that permeated the first half of the nineteenth century. Men and women in the free African-American community such as Robert and Harriet Forten Purvis, Frederick Douglass, Sojourner Truth, Henry Highland Garnet, and Harriet Tubman joined the efforts of white abolitionists such as William Lloyd Garrison, Lydia Maria Child, Lucretia Mott, and Wendell Phillips to agitate for the freedom of the enslaved. Few Americans heeded their appeal. Neither proslavery nor problack, most white Americans generally acceded to the South's claims to the right of ownership of human beings. Often when they did raise their voices against the institution it was not done in support of the enslaved but in defense of the rights of white men who were forced to compete with slave labor. Hence, when the war came, few stood ready to recognize its potential for black freedom, except, of course, black men and women themselves.

LINCOLN'S POSITION ON SLAVERY

I am naturally anti-slavery. If slavery is not wrong, nothing is wrong. I can not remember when I did not so think, and feel.
—ABRAHAM LINCOLN, April 4, 1864

For most of his public life, Abraham Lincoln's stance on the issue of slavery was more demonstrative than that of most white Americans, but his views fell short of the abolitionist creed. While he had acknowledged early in his political career the inhumanity of the institution, his reverence for the constitutional guarantees of protection of private property and his adherence to the laws of the land placed him at odds with the abolitionists. This commitment to the Constitution allowed him to represent the slaveholder Robert Matson, who in the fall of 1847 sued for the return of his fugitive property. The owner of plantations in Kentucky and Illinois, Matson circumvented the laws of the latter, which prohibited slavery, by keeping his enslaved laborers in the state for only a few months at a time. He became legally entangled when he kept one slave family in Illinois for two years. When the family fled its bondage and secured the support of an abolitionist, Matson sought their return. Lincoln defended the slaveholder, arguing that since Matson had not intended to domicile his laborers in Illinois permanently, he was within his rights to recover his property. The court decided in favor of the defendants, and eventually the family left the country and settled in Liberia.[8]

Lincoln's personal views of enslaved people, in particular, and of African Americans, in general, made him a somewhat improbable champion of the unfree. He exhibited a propensity for recounting racially insensitive jokes and held less than complimentary opinions on the mental and moral capacity of people of color. Apologists insist that his storytelling and racial views mirrored the attitudes and customs of his day. Indeed, Lincoln's willingness to employ racially offensive language in the 1858 Illinois senatorial debates with his bigoted opponent Stephen A. Douglas only added to the future president's acceptability as a politician. And his yarns found willing listeners in the gathering places at home in Springfield as well as in the halls of official Washington.

But in many ways, Lincoln was an atypical nineteenth-century American. The nation in his day was rife with bigotry and intolerance and awash with racial hatred. Even some of the most ardent abolitionists held biased views of black men and women, considering them inherently inferior, unprepared for freedom, and unable to discern what was in their best interest.[9] Although Lincoln generally subscribed to these views, to his credit he also believed in the fundamental right of all people to enjoy equality of opportunity. He recognized that as long as slavery prevailed in any part of the nation, as long as freedom was denied to any, the promise of the Declaration of Independence—the right of all people to "life, liberty, and the pursuit of happiness"—would remain unrealized.

Despite these seeming contradictions, most scholars agree that when he took office in March 1861, the new president brought with him a long-standing aversion to slavery. Whether or not one accepts William H. Herndon's assertion that Lincoln once quipped, "If ever I get a chance to hit that thing, I'll hit it hard,"[10] there can be little doubt concerning his views on the South's preeminent institution. Since the 1830s, Lincoln had in myriad ways publicly communicated his position on slavery. While a member of the Illinois legislature in 1836–37, he had joined with fellow legislator Dan Stone to declare that the institution was "founded on both injustice and bad policy."[11] While serving in Congress more than a decade later, he proposed (but never formally introduced) a bill calling for abolition in the federal city. In 1848 (the year before he proposed the bill), seventy-seven enslaved Washingtonians made an unsuccessful attempt to escape their bondage by absconding on the schooner *Pearl*.[12] The incident had illuminated slavery in the nation's capital and, perhaps, had encouraged Lincoln to take action. In any case, for the next several years, he solidified his antislavery position. In eloquent and impassioned speeches, he opposed the Kansas-Nebraska Act, which nullified the Missouri Compromise of 1820, thus reopening federal territory to the institution. In 1857, he spoke out against the Dred Scott decision, which suggested that a slave owner could take his human property wherever he wished—as residence in a free state or territory did not make one free—and that African Americans were not citizens. And in his senatorial race against Stephen A. Douglas, Lincoln argued against slavery on moral and economic grounds and asserted that it violated the principles of the Declaration of Independence. "Certainly, the negro is not our equal in color," he argued, but "in the right to put into his mouth the bread that his own hands have earned, he is the equal of every other man, white or black. In pointing out that more has been given you, you can not be justified in taking away the little which has been given him. All I ask for the negro is that if you do not like him, let him alone. If God gave him but little, that little let him enjoy."[13] Lincoln's words failed to garner sufficient support to win the senate race, but the campaign increased his national stature.

Despite such statements, Lincoln was no abolitionist. He believed that states had the right to control their own domestic institutions and that the Constitution prevented any meddling in this regard. Wedded as he was to this "sacred" document, he was left with little alternative but to embrace the idea of containment, or prohibiting the extension of slavery into the territories. Absent the ability to expand, he presumed, the institution would die a natural death.

In a speech delivered at the Cooper Union in New York in February 1860, Lincoln argued in favor of checking the spread of slavery. He espoused the view that the intent of the majority of the founding fathers did not preclude the federal government from controlling the institution in the territories.[14] The speech won for him support from those in the North who had previously been unaware of him or, at best, were lukewarm to his candidacy for the presidency. Hence, when in May 1860, the new Republican Party met to choose its presidential candidate from among a group of individuals with seemingly extreme positions, the moderate Lincoln won nomination on the third ballot. A hopelessly divided Democratic Party failed to coalesce around a single candidate, and hence lost the presidential election to the "rail splitter from Illinois."[15]

NONINTERFERENCE WITH SLAVERY: *Appeasing the Slave States*
I have no purpose, directly or indirectly, to interfere with the institution of slavery in the States where it exists. I believe I have no lawful right to do so, and I have no inclination to do so.
—ABRAHAM LINCOLN, March 1861

When he took office in March 1861, ending slavery did not loom large in the president's thinking. Seven slave states had already left the Union; reassurances to those remaining that there would be no interference with domestic institutions (including slavery), was crucial to arrest secession, Lincoln believed. Hoping for a swift resolution to the conflict, in the first few months of the war he pursued a policy of appeasement toward the loyal slave states and those in rebellion. He pledged to uphold all laws, including the Fugitive Slave Act of 1850, which required Americans to aid in the apprehension of fugitives and fined them if they refused or thwarted the recovery of runaways. The law gave unfair advantage to the slaveholder, in that it provided for payment in the amount of ten dollars to the commissioners adjudicating the case if the fugitive was handed over to his alleged owner, but only five dollars if released.[16]

Neither bound by constitutional constraints nor inclined to sympathize with Lincoln's predicament, enslaved people fled at every opportunity. Their assault on slavery was as emphatic as was the president's determination to leave the institution untouched. Even before hostilities commenced, enslaved people struck out in pursuit of freedom. On the morning of March 12, 1861, four fugitives from bondage arrived at Fort Pickens in Florida "entertaining the idea that [Union troops] were placed here to protect them and grant them their freedom," Lt. Adam J. Slemmer reported to his superiors.[17] Unlike Butler's acceptance of the fugitives arriving at Fortress Monroe two months later, Slemmer had the men taken to Pensacola and eventually they were returned to their owners.

Despite the possibility of having their actions thwarted, once armed conflict was underway enslaved people lost little time in making it a war for their liberation. Wherever, with the help of impressed enslaved laborers, the Confederacy threw up breastworks, along the borders between free and enslaved states, and whenever the Union forces drew near plantations and farms under the jurisdiction of the rebels, enslaved people made their way to freedom. They came singly and in groups of a few hundred, on foot and by wagon, over land and along the waterways. Men tended to predominate, but fugitives of both genders and all ages—from infants in arms to the superannuated—sought refuge within the Union lines.[18]

Even as southern planters attempted to continue the practices that had kept slavery firmly established before the war, enslaved people used the conflict's disruption to their advantage. Upon returning from patrol duty in early May 1861, John T. Washington of King George County, Virginia, discovered that five of his enslaved laborers had packed their meager belongings and fled his plantation. When he made inquiries, Washington learned that several of his neighbors had lost their bondsmen in similar fashion.[19] Despite efforts to "intercept and recover" the fugitives, the slaves avoided capture and presumably made their way to the Union lines.[20]

The problem of flight proved especially acute along the waterways, which enslaved people used as their own personal highways to freedom. In places such as Bertie County, North Carolina, Liberty County, Georgia, and Charles City County, Virginia, Union gunboats plied the rivers and waterways, beckoning the large black populations as they went.[21] Owners of such "property" lamented their financial losses and feared that certain areas—especially the coastal regions—would become depleted of enslaved laborers needed to work the staple crops and raise provisions for the Confederate military forces. Equal concern was expressed in regard to valuable information fugitives supplied to the Union. "The absconding negroes hold the position of traitors, since they go over to the enemy and afford him aid and comfort by revealing the condition of the districts and cities from which they come," a group of men from Liberty County, Georgia, complained to the military authorities in their district. Moreover, they argued, fugitives aided the Union cause by erecting fortifications and by raising provisions.[22]

Frustrated by black flight, the men of Liberty County proposed the surrender of their near-sacred belief in the right of owners to dominion over their property. Their appeal to Brig. Gen. H. W. Mercer, commander of the District of Georgia, alluded to the great loss of property—20,000 slaves—valued at from 12 to 15 million dollars, as well as the damage done through providing aid and comfort to the enemy. Liberty County residents feared that failure to halt the escapes would result in an inability to provision armies along the coastal areas and could produce "an army of trained Africans for the coming fall and winter campaigns."[23] Contending that existing state law was ineffective in punishing those who ran away or enticed others to do so, the residents asked for intervention under military law. They called for an order that would permit the execution of those caught in the process of fleeing, abetting the escape of others, or returning after having fled.[24] Such thinking, along with the Confederate government's policies regarding impressments of enslaved laborers, helped to weaken the very institution that southerners fought to preserve.

Union commanders understood that Lincoln had declared a hands-off policy regarding enslaved people, but with no clear guidelines in place regarding runaways, they responded to the situation according to their own proclivities. Some of them took the position of Col. Harvey Brown, who by June 1861, was commanding at Fort Pickens. Disregarding the Fugitive Slave Act of 1850, Brown wrote to Lt. Col. Edward D. Townsend (Assistant Adjutant-General, Washington, D.C.): "I shall not send the negroes back as I will never be voluntarily instrumental in returning a poor wretch to slavery but will hold them subject to orders."[25] Other commanders, however, thought nothing of returning fugitives to their owners. Hence, Gen. George B. McClellan sought to reassure western Virginia Unionists that "Your homes, your families and your property are safe under our protection. All your rights shall be religiously respected . . . not only will we abstain from all such interference but we will on the contrary with an iron hand crush any attempt at insurrection on [the slaves'] part."[26]

Because of its strategic position and as the symbol of Unionism, the District of Columbia was overwhelmed by runaways from Virginia. Holding steadfastly to his pledge to uphold the laws (and eager to appease loyal Virginians), Lincoln in mid-July 1861 inquired of General-in-Chief Winfield Scott, "Would it not be well to allow owners to bring back [slaves] which have crossed the Potomac" with Union troops?[27] In response to the president's query, Scott directed the Department of Washington's commander, Gen. Joseph Mansfield, to take action. Mansfield responded by banning runaways from the camps and prohibiting them from accompanying troops on the move.[28]

Fugitives from professedly loyal states such as Maryland created even greater problems for the president. Since slavery's abolition in the District of Columbia in April 1862, fugitives from Maryland (and Virginia) had sought freedom in the city. Before District emancipation, the marshal's office had routinely detained such runaways and placed them in the notorious "Blue Jug" or city jail, where they awaited the arrival of their owners or were sold to defray the cost of incarceration. The marshal for the District of Columbia, Ward Hill Lamon (a close friend of Lincoln), justified the practice as a requirement of the Fugitive Slave Act, which had yet to be repealed. By late 1861, such imprisonments and abuse in the city jail had embroiled Lamon in a dispute with certain Republican senators and congressmen.[29] Lincoln himself became involved in the dispute when he stood steadfast against pressure to fire Lamon and then refused to accept the embattled marshal's resignation when he offered it.

After emancipation in the District of Columbia, Maryland slaveholders charged, with some degree of justification, that their fleeing property found refuge among the abolitionist soldiers stationed in the city. In May 1862, a delegation of slaveholders from adjacent Prince George's County visited the president and complained that a rumor suggesting that the government had forbidden the marshal's office from detaining fugitives had encouraged their property to abscond. They were particularly scornful of the military governor for the District, James S. Wadsworth, a well-known antislavery man. Wadsworth's failure to enforce vigorously the Fugitive Slave Act, they contended, had caused them to lose 800 to 1,000 laborers, only 12 of whom had been recovered. Lincoln promised that "no injustice" would be done to the slaveholders.[30]

Abolitionists countered, however, that the government engaged in "friendly" treatment of suspected rebels, whose slave property Union troops secured while authorities sought to ascertain the guilt or innocence of their owners. George Stephens, an African-American reporter, related such an incident to his readers. A planter by the name of "Big Dick" Posey had earned a reputation as "the king rebel of Charles County," Maryland. When he was arrested for aiding the Confederacy in October 1861, Union authorities sought to avert the flight of his enslaved laborers by placing them under guard. "[African Americans] see the Union troops holding [Posey's] slaves while he undergoes the form and ceremony of government arrest," Stephens wrote. "It is hard to convince these people that we are on the side of freedom."[31]

Adherence to the letter of the law sometimes resulted in deadly consequences for enslaved people. The case of Jack Scroggins provides a particularly egregious example. Scroggins was the enslaved laborer of Samuel Cox, a prominent southern Maryland planter well known for his Confederate sympathies and strongly suspected of trading with the secessionists.[32] Scroggins had alerted military authorities camped in the vicinity of Cox's home to his owner's possession of a large quantity of arms and ammunition. When the troops left the area, Scroggins, believing that a grateful nation would reward him for his heroism (and doubtless fearing retaliation from his owner) went with them. Cox subsequently entered the Union camp and attempted to claim his property, but the soldiers refused to surrender the enslaved man. Under the threat of being shot by one of their officers if they persisted, the men handed over the doomed slave to his owner. As Stephens relates the story, Cox dragged Scroggins behind a galloping horse for eleven miles, and then with the aid of two other men, beat him to death.[33] "Thus perished a loyal negro at the hands of a traitor," Stephens wrote. "What a terrible reward for patriotism; death in its worst, and hideous form, by torture! Yet the villain who did this is at liberty! This is the way United States officers treat traitors."[34] Ironically, in the aftermath of the Lincoln assassination, Cox was implicated in assisting John Wilkes Booth in his escape through southern Maryland and across the Potomac.[35]

The return of fugitive slaves to their owners and Lincoln's unwillingness to attack slavery earned the president the ire of the abolitionists. "Every instance of sending back poor fugitive slaves has cut into my heart like the stab of a bowie-knife, and made me dejected for days," wrote Lydia Maria Child in July 1861.[36] Abolitionists had hoped at the beginning of the war that it would be waged as both a return to Union and an assault on slavery. This sentiment led some to support the Lincoln administration and to discourage criticism of the government. They urged the president to emancipate under the war powers provision of the Constitution. Wendell Phillips, William Lloyd Garrison, and others pressed to show that slavery was the cause of the conflict and only its eradication could restore peace and union. Others pointed to the indispensability of enslaved labor to the Confederacy. As long as the Union refrained from attacking the institution, it gave the rebels an advantage in prosecuting the war.[37] But as Lincoln maintained a conservative policy in regard to slavery, some within the abolitionist ranks grew weary of waiting for the administration to see the justness of their cause.

Standing to benefit the most from a war against slavery, African Americans made the most fervent appeals to the president and the nation. "The Union's danger is the slave's deliverance," the *Weekly Anglo-African* declared. "No adjustment of the nation's difficulty is possible until the claims of the black man are first met and satisfied . . . his prostrate body forms an impediment over which liberty cannot advance . . . His title to life, to liberty and the pursuit of happiness must be acknowledged, or the nation will be forsook; and being so, incur the dreadful penalty of permanent disunion, unending anarchy, and perpetual strife."[38]

Lincoln's policies received significant and sustained challenge from Frederick Douglass, whose hatred for slavery developed from firsthand knowledge of the institution. Born into bondage in southern Maryland in 1818, Douglass had fled as a young man to the relative freedom of the North and had soon thereafter joined the abolitionist camp of William Lloyd Garrison. The impassioned orator became a favorite on the antislavery lecture circuit. When the war came, he immediately saw the implications for his people: "On behalf of our enslaved and bleeding brothers and sisters, thank God!—The slaveholders themselves have saved our cause from ruin! They have exposed the throat of slavery to the keen knife of liberty, and have given a chance to all the righteous forces of the nation to deal a death-blow to the monster evil of the nineteenth century." He urged African Americans to strike a blow for freedom. "Let the long crushed bondman arise! And in this auspicious moment, snatch back the liberty of which he has been so long robbed and despoiled. Now is the day, and now is the hour!"[39] By liberating the bondsman, allowing him to don the Union blue, and placing him in defense of the nation, Douglass argued, the government at Washington could secure freedom and union and end the conflict.

When the Lincoln administration failed to prosecute the war effectively, Douglass excoriated the president in his newspaper *Douglass' Monthly*. "An administration without a policy is confessedly an administration without brains," he chided. "I hold that the rebels can do us no serious harm unless it is done through the culpable weakness, imbecility or unfaithfulness of those who are charged with the high duty of seeing that the Supreme Law of the land is everywhere enforced and obeyed."[40]

Voices raised against making the war an avenue for black freedom reached Lincoln's hearing as well. A great deal of resistance to abolitionist aims emanated from certain factions of the Democratic Party and from those Republicans who had no desire to tamper with southern institutions, least of all slavery.[41] Many northern Democrats opposed the war itself and, fearful of being overrun by unassimilatable freedmen, were vociferous in their objections to linking the conflict to the liberation of enslaved people.[42] Border-state politicians and southern unionists were equally opposed. In late July 1861, congressman John J. Crittenden of Kentucky and senator Andrew Johnson of Tennessee supported Lincoln's position on the war by proposing a joint resolution disavowing any intent of the federal government to wage war that interfered with southern rights and institutions. Instead, the resolution declared, the purpose of the war was defense of the Constitution and preservation of the Union. The passage of the resolution in both houses reflected the conservative thinking on the subject of emancipation and revealed that Lincoln's views were attuned to public opinion.[43]

The northern white masses were, at best, ambivalent about the possibility of freedom for the enslaved. Since the advent of the emancipation that followed the American Revolution, people of color and whites had experienced a tenuous coexistence in northern cities. Abolition failed to erase the belief that African Americans were racially inferior or that they were incapable of contributing politically or socially to the communities in which they resided. While in certain jurisdictions the black man had been granted suffrage in the egalitarian spirit that followed the war with England, some northern states retreated from this position by the turn of the century and barred African Americans from voting or placed other restrictions on political participation. In several of the midwestern and far-western states they were denied the opportunity to testify against whites in courts of law and were nearly universally prevented from serving on juries. As poor white men gained greater acceptance in politics during the antebellum period, blacks found their political voices silenced by property qualifications and residency requirements.[44]

African Americans who resided in the North experienced social disadvantages as well. Certain northern states—specifically those in the newly settled areas of the Old Northwest (from Ohio to Wisconsin)—discouraged black emigration by law and custom; others banned African Americans outright. In addition, people of color in the North witnessed daily discrimination in hotels and other public accommodations (especially in entertainment and transportation). Even Frederick Douglass had experienced such treatment when he attempted to assert himself as a free man in Massachusetts and as he traveled throughout the North and Midwest on the antislavery lecture circuit.[45] African Americans found it difficult as well to secure adequate housing for their families, even when they possessed the financial capability. And their children often suffered inadequate, segregated schools or received no public instruction at all.

Similarly, the economic positions of African Americans proved tenuous at best. Black men found it difficult to secure positions in skilled labor and, as they faced competition from newly arriving immigrants, even unskilled work on the docks and the railroads proved elusive. Left to occupy the most menial forms of day labor, African Americans sought the least desirable but most affordable housing then available to them—that which was found in the overcrowded, disease-infested communities of the poor. Northern whites had no desire to see these communities swell with new arrivals from southern emancipation.

Given these considerations, Lincoln held little optimism that northern whites would embrace universal emancipation or that race relations would improve with time. But the exigencies of war forced Lincoln and the northern people ultimately to embrace a policy that would lead to a united nation and an ostensibly free one. President and country came to realize that war could be pursued effectively only by eliminating the crucial role black men and women played as involuntary support to the Confederate effort and by utilizing the services of men eager to fight for the Union cause.

From the outset of war, the Union forces had steadfastly rejected the services of black men. Those designated as contraband-of-war had been put to work as military laborers, but soldiering was limited to the few who found their way either clandestinely or otherwise into the ranks, or who served in the seemingly more inclusive navy. African-American efforts to raise and provision military units had failed to win the approval of the Lincoln administration. At the same time, Confederate forces made ample (if noncombatant) use of enslaved laborers on the plantations. After having first impressed free black men into service for the Confederacy, the rebels secured (initially through voluntary effort of the owners and later through impressment) the labor of enslaved men to facilitate their prosecution of the war. Black men threw up breastworks and served as teamsters, boatmen, blacksmiths, wheelwrights, carpenters, cooks, and musicians.[46] Others constructed military roads and cut wood or served as nurses and orderlies in hospitals or as laborers in heavy industries such as foundry smithing.[47] Those on the home front continued to grow crops and worked in the various industries that supported the war effort. Neither Congress nor the president could long ignore the assistance that enslaved labor rendered the Confederate cause, especially after the war continued beyond the three months most Americans had anticipated.

PRESIDENTIAL PREROGATIVE

I further make known that whether it be competent for me, as Commander-in-Chief of the Army and Navy, to declare the Slaves of any state or states, free . . . I reserve to myself.

—ABRAHAM LINCOLN, May 19, 1862

In the first several months of the war, Lincoln's belief that the Constitution limited his authority to address the issue of slavery placed him in the position of reacting to congressional mandates and the field proclamations of his generals rather than initiating policy himself. In the aftermath of the humiliating defeat at Bull Run in late July, Congress dared to do something about Confederate use of its slave labor force by enacting a measure designed to legalize what General Butler had already implemented at Fortress Monroe. A confiscation act, passed in August 1861, authorized the seizing of rebel property (including enslaved laborers) that had been used to promote the Confederate struggle against the Union. The vote on the measure polarized Congress, with Democrats and border-state representatives generally opposing it while the vast majority of Republicans lent their support. Ever mindful of the fraying cord that bound the border states to the Union, Lincoln feared that this attack on slave property would provide additional stress. With some reluctance, he signed the bill anyway, influenced by the argument that the South must be denied use of its enslaved laborers.[48]

Lincoln drew clear distinctions between the *confiscation* of the property of rebels and the *freeing* of enslaved people. When nearly a year after implementation of the First Confiscation Act Congress passed a second measure that freed slaves of disloyal owners (regardless of whether or not they had been used against the Union), Lincoln urged the federal legislature to modify it or face his veto. Congress complied, but the president elected to send his official objections to the original document anyway. He expressed his continued concern that constitutional guarantees be protected, even for those who had waged war against the nation. In his message to Congress in July 1862, he acknowledged that those who were responsible for an unwarranted war should be required to pay its cost but contended that "the severest justice may not always be the best policy." Rather, it would be better to convince those in rebellion that they have "something to lose by persisting . . . and something to gain by desisting."[49] He also objected to the idea that enslaved property would be forfeited beyond the life of the owner, insisting that such a punishment for treason was unconstitutional: "This act, by proceedings *in rem*, forfeits property, for the ingredients of treason, without a conviction of the supposed criminal, or a personal hearing given him in any proceeding. That we may not touch property lying within our reach, because we can not give personal notice to an owner who is absent endeavoring to destroy the govern [ment,] is certainly not very satisfactory."[50]

The president showed similar concern regarding the decision of certain military commanders to formulate and execute plans of emancipation. When generals John C. Frémont and David Hunter proclaimed freedom in Missouri and the Department of the South, respectively, Lincoln restrained them with stern rebukes. On August 30, 1861, Frémont declared martial law in Missouri and freed the enslaved laborers of "those who shall take up arms against the United States, or who shall be directly proven to have taken an active part with their enemies in the field."[51] Lincoln considered Frémont's decree as exceeding the provisions of the First Confiscation Act, since it did not require such confiscated property to have been used to aid the rebellion. Moreover, where Congress had been silent on the future status of these enslaved people in its confiscation plan, Frémont had proclaimed them free. The general's edict came at a time when the Kentucky legislature was in the midst of deciding if the state would remain loyal or join her slaveholding sisters. Fearing that Frémont's proclamation would "alarm our Southern union friends, and turn them against us—perhaps ruin our rather fair prospect for Kentucky," Lincoln requested and later ordered the intractable general to bring his proclamation of freedom into conformity with the congressional measure.[52]

Lincoln responded similarly to the actions of David Hunter who in May 1862 declared martial law in the Department of the South, which included portions of South Carolina, Georgia, and Florida. Asserting that "slavery and martial law in a free country are altogether incompatible," he attempted to free the slaves as well. Perturbed by Hunter's actions, Lincoln nullified the order ten days later. In so doing, he declared that Hunter had acted without authorization and asserted that he reserved the right to determine whether or not as commander-in-chief he had the authority to emancipate enslaved people in any state.[53]

The revocation of the Frémont and Hunter proclamations drew intense criticism from Lincoln's friends as well as his foes.[54] When Illinois senator Orville H. Browning penned a letter to Lincoln chastising him for the Frémont affair, Lincoln used his reply to quell the mounting discontent with his policies. "Genl. Frémont's proclamation, as to confiscation of property, and the liberation of slaves, is *purely political,* and not within the range of *military* law or necessity," he replied to Browning. "If a commanding General finds a necessity to seize the farm of a private owner, for a pasture, an encampment, or a fortification, he has the right to do so, and to so hold it, as long as the necessity lasts . . . But to say the farm shall no longer belong to the owner, or his heirs forever . . . is purely political, without the savor of military law about it. And the same is true of slaves."[55] Again, Lincoln argued that such actions would encourage the border states to abandon the Union. "I think to lose Kentucky is nearly the same as to lose the whole game. Kentucky gone, we can not hold Missouri, nor, as I think, Maryland. These all against us, and the job on our hands is too large for us."[56]

The president's revocation of the Hunter proclamation provoked protest as well, especially within the African-American community. Douglass charged, "whatever may have been his intentions, the action of President Lincoln has been calculated in a marked and decided way to shield and protect slavery from the very blows which its horrible crimes have loudly and persistently invited."[57] But others were somewhat more charitable in their assessment of the Hunter affair. The New York *Daily Tribune* recognized that it was the president's duty to render decisions based on the interests of the entire nation, rather than a small portion of it. Yet, it encouraged Lincoln to take the opportunity to formulate and state a clear policy regarding the disposition of fugitive slaves. Unless he did so, confusion and clashing policies would continue to characterize Union efforts to pursue the war.[58]

Some antislavery proponents took comfort in words in the Hunter revocation that suggested the president was not unmindful of slavery's significance in the war. Lincoln had appealed for gradual, compensated emancipation led by the border states. "I beseech you to make the arrangements for yourselves. You cannot if you would, be blind to the signs of the times," he had warned them.[59] Proponents of freedom fastened their hopes to these words, assured that Lincoln was moving closer to ending slavery.

COURTING THE BORDER STATES

Believing that you of the border states hold more power for good than any other equal number of members I feel it a duty . . . to make this appeal to you.

—ABRAHAM LINCOLN, July 1862

Lincoln's objections to the emancipationist aims of some of his generals in the early stages of the war reflected more than simply a desire to appease the border states and to bring the conflict to a quick resolution. And it did not signal any intention to protect slavery (as has been suggested by certain recent scholarship).[60] From the beginning, he had recognized the centrality of the institution in causing the war. When a speedy end failed to occur, he concluded that the best hope for the nation was eradication of the blight. But he came to this position more slowly and from a markedly different perspective than did abolitionists, many in Congress, and the enslaved themselves.

Given what he perceived to be the legal, political, and social constraints to emancipation, Lincoln championed a plan that included provisions for a gradual, compensated approach that would encourage African Americans to surrender their birthright. The Constitution's protection of property, Lincoln believed, required that abolition could be secured (with limited exception) only through the consent of the slave owners, who must be compensated for their loss. Hence, funds would be appropriated and the expense shared equally by the various states. In addition, abolition would be achieved over an extended period of time, so as to "[save the slaves] from the vagrant destitution which must largely attend immediate emancipation."[61] Lincoln also believed that abolition would be more palatable to whites if freed blacks could be convinced to find a more "suitable" home beyond America's shores. His colonization efforts revealed a certain degree of pessimism regarding the likelihood of free black men and women succeeding in America. Although his was a cynicism born of

astute observation and a clear understanding of the racist attitudes and limitations of his countrymen, Lincoln failed to fully comprehend or appreciate the resolve of African Americans to remain
in the country of their birth, despite its shortcomings. Confessing that had he the power to do so,
he would not know how to get rid of slavery, he suggested that his "first impulse would be to free
all the slaves, and send them to Liberia—to their native land." With this logistically impossible, he
pondered: "What then? Free them all, and keep them among us as underlings? Is it quite certain that
this betters their condition? . . . Free them and make them politically and socially our equals? My
own feelings will not admit of this, and if mine would, we well know that those of the great mass of
white people will not."[62] Lincoln understood well the influence of public opinion. Voicing a belief
that guided him throughout the war, he offered: "A universal feeling, whether well or ill-founded,
can not be safely disregarded."[63] Given the sentiment against them, therefore, black people could not
(in Lincoln's estimation) be made equal.

The focus of Lincoln's emancipation plans would be the border states, where the demise of slavery would signal to the seceded states that their Unionist slaveholding sisters would never join the
Confederacy. His appeal to the border states also allowed Lincoln to remain faithful to the idea that
the will of the people must be reflected in the emancipation process. Hence, in November 1861 he
sought to implement this gradual, compensated plan of freedom by courting Delaware, a state with
fewer than 2,000 enslaved people. He drafted two bills, which outlined a likely process of abolition
and the method by which owners could be compensated for their loss of property. The first proposed
an elaborate program that would free a few hundred adults each year until 1867, when children and
all remaining men and women would be freed. The second proposal—the one Lincoln purportedly
preferred—called for the elimination of slavery by 1893. Children born after passage of the bill and
all persons over thirty-five would enjoy immediate freedom; others would be freed as they reached
that age.[64] The proposal would have sanctioned slavery in Delaware for another three decades and
prolonged the bondage of an entire generation of African Americans. Lincoln also advised that the
states could (if they so chose) implement a system of apprenticeship for the children of those whose
mothers were still enslaved when they were born. Customarily, indentures were in effect until age
twenty-one for men and eighteen for women.[65] And while not bondage, abuse of the system could
and did approximate quasi-slavery. Even at its best, apprenticeship did little to prepare black children
for economic independence. Nor did it provide them the skills to establish institutions that would
support a community of free people.

Despite his efforts, Lincoln's Delaware plan never reached the state's legislature because the slaveholding power there rejected his overtures. Undeterred, Lincoln's message to Congress on March 6,
1862, proposed the adoption of a joint resolution pledging the government's cooperation with any
state attempting to implement gradual abolition. Help would be offered in the form of "pecuniary aid
. . . to compensate for the inconveniences public and private, produced by such change of system."[66]
On April 10, Congress responded favorably to the president's proposal by passing the joint resolution.
But no border state came forward to seek aid or to initiate freedom.

Meanwhile, Congress continued to pursue its own course of emancipation. Because the District
of Columbia was under its jurisdiction, the federal legislature had the authority to abolish slavery
within its borders. The notorious slave markets that traded in human beings had been eradicated as

a consequence of the Compromise of 1850 (which abolished the slave trade in the federal city), but bondage itself remained. On April 11, Congress gave hope to the "lovers of freedom" by passing a bill that provided for emancipation (with compensation to owners) of the more than 3,100 persons enslaved in the District.[67] Concerned that city residents had been excluded from exercising a political voice in the matter, Lincoln delayed signing the bill for several days. Both proponents and detractors of the measure visited him to lobby for their respective positions, but Lincoln refused to reveal his intentions to either group. Finally, on April 16, he penned a note to Congress, approving the bill and expressing gratification that "the two principles of compensation, and colonization, are both recognized, and practically applied in the act."[68]

The legislative body's momentary assumption of leadership in the emancipation process failed to deter Lincoln from his own effort to convince the border states to abandon slavery. Believing that a direct appeal to their congressional representatives might be successful, he invited them on July 12 to the White House, where he sought to convince them that they held the power to bring "speedy relief" to a country "in great peril." Lincoln warned, "If the war continue long, as it must, if the object be not sooner attained, the institution in your states will be extinguished by mere friction and abrasion—by the mere incidents of the war."[69] Better, then, to agree to a gradual emancipation, end the horrible conflict, and secure compensation for the loss of property. As for the disposition of the liberated blacks, new homes could be found for them in South America, "and when numbers shall be large enough to be company and encouragement for one another, the freedpeople will not be so reluctant to go."[70] With pressure mounting in the North to force emancipation in the seceded states, he argued, only voluntary action on the part of the border states would stem the unrelenting drive and end the war.

Calls for Lincoln to emancipate the slaves in the seceded states increased significantly by the second year of the war. During the summer of 1862 various profreedom groups made direct appeals to the president to strike a blow against slavery. In June, Lincoln met with a group of Quakers—Progressive Friends—who presented him with a memorial encouraging him to free the slaves. Still exhibiting a sense of humor, despite the disappointing course the war had taken, Lincoln joked that he was relieved that the delegation did not consist of "applicants for office." On the cause of their visit, he pointed out the ineffectiveness of a proclamation of freedom, since even the Constitution could not be enforced in the South.[71] Not to be put off, the delegation expressed its desire that Lincoln would rely on God's "divine guidance" to bring about an end to slavery.

As the summer advanced, impatience at the president's refusal to emancipate grew, especially among African Americans. In August Douglass took the administration to task for failing to enforce the provisions of the Second Confiscation Act, which declared free the enslaved property of disloyal owners. "The Legislature has put a sword into the hands of the President, with the general approbation of the country, and every body is wondering why he delays to strike," Douglass wrote.[72] "Mr. Lincoln and his Cabinet will have by and by to confess with many bitter regrets, that they have been equally blind and mistaken as to the true method of dealing with the rebels—They have fought the rebels with the Olive branch. The people must teach them to fight them with the sword. They have sought to conciliate obedience. The people must teach them to compel obedience."[73]

Pressure to emancipate also mounted from the Union's failure to achieve sustained military success. McClellan's Peninsula campaign had not brought the victories the North needed so desperately to put an end to the war, and no "turning of the tide" seemed imminent. Richmond had been secured by the determination of Confederate forces under the command of Robert E. Lee, who, unlike McClellan, had the will and the commitment to prosecute the war. Confederate success and Union defeat in the summer of 1862 ensured that the conflict would drag on indefinitely. The thought demoralized the troops in the field as well as civilians at home.

His plan of gradual, compensated emancipation initiated by the border states having failed, pressure intensifying from certain quarters to emancipate, and military gains unimpressive or nonexistent, Lincoln pursued the only course left to a man committed to preservation of the Union. In a reply to Horace Greeley's *New York Tribute* editorial chiding him for being "unduly influenced by the counsels . . . of certain fossil politicians hailing from the Border Slave States,"[74] Lincoln reiterated his position on emancipation while preparing the nation for a radical departure from his earlier efforts. Indicating that he would free all, some, or none of the slaves, depending on what was required to save the Union, he declared, "What I do about slavery, and the colored race, I do because I believe it helps to save the Union. I shall do less whenever I shall believe what I am doing hurts the cause, and I shall do more whenever I shall believe doing more will help the cause."[75]

By July 1862, Lincoln stood ready to do more. When he met with his cabinet on the twenty-second, he surprised them with news that he was contemplating a proclamation of freedom. The response to his declaration was mixed, with some favorably disposed to immediate action, while others expressed fear of injury during the fall elections, or anxiety that the president's decision would seem rash and desperate. After careful consideration of the cabinet's concerns, he decided to withhold the proclamation until the Union secured a victory. Given the general ineptness of certain Union generals, Lincoln must have wondered if the nation could endure that long. But the opportunity finally arrived when on September 17 Union forces under McClellan's command pushed back the Confederates under Robert E. Lee at Antietam Creek near Sharpsburg, Maryland. The victory, although slight, provided the opportunity Lincoln had been awaiting. From this point on, the war became what African Americans always believed it should be—one with the dual aims of preservation of the Union and freedom.

ISSUING THE EMANCIPATION PROCLAMATION

[It] is the central act of my administration and the great event of the nineteenth century.
—ABRAHAM LINCOLN, February 1865

The pronouncement issued in September was an ultimatum, a final demand to the Confederacy for a return to reason. Lincoln's policies heretofore had not produced the effect he had sought, and now (as he had indicated to Greeley) he aimed to save the nation by removing the source of its tension. In the opening lines of the document, the president reconfirmed his commitment to "restoring the constitutional relation between the United States, and each of the states, and the people thereof."[76] Furthermore, the preliminary proclamation revealed that he would continue to pursue voluntary emancipation by any state, along with a plan of colonization of the freed people. Finally, the document declared that on January 1, 1863, "all persons held as slaves within any state, or designated part of a state the people whereof shall then be in rebellion against the United States shall be then, thenceforward, and forever free." Lincoln pledged the assistance of the military in maintaining the freedom of the liberated and forbade Union forces from hindering enslaved people seizing their freedom.[77] Designation of the areas to be included in the emancipation would be decided when the proclamation took effect in one hundred days.

The president's action evoked mixed sentiment in the North. Already concerned that, once freed, African Americans would set out for opportunities in northern climes, white Union men and women voiced their objections to waging a war of liberation. The Democrats, as expected, damned it as tyrannous and as signaling the beginning of barbarous insurrection.[78] Believing that it would prolong the war, they lost little time in capitalizing on the discord caused by Lincoln's edict. Using their condemnation of the proclamation as a rallying cry, Democrats (as Lincoln and the Republicans had feared they might) won significant victories in the 1862 elections.[79]

Most Republicans, especially those vehemently opposed to slavery, generally responded favorably to the decree, although some questioned the constitutionality of the document and the wisdom of pronouncing freedom at that time.[80] The abolitionists, for the most part, were elated by the surprise announcement. Most welcomed it as heralding the end of the war, a return to Union, and an affirmation of America's place among civilized nations.[81]

The response of African Americans to news of the proclamation reflected the dissolution of centuries of pent-up anguish. "Common sense, the necessities of the war, to say nothing of the dictation of justice and humanity have at last prevailed," Frederick Douglass proclaimed. "We shout for joy that we live to record this righteous decree."[82] Henry Highland Garnet, the firebrand who earned the ire of some when in the 1840s he advised enslaved people to rise up and slay their masters, agreed with Douglass's assessment of the proclamation's significance. Unwilling to wait until the pronouncement took effect, Garnet organized a celebratory gathering at his Shiloh Presbyterian Church in New York. Fellow minister and abolitionist Henry M. Turner, pastor of Washington, D.C.'s Israel Bethel Church (and later bishop of the African Methodist Episcopal denomination) used the occasion of the preliminary proclamation to urge his people to assist the contraband who were swelling the ranks of the poor in certain cities. While African Americans had been reluctant to "lavish charitable expenditures on human chattel" who might be destined for a return to slavery, Turner argued, "the proclamation of President Lincoln has banished the fog, and silenced the doubt. All can now see that the stern intention of the Presidential policy is to wage the war in favor of freedom, till the last groan of the anguished heart slave shall be hushed in the ears of nature's God. The definition of the policy bids us rise, and for our-selves think, act, and do. We have stood still and see the salvation of God while we besought Him with teary eyes and bleeding heart; but the stand still day bid us adieu Sept. 22, 1862."[83] While little is known about the reaction of enslaved people themselves to the preliminary proclamation, evidence suggests that it may have encouraged an alleged conspiracy between free blacks and bondsmen which was uncovered in Culpeper, Virginia, in early October 1862. When arrested, some of the men were in possession of northern newspapers that had printed the proclamation. The connection was unmistakable to Confederates already suspicious of the blacks in their midst and expecting revolt at any minute. As a consequence, seventeen black men were executed.[84]

As elated as they were, supporters of Lincoln's emancipation policy worried that he might change his mind before the final proclamation took effect on January 1. Shortly after the September 22 pronouncement, Douglass wondered if the president—swayed by public sentiment and political considerations—might retract the edict. Overjoyed by the prospect of black freedom, Douglass comforted himself with the thought that "events greater than the President" and Lincoln's own integrity would prevent such an occurrence. But within days of the final decree, the man who had fought against slavery his entire life suffered renewed doubts. Declaring that there was "reason for both hope and fear," Douglass's anxiety was fueled by the proclamation's tone: "His words kindled no enthusiasm. They touched neither justice nor mercy. Had there been one expression of sound moral feeling against Slavery, one word of regret and shame that the accursed system had remained so long the disgrace and scandal of the Republic, one word of satisfaction in the hope of burying slavery and the rebellion in one common grave, a thrill of joy would have run round the world."[85]

This pessimism followed Lincoln's December message to Congress. Just one month before the Emancipation Proclamation was due to take effect, the president recommended that the nation adopt a new constitutional amendment that would provide for compensation for any state seeking to end slavery before January 1, 1900. Each state would decide how long and what method of emancipation would be implemented. This gradual plan, he recognized, would permit slavery to exist for another thirty-seven years but would ultimately eliminate it throughout the land by going beyond the provisions of the preliminary Emancipation Proclamation. He justified gradual emancipation as a way to "spare both races from the evils of sudden derangement." Furthermore, it would ensure that those who objected most vociferously to freeing the enslaved would have "passed away before its consummation." To those who would oppose delaying freedom, who "will feel that it gives too little to the now living slaves," Lincoln argued (rather unconvincingly) that gradualism "really gives them much. It saves them from the vagrant destitution which must largely attend immediate emancipation . . . gives the inspiring assurances that their posterity shall be free forever."[86]

In proposing to compensate slave owners, Lincoln was acknowledging a legal reality. Slaves were property, "acquired by descent, or by purchase, the same as any other." Since emancipation would destroy these chattels, it fell to the entire nation—North as well as South—to make restitution for such losses. In arguing the economic advantage of compensated freedom, since it would ultimately end the war, Lincoln proposed to commit later generations to sharing the financial burden that such an undertaking would entail.[87]

The third component of the proposed amendment saw Lincoln advocating voluntary removal of those who would be freed by the gradual, compensated program. The possibility of colonization, he thought, might allay the fears of northern whites who envisioned hordes of the newly emancipated descending on them in search of employment. Lincoln thought it unlikely that white laborers would suffer economically from the presence of free blacks, but he realized that the perception that it would might cause whites to resist his plan of emancipation.[88]

In an effort to convince African Americans of the benefit of emigration, Lincoln had arranged four months earlier to meet at the White House with a committee of five men of color—four were recently released from slavery and one newly arrived in the city—to discuss his views on colonization. Once assembled, the men listened politely as Lincoln attempted to persuade them of the logic of his proposal. His appeal to the delegation emphasized the incompatibility of the two races and cited the physical differences as a "great disadvantage to us both . . . your race suffer very greatly, many of them by living among us, while ours suffer from your presence. Without the institution of Slavery and the colored race as a basis," Lincoln declared, "the war could not have an existence."[89] Pointing to the illusion of freedom the free born and freed people of color experienced, he observed, "Even when you cease to be slaves, you are yet far removed from being placed on an equality with the white race . . . not a single man of your race is made the equal of a single man of ours. Go where you are treated the best, and the ban is still upon you."[90]

Edward M. Thomas, the principal spokesman for the committee of blacks, later wrote to Lincoln promising to confer with black leaders throughout the North and encouraged the president in Thomas's belief that African Americans would "join heartily in sustaining such a movement."[91] But Lincoln's ill-conceived colonization plan found scant support in the African-American community. His proposed plan of emigration may have been an astute political maneuver, but for black men and women, it was a denial of their capacity for progress. Although certain black leaders such as Henry Highland Garnet, H. Ford Douglas, and William Wells Brown had urged emigration at one time or another, most people of color rejected the notion that their future lay in a foreign land. A. P. Smith, a resident of Saddle River, New Jersey, aptly conveyed the sentiment of many African Americans when he wrote to Lincoln: "But were all you say on this point true, must I crush out my cherished hopes and aspirations, abandon my home, and become a pander to the mean and selfish spirit that oppresses me? Pray tell us, is our right to a home in this country less than your own, Mr. Lincoln? . . . Are you an American? So are we. Are you a Patriot? So are we. Would you spurn all absurd, meddlesome, impudent propositions for your colonization in a foreign country? So do we."[92]

Had he read Smith's letter, Lincoln doubtless would have understood black men and women's legitimate assertions of an American birthright. But the legitimacy of black claims was not what most occupied his thinking when he met with the black delegation or months later when he proposed the constitutional amendment. Rather, as always, he was focused on preservation of the Union. By the end of 1862, however, he recognized that Union and freedom were inseparable. Thus, he closed his December address to Congress with an impassioned appeal: "Fellow citizens, *we* cannot escape history . . . The fiery trial through which we pass, will light us down, in honor or dishonor, to the latest generation . . . We know how to save the Union . . . In *giving* freedom to the *slave*, we *assure* freedom to the *free*—honorable alike in what we give, and what we preserve. We shall nobly save, or meanly lose, the last best, hope of earth."[93]

A constitutional amendment required the agreement of two-thirds of the Congress and ratification by three-fourths of the states, including at least seven of the slave states.[94] Although Lincoln suggested that "timely adoption" of his plan would lead to restoration of the Union, the end of war, and withdrawal of the preliminary proclamation, he knew that circumstances did not favor ratification. In taking the opportunity to outline an alternative to immediate, uncompensated emancipation without the consent of the people (what the Emancipation Proclamation represented), he was reaffirming his commitment to moderation while seeking political cover.

When, on January 1, 1863, Congress failed to implement the proposed constitutional amendment and the states in rebellion ignored his ultimatum, Lincoln issued a proclamation of freedom. He pledged the Union military and naval authorities to ensure that freedom was recognized and maintained. The newly emancipated were directed to "abstain from all violence, unless in necessary self-defence."[95] A revision of the preliminary document of September 22, the decree no longer mentioned colonization. Nor did it suggest the gradualism that Lincoln had embraced previously or provide for compensation to slaveholders.[96]

Taken as "a fit and necessary war measure," Lincoln's actions were limited in scope. He exempted those areas already under Union control: the city of New Orleans as well as several parishes in Louisiana; the forty-eight northwestern counties formerly in Virginia that now comprised West Virginia; several counties in eastern Virginia and the cities of Norfolk and Portsmouth; the state of Tennessee; and the border states of Missouri, Kentucky, Maryland, and Delaware. While some 800,000 enslaved African Americans were excluded from its provisions, the proclamation declared that 3 million "henceforward shall be free."

Perhaps better than anyone else, Lincoln understood (and intended) the proclamation's limitations. Citing "military necessity," the decree was a tacit recognition that gradualism would not bring about the ultimate goal he sought. He had attempted to avoid using the war powers granted by the Constitution, but circumstances had left him with few alternatives.

In addition to wanting to deprive the Confederacy of its indispensable labor force, Lincoln was motivated by the need to dissuade European recognition of the Confederacy as a legitimate polity. Britain, especially, posed a serious threat in this regard. Despite its abolition of slavery in the West Indian possessions in the 1830s, economic self-interest (reliance on southern cotton) could have prompted it to side with the Confederacy. Emancipation would complicate the British position. Once freedom was declared, Lincoln believed, the English people would eschew an alliance with the secessionists. As he predicted, with the issuing of the proclamation, the Confederacy found itself absent the essential support it needed.[97]

Finally, the proclamation enabled Lincoln to move more effectively to acquire fighting men to supplement the forces in the Union army that had been depleted by a war of attrition. He hoped to alleviate the pressure on the Union forces by authorizing men "of suitable condition" to "be received into the armed service . . . to garrison forts, positions, stations, and other places, and to man vessels of all sorts in said service." This provision facilitated activity that was already underway as a consequence of the Militia Act of 1862. It was the kind of action African Americans had sought since the conflict began, but their initial pleas for inclusion in the fight had been rebuffed by an administration and a northern people determined to keep it a white man's war. Wishing to take part in an army of liberation, some 186,000 black men would ultimately serve in the army and navy, thus joining the countless others who had supported the cause of union and liberty all along by serving as nonsoldiering military laborers.

Northerners responded to Lincoln's final decree according to political considerations and individual sentiment. The abolitionists, generally, were pleased if not totally satisfied because emancipation was not universal. Most praised Lincoln for taking the initial steps that they believed ultimately would lead to freedom for all. Just as with the preliminary proclamation, some were put off by the cold tone of Lincoln's decree. Robert Hamilton, the editor of the *Anglo-African,* declared the proclamation "simply a war measure . . . It is an instrument for crushing, hurting, injuring, and crippling the enemy. It is per se no more humanitarian than a hundred pounder rifled cannon. It seeks to deprive the enemy of arms and legs, muscles and sinews, used by them to procure food and raiment and to throw up fortifications."[98] With a hint of sarcasm, Hamilton feigned astonishment that "the skill of our generals . . . the bravery of our soldiers . . . the strength of our resources" had not brought the victory the North sought. As a last resort, "our tried and trusted ruler calls upon the negro 'to come to the rescue.'"[99] Certain critics charged that Lincoln freed the slaves where he had no authority and kept enslaved those held in the Union. The more optimistic believed, however, that a proclamation liberating enslaved people in one state would ultimately sound the death knell of the institution in adjoining jurisdictions.[100] And those who had questioned the constitutionality of such a decree when Lincoln first made his pronouncement in September were even more strident in their objections to the final proclamation.

Lincoln had feared that any action taken on behalf of emancipation would push the border states into the beckoning arms of the Confederacy. Indeed, shortly before the final proclamation was issued, military officials received word that if Lincoln proceeded as planned, "the Legislature of Kentucky . . . will legislate the State out of the Union."[101] Although no border state seceded, many within the slave-holding Union soundly condemned the president's actions.[102] Serious opposition to the proclamation surfaced throughout the North and West as well. Common folk and political partisans were equally demonstrative in their disdain for Lincoln's decree. Military recruitment slowed significantly, and loud grumbling about having to fight for the freedom of blacks was accompanied by increased desertions in the months following the pronouncement. Especially in the west, a fear of "Negro equality" led to rioting and resistance to conscription.[103]

AFRICAN AMERICANS CELEBRATE FREEDOM
Cry out and shout all ye children of sorrow,
The gloom of your midnight hath passed away . . .
—Song of Freedom, 1863

African Americans did not allow the displeasure of these Union men and women to deter their enthusiasm for the proclamation. For free blacks in the North, the issuing of the final proclamation provided an opportunity for reflection and recommitment. In every major city throughout the Union—from New York to Chicago and from Boston to the District of Columbia—they remembered the sacrifices sustained in the struggle for freedom and pledged to continue to press for universal emancipation.[104] People who gathered at Chicago's Quinns Chapel on January 1 were treated to the oratory of Osborne Perry Anderson, the sole black survivor of the Harpers Ferry raid. Anderson reminded his audience of the tireless devotion of John Brown and assured them that the war was "God's vindicating the principles of that old man . . . who fought and died for the right."[105] Sharing the podium with William Wells Brown, John Rock, and other prominent abolitionists, Frederick Douglass spoke to a crowd of over 3,000 at Boston's Tremont Temple.[106] In Washington, D.C., Henry McNeil Turner rushed from the newspaper office to deliver the emancipation message to his congregation. Out of breath, he handed the article proclaiming freedom to someone else to read. Later, he wrote that "the first day of January, 1863, is destined to form one of the most memorable epochs in the history of the world . . . The seeds of freedom . . . have now been scattered where despotism and tyranny ranked and ruled."[107] Although exempted from the proclamation, black men and women in Norfolk celebrated because they believed that eventually they would be free as well.

Emancipation celebrations continued to occupy the attention of African Americans in the North long after the great day. One of the largest such gatherings occurred at Cooper Union on the night of January 5. As the *Anglo-African* reported, "Churches suspended their usual Monday night meetings, societies closed their doors, friends put off their social gatherings on that night, and the general cry was "ho for the Cooper Institute." Hosted by the Sons of Freedom, the affair drew people from towns and cities throughout New York and from a few of the surrounding states. The program opened with the playing of the "Star Spangled Banner," followed by the audience's participation in the singing of a song penned in commemoration of freedom:

> Cry out and shout all ye children of sorrow,
> The gloom of your midnight hath passed away,
> Bright is the bow which now beams on your morrow,
> Fruition's new glories o'ershadow to-day.
> Let people and nations aroused from their slumber,
> Rejoice in the severance of Slavery's chain,
> While voices and instruments mightily in number,
> Sound praises to him who removed the dark stain.[108]

In the celebrations cheers were given to God and Lincoln, to flag and country, and to the abolitionists—collectively and individually.[109] Overjoyed, African Americans tempered their criticism of the president's path toward emancipation, and in some instances they forgot their reservations about him altogether. When Garnet, presiding at the Cooper Union celebration, praised Lincoln as "an advancing and progressive man . . . the man of our choice and hope," he doubtless spoke for many African Americans who were more than ready to credit the president with taking a decisive step toward ending slavery.[110]

Southern blacks, if not as ebullient as their northern brothers, nevertheless grasped the proclamation's potential for altering their lives. Despite Confederate efforts to conceal news of the document from those in bondage, the enslaved population of the South soon learned by grapevine and through fragments of overheard conversation that their "day of jubilee" had come. Believing at the outset that the war would bring them freedom, they rejoiced that circumstances had led finally to the day of deliverance. Prayers of thanksgiving to God and to Abraham Lincoln were offered throughout the South, as men, women, and children, singly and collectively, demonstratively and quietly, celebrated the legal transition from chattel to humankind. The freed people spoke reverently of the president and believed that the man who "dispersed their masters" would look out for them.[111]

The celebration of freedom at Camp Saxton in South Carolina typified the spirit of inclusion that black men and women now felt. Freed people in the area celebrated the proclamation with the First South Carolina Volunteers, the first regiment of former slaves raised on southern soil. In chronicling the festive atmosphere of the day, their commander, Col. Thomas Wentworth Higginson, singled out one special moment for its extraordinary impact on everyone present:

Then the President's Proclamation was read by Dr. William H. Brisbane . . . a South Carolinian addressing South Carolinians, for he was reared among these very islands, and here long since emancipated his own slaves . . . Then followed an incident so simple, so touching, so utterly unexpected and start-ling that I can scarcely believe it on recalling, though it gave the keynote to the whole day. The very moment the speaker had ceased, and just as I took and waved the flag, which now for the first time meant anything to these poor people, there suddenly arose, close beside the platform, a strong male voice (but rather cracked and elderly), into which two women's voices instantly blended, singing, as if by an impulse that could no more be re-pressed than the morning note of the song-sparrow—

> "My country, 'tis of thee,
> Sweet land of liberty,
> Of thee I sing!"

"Just think of it!" Higginson exclaimed. "The first day they had ever had a country, the first flag they had ever seen which promised anything to their people."[112]

Lincoln understood that the proclamation would be effective only if the Union army occupied secessionist territory or if his decree "[induced] the colored people to come bodily over from the rebel side to ours."[113] And they did. Robert Hamilton likened the proclamation to "a pillar of flame, beckoning [enslaved men and women] to the dreamed of promise of freedom! Bidding them leap from chattel-hood to manhood, from slavery to freedom!"[114] They had been fleeing bondage since the war commenced, but this time they did so with the authorization and encouragement of the president and with the aid of the federal forces.

At Fortress Monroe, where Mallory, Baker, and Townsend had sought and found refuge in May 1861, Capt. Charles Wilder, assistant quartermaster and superintendent of the contrabands, estimated that approximately 10,000 fugitives had come under the control of his forces. Testifying before the American Freedmen's Inquiry Commission, an agency established to investigate the condition of the freed people and to ascertain the best means to facilitate their protection and improvement, Wilder reported that "They came here from all about, from Richmond and 200 miles off in North Carolina . . . Some men who came here from North Carolina, knew all about the Proclamation and they started on the belief in it."[115]

Flight to the Union forces often proved perilous for the fugitives. When possible, owners or their agents pursued and dragged slaves back to the plantation where they invariably received punishment. Even when successful in eluding patrols or Confederate authorities, flight could prove deadly. For instance, when a small boat of contrabands sailing off the coast of Wilmington, North Carolina, attempted to rendezvous with the steamer *Governor Buckingham,* an accident ensued which propelled the boat's occupants into the sea. Before assistance could be rendered, a woman and three children had drowned.[116]

Naval commanders took the proclamation seriously, often sending parties ashore and venturing onto land to rescue fleeing slaves. When in May 1863, the commander of the U.S.S. *South Carolina* observed on Bull's Island Beach a group of people "resembling negroes," he sent two boats to shore to bring them back to the ship. The island was known to be sometimes occupied by Confederate forces, but in an attempt to "carry out the spirit of the President's proclamation," its commander took the risk and rescued thirteen men, women, and children from slavery.[117]

Although generals in the field informed him that the proclamation was a great boon to the Union cause, Lincoln worried that a peace settlement might be forced upon him before the masses of enslaved people had an opportunity to escape their bondage. In preparation for such an occurrence, in late August 1864 he invited Frederick Douglass to the White House, where he requested assistance in devising "means most desirable to be employed outside the army to induce the slaves . . . to come within the Federal lines."[118] On August 29, Douglass proposed the employment of agents and subagents who would travel to various parts of the South where Union troops were engaging the Confederate forces and coax slaves into the Union lines.[119] Douglass's plan became unnecessary as an increasingly victorious Union military force quieted the clamor for peace.

THE CONFEDERACY RESPONDS

President Lincoln has sought to convert the South into a San Domingo by appealing to the cupidity, lusts, ambition, and ferocity of the slave.

—Address of Congress to the People of the Confederate States (1864)

To those accustomed to holding human beings as property, the Emancipation Proclamation was an abomination. Although initially the South claimed the decree was "a mere *brutum fulmen*" (a harmless threat), they understood its potential for damaging the Confederate cause. Far from being seen as a legitimate instrument of warfare, the proclamation was viewed as an affront to civilized society. History would "hereafter pillory those who committed and encouraged such crimes in immortal infamy," southerners believed.[120]

In his address to the seceded states' congress on January 12, 1863, Confederate president Jefferson Davis reviled Lincoln and the Union for the proclamation. Calling Lincoln's action "the most execrable measure recorded in the history of guilty man," Davis argued that the edict encouraged slaves to kill their owners.[121] He threatened to charge captured U.S. commissioned officers who commanded black units with "enticing servile insurrection" and to turn them over to the states for punishment according to their statutes. The proclamation, Davis contended, proved the North's intention all along had been to end slavery and that it "afford[ed] the fullest guarantee of the impossibility" that the union could be mended.[122]

Even before issuance of the final proclamation, slave owners had been compelled to remove their chattel from the coastal areas and regions accessible to Union lines. Individual states issued ordinances that outlined procedures and conditions for "refugeeing" as well as plans for housing and maintenance of the removed. Such ordinances made it clear that slaveholders would be obliged to follow the dictates of military authorities.[123] Once the Union accepted black men into military service as soldiers, the Confederates, fearing that absconding men would swell the enemy's ranks, intensified their efforts to hinder flight. In Mississippi, Gov. John J. Pettus informed the state legislators that "every able-bodied negro man that falls into the hands of the enemy is not only a laborer lost to the country in the production of supplies for the support of our armies in the field, but he is also, under the present policy of the United States Government, a soldier gained to its Army."[124] Pettus pressed the state legislature to pass a law removing all able-bodied blacks from the more exposed districts of the state.

Confederate authorities and private individuals stood ready to use any methods at their disposal to stop the drain of black labor from the South, including sanctioning murder. Union general William T. Sherman wrote incredulously from the Military Division of the Mississippi that a woman in Canton, Tennessee, "thank[ed] her God that her negroes, who had attempted to escape into our lines at Big Black, had been overtaken by Ross' Texas brigade and killed . . . All the people of the South," he reported, "old and young, rich and poor, educated and ignorant, unite in this that they will kill as vipers the whites who attempt to free their slaves, and also the 'ungrateful slaves' who attempt to change their character from slave to free."[125]

Fearing that freedom would alter the social and political climate as well as restructure economic relationships, white southerners redoubled their efforts to be victorious. They were warned that failure to answer the call to military service would result in "the elevation of the black race to a position of equality—aye, of superiority, that will make them your masters and rulers."[126] Better that the young men die in defense of the rights and liberties that had been granted by God, and old men, women, and children engage in mass suicide, than that the former slaves should be placed on an equal footing with whites.

Others in the Confederacy realized that white conscription alone would not ensure victory. Exactly a year and a day after the Emancipation Proclamation authorized the use of black troops in the Union army, a group of Confederate officers sent a letter to the commanding general and fellow officers of the Army of Tennessee. The men sought discreetly to air their views regarding the state of affairs confronting them since the Union expanded the goal of the war to include freedom for the enslaved. "If this state continues much longer we must be subjugated," they wrote. The solution was to "immediately commence training a large reserve of the most courageous of our slaves, and further that we guarantee freedom within a reasonable time to every slave in the South who shall remain true to the Confederacy in this war."[127] Borrowing from Lincoln's own reasons for issuing the Emancipation Proclamation, the men argued that southern emancipation would not only increase the South's inferior troop strength but would also secure the sorely needed assistance of England and France, who heretofore could not supply material aid because of their commitment to freedom. Furthermore, it would solve the problem of the South's vulnerability from within: "The approach of the enemy would no longer find every household surrounded by spies . . . There would be no recruits awaiting the enemy with open arms, no complete history of every neighborhood with ready guides, no fear of insurrection in the rear . . . The chronic irritation of hope deferred would be joyfully ended with the negro and the sympathies of his whole race would be due to his native South."[128] In arming the slaves, care would have to be taken to bind them to the Confederate cause. Hence, the officers proposed not only to free the would-be soldiers but also to emancipate the race. As a good faith gesture, they suggested that the Confederacy "immediately make [the slave's] marriage and parental relations sacred in the eyes of the law and forbid their sale."[129] The officers worried that this "concession to common sense" might come too late if Confederate leaders did not act quickly.

The men need not have worried that their views would be received as too radical a departure from policy, as members of the Confederate cabinet held similar sentiments. In response to an inquiry regarding the use of black troops, Secretary of State Judah P. Benjamin agreed that it was a reasonable consideration and suggested that "If they are to fight for our freedom they are entitled to their own." Like Lincoln, he preferred that emancipation be gradual, "after an immediate stage of serfage or peonage." Such gradualism, he concluded, would allow the South to maintain its belief that people of color were inferior and "unfitted for social or political equality with the white man." The transition period would serve to "modify and ameliorate the existing condition of blacks by allowing them to acquire property, enjoy personal liberty, and protect their families."[130]

THE DESTRUCTION OF SLAVERY

Those who shall have tasted actual freedom I believe can never be slaves or quasi slaves again.
—ABRAHAM LINCOLN, July 1863

As the states in rebellion suffered greater military losses, support of Confederate enrollment of black troops and for some measure of emancipation swelled. Finally, the Confederate congress debated the issue and agreed to a plan of action. By this time, however, "the mere friction of war" (as Lincoln had warned in his address to the border-state representatives in 1862) had begun the erosion of slavery. All over the South, the institution experienced challenges, largely from enslaved people themselves. Not only did loss of human property compromise the Confederate cause, but flight by comrades-in-bondage and the presence of Union forces encouraged insolence among those enslaved people who stayed behind. Traditional assumptions were reassessed and relationships transformed by wartime circumstances. Left behind as husbands, sons, and overseers went off to war, white women and older men found themselves surrounded by blacks who refused to labor or did so sullenly. In those areas abandoned by rebels fleeing the Union advance, former slaves pressed for control. In Mississippi, Governor Pettus reported in November 1863 that "marauding bands of these freed negroes are desolating neighborhoods in the Valley of the Mississippi, and citizens of Mississippi have been murdered at their homes by them."[131]

The slaveholders' need to maintain authority over their bondsmen sometimes clashed with the interests of the Confederate military. By the fall of 1863, Maj. Gen. J. Bankhead Magruder's Headquarters District of Texas had been overwhelmed by requests for the detailing of overseers—between 200 and 300 applications in all. In some instances, groups of women—as many as 100 to 200—collaborated by endorsing a single petition for assistance, declaring that there were no men in their vicinity to help control the slaves. Despite sympathetic statements, Magruder declined to release individuals to the fields but offered to send troops to quell any disturbances.[132]

The presence of free blacks posed similar problems for the Confederacy. Having faced economic dependence and denial of social and political equality, and suffering from violence and intimidation, their lives under the domination of the slaveocracy had been proscribed nearly as much as that of their enslaved counterparts.[133] Union victory, especially after the issuing of the Emancipation Proclamation, promised to ensure their freedom and secure their rights. Caught in the precarious position between needing to appear loyal in the presence of their secessionist neighbors and a desire to see slavery ended, they played a dangerous game that included cooperating with the Confederate army while offering aid to the Union cause. In some instances, their enthusiastic support of Union victory emboldened them. In Virginia, Confederate authorities complained of inadequate laws for the management of free people of color who were guilty of "many outrages upon persons and property . . .

They are sometimes found co-operating with the enemy, and occasionally indulging in the utterance of treasonable sentiments and threats against our fellow-citizens."[134]

In those areas exempted from the proclamation, slavery began to die just as surely as in the Confederacy. By August 1863 in some areas of Union-occupied Louisiana, for instance, unsupervised blacks gained possession of horses and mules and purportedly terrorized surrounding plantations.[135] Gen. Lovell H. Rousseau, headquartered in Nashville during the winter of 1863–64, reported that African Americans were causing considerable trouble in areas under his command. "Slavery is virtually dead in Tennessee," he reported, despite the state's exemption from the provisions of the Emancipation Proclamation. "Many straggling negroes have arms obtained from soldiers, and by their insolence and threats greatly alarm and intimidate white families, who are not allowed to keep arms, or who would generally be afraid to use if they had them . . . In many cases negroes leave their homes to work for themselves, boarding and lodging with their masters, defiantly asserting their right to do it."[136]

The Union encouragement of black men to enlist in the federal forces hastened the destruction of slavery in the border states. As Ira Berlin and his co-editors at the Freedmen and Southern Society Project have ably shown, the Emancipation Proclamation compromised slavery in the loyal slaveholding states, as enslaved men found ways to use federal laws regarding enlistment to their advantage. Benefiting from provisions that prohibited the return of fugitives to alleged owners or even assessing the validity of such claims, and taking advantage of laws that granted freedom to those willing to work for the Union military, slaves who remained in bondage were able to alter their condition. Hence, as Douglass had predicted when he learned of the exemption of the border states in Lincoln's decree, Maryland and Kentucky could not remain enslaved once Virginia was declared free.[137]

As black men in the border states seized their freedom by enlisting in the Union army, families were left behind at the mercy of owners. In territory exempted from the proclamation, enslaved men were obliged to seek permission from their owners to join the army. However, Union recruiters often ignored the rights of slaveholders, and enslaved men facilitated this blindness by claiming to be owned by disloyal persons. In any case, as men abandoned the fields, owners sought to punish the workers' wives and daughters by making them do the men's work. Hence, in March, 1864, an assistant provost-marshal stationed in Mexico, Missouri, inquired of his superior what should be done with a black family consisting of an elderly woman, her two daughters, and two grandchildren, who had fled their owner after their husbands enlisted. The owner threatened to split up the family and hire the women out to renters who would put them to work in the fields, contrary to their customary labor. One provost-marshal in Missouri thought he had come upon a solution when he inquired of the acting provost-marshal-general if he might give passes to Saint Louis to those black women "who come to this post, when their masters come after them and they refuse to go home . . . masters disloyal." In the curtest language, the provost marshal-general prohibited the local provost-marshal from granting passes to black women for admission to the city, hence potentially exposing them to abuse by their owners.[138]

Nor was black freedom secure after Union forces occupied formerly Confederate-held territory. Such was the case with the enslaved property of one Fountain Brown, minister and presiding elder in an Arkansas Methodist church. A locally respected citizen of Flat Bayou, Brown had owned two enslaved families—four adults and six children—when the Emancipation Proclamation took effect. After Union forces arrived in town, Brown informed his slaves that they were free to leave, but the freed people decided to stay. In the meantime, a local man sought Brown's help in spiriting the freed people beyond Union lines, where he intended to reenslave and transport them to Texas. After initially refusing, Brown succumbed to the enticement of $7,000 for the two women and their children. He received $4,000 in cash and accepted the purchaser's promise to remit the remaining $3,000 at a later date. When the husband of one of the women returned home after a brief absence and found his family gone, the minister reported what he knew of their disappearance to the authorities and asked for exemption from prosecution. Nevertheless, a military commission found him guilty of "selling into slavery persons of African descent, made free by the President's proclamation." The good citizens of Flat Bayou then petitioned Lincoln to pardon the minister and set aside his sentence of five years imprisonment. But Judge Advocate Gen. Joseph Holt was unmoved by their entreaties. In his recommendation to the Secretary of War, Holt declared that the proclamation was "a solemn law of the land, upheld by the inherent war powers of a nation struggling for self preservation, sanctioned by reason, and sanctified by precious blood." Brown's pardon, he believed, would suggest to the "traitorous adherents of slavery" that the government was unwilling to sustain the document.[139] Although Lincoln denied the petition for pardon, a second memorandum was presented to Holt in November 1864. The judge advocate general reiterated his position on the matter and admonished the military authorities for failing to carry out Brown's sentence.[140]

Freedom became especially tenuous as the Union army withdrew from certain areas. Those freed by the Emancipation Proclamation sometimes faced reenslavement when they followed the army into border state territories. These freed people mingled with fugitives who had not been included in the proclamation, which made it difficult for local authorities to distinguish between them. Swayed by the potential for financial gain, some ostensibly loyal whites thought nothing of declaring any black person a fugitive, having him jailed until the owner could be notified, and placing him on the auction block if no owner appeared. The practice became so notorious in Kentucky that Lincoln instructed Gen. Ambrose Burnside, then commanding the Department of the Ohio, to ensure such persons were protected from reenslavement.[141] Kentuckians continued the practice, however, and even those freed people who had passes or were under white guardianship did not escape the threat of reenslavement.

SEEKING AND SECURING FREEDOM IN THE MIDST OF WAR

[The freed people] have shown that they can appreciate freedom as the highest boon; that they will be industrious and provident with the same incitement which stimulates the industry of other men in free societies; that they understand the value of property and are eager for its acquisition, especially of land.

—BRIG. GEN. RUFUS SAXTON, December 30, 1864

As the proclamation beckoned increasing numbers of enslaved people to abandon the fields, they became problematic for the Union forces, on land and sea. In March 1863, Charles Boggs, captain of the U.S.S. *Sacramento* requested instructions from his superiors regarding the disposition of con-trabands who had escaped to his ship sailing off of Wilmington, North Carolina. "Some have come off and many more may be expected, both women and children," he warned. "Are we obliged by any law or regulation to receive all contrabands that may ask asylum?"[142] In June, Henry Walke, captain of the U.S. gunboat *Lafayette,* complained to his superiors that "some 200 contrabands have come to me for protection, whom I was obliged to receive . . . and I can feed them but a few days longer."[143] While some vessels were able to absorb a number of the able-bodied fugitive men who came aboard, none willingly accepted the burden posed by women, children, and elderly men.

As these examples attest, the escape of freed people generally challenged the ability of the Union to implement a workable solution for their care. Able-bodied men were recruited as soldiers and as military laborers, but the aged and infirm and women and children could not be similarly absorbed. Hence, the government established contraband camps to house them. In these settlements the freed people experienced the hard realities of their new status. Surrounded by squalor and harassed by Union soldiers, they were made to follow a code of conduct that hardly differed from the one that had characterized their bondage.[144]

In certain areas freed people were settled on government established plantations, where they cultivated staple crops in labor gangs under the supervision of an overseer or they worked on shares for northern speculators who had acquired abandoned lands. In his annual report to the Secretary of State, Gen. Rufus Saxton, who was in charge of overseeing the affairs of freed people in the Sea Islands off the coast of South Carolina, reported the abuses resulting from these wartime policies: "There was a general disposition among the soldiers and civilian speculators here to defraud the ne-groes in their private traffic, to take the commodities which they offered for sale by force, or to pay for them in worthless money. At one time these practices were so frequent and notorious that the negroes would not bring their produce to market for fear of being plundered. Other occurrences have tended to cool the enthusiastic joy with which the coming of the 'Yankees' was welcomed."[145]

In fact, such deprivations were a continuation of the unofficial policy pursued by military forces since the beginning of the war. The appropriating of goods essential to the army was common and legal (with vouchers), but frequently such foraging raids (carried out by both armies) proved to be little more than pillages. Henry Jenkins of South Carolina recalled that "money, silver, gold, jewelry, watches, rings, brooches, knives and forks . . . was took and carried 'way by a army dat seemed more concerned 'bout stealin' than they was 'bout de holy war for the liberation of de poor African slave people."[146] Black southerners received no consideration during these raids. Able-bodied men became victims of impressment as the Union military, always eager to find ways to strengthen its numbers, forced them to enlist. What little property enslaved people had became the possession of pilfering troops. Black women, long the victims of southern white men's lust, now fell prey to northern men. In condemning the unlawful behavior of Union troops, some of their commanders expressed more concern for the injured sensibilities of white "ladies" (many of them secessionists) than physical abuse of black women.[147]

Despite assaults on their persons and property, however, African Americans who lived and la-bored in contraband camps and on government-run plantations learned to negotiate the divide be-tween chattelhood and freedom. Through hard work and individual circumstance, a few had been able to acquire personal and real property. In the Sea Islands, lands that had been abandoned by fleeing rebels or were delinquent in tax payments were confiscated and sold at auction. Men and women who had spent their entire lives on these properties sometimes acquired the legal owner- ship that had been purchased emotionally long before by their own labor and that of their ancestors. Failure of the tax commissioners to make adequate lands available to the freed people at reasonable rates, however, resulted in most of the property falling into the hands of speculators. A poignant letter from a would-be purchaser conveys the frustration and hunger for land that the freed people experienced and suggests that they looked to the president to help them secure it: "Tell Linkum dat we wants land—dis bery land dat is rich wid de sweat ob we face and de blood ob we back. We born here; we parents' graves here; we donne oder country; dis yere our home . . . Our men—ebery able bodied man from we island—bin a fight for dere country in Florida, at Fort Wagner; any where dat Govment send um. But his dere country. Dey want land *here*."[148]

Along the coastal areas of South Carolina, Georgia, and Florida—from Charleston to Jacksonville and inland for thirty miles—Major General Sherman's Special Order Number 15 temporarily an- swered the prayers of black men and women eager to embrace economic independence. It made lots of up to forty acres available to black families through a grant of "possessory title." The order followed a meeting Sherman attended in January 1865 with Secretary of War Edwin Stanton and members of the black community—mostly ministers, many of whom had been enslaved at one time. In the in- terview that transpired, the men expressed their opinions on a variety of issues affecting themselves and black people, including how they might survive economically. They indicated that they wanted land that they could till with their own labor, and they suggested that while the young men went off to war to win Union victory, the women and children would work the land "until we are able to buy it and make it our own."[149] General Saxton had proposed the same solution a few weeks earlier. "I was early convinced . . . that to lay a sure basis for the substantial freedom and permanent improvement of the negroes, that they should be owners of the land they cultivate," he reported. "In view of their past wrongs . . . it seemed to be the dictate of simple justice that they have the highest right to a soil they have cultivated so long under the cruelest compulsion."[150] Given years of uncompensated toil, the freed people, he felt, had already paid for the land several times over.

AFRICAN AMERICANS DEFINE FREEDOM
We ask only even handed justice, and all of our wrongs will be at an end by virtue of that act.

—JOHN JONES OF ILLINOIS, November 1864

African Americans concurred with Saxton's sentiment. In addition, they believed that the Emancipa- tion Proclamation committed the nation to ensuring the justice about which Saxton spoke and to guaranteeing to blacks those rights enjoyed by other free men and women. The decree, revolution- ary enough in its declaration of freedom, held even greater significance because of this perceived promise.

African Americans believed that the proclamation's authorization of the use of black men as sol- diers was a major step toward securing those rights enjoyed by the rest of the nation. According to

Francis Carpenter, who resided in the White House for six months while he painted the president's portrait, Lincoln had expressed concern over the timing of the proclamation. "It may be viewed as the last measure of an exhausted government, a cry for help; the government stretching forth its hands to Ethiopia, instead of Ethiopia stretching forth her hands to the government," Carpenter reported him saying.[151] Indeed, from the perspective of Ethiopia, the government *was* asking for its assistance. And African Americans expected a *quid pro quo* for their efforts. Lincoln himself had recognized the justice of acknowledging their services to the nation. In a letter to Illinois friend and fellow Republican James C. Conkling, Lincoln outlined why the proclamation could not be retracted: "Negroes, like other people, act upon motives. Why should they do any thing for us, if we will do nothing for them? If they stake their lives for us, they must be prompted by the strongest motive—even the promise of freedom. And the promise being made, must be kept."[152] But African Americans defined freedom more broadly than did Lincoln and many other Americans at that time. Freedom for them was hollow absent the dignity that came with economic independence, political rights, and social equality.

Even before the proclamation was issued and they were accepted into the military, African-American men had tied their willingness to go to war to the receiving of certain rights. Some northern blacks counseled that people of color should eschew taking sides in the conflict, but "ever praying for the success of that party determined to initiate first the policy of justice and equal rights."[153] Others vowed that until they acquired those rights, "we are in no condition to fight under the flag which gives us no protection."[154] Soon after the proclamation was issued, the State Central Committee of Colored Men of Michigan met to discuss their lack of a political voice and their treatment under "odious and unjust laws."[155] The men decided to petition the Michigan legislature for abolition of laws that made references to color and for removal of the word *white* from the state constitution. Linking their willingness to provide military service to their treatment, they indicated their readiness to "obey our country's call . . . But as residents of the State of Michigan, we cannot feel willing to serve a State while it concedes all that is due to others and denies much, if not the most, that is due to us."[156]

Frederick Douglass confirmed the black perception that there was a connection between military service and the granting of full citizenship. "Once let the black man get upon his person the brass letters U.S.," Douglass averred, "let him get an eagle on his button, and a musket on his shoulder, and bullets in his pocket, and there is no power on the earth or under the earth which can deny that he has earned the right of citizenship in the United States."[157] African Americans pressed for those rights as they fought to free the enslaved. Encouraged by suffering and sacrifice on the battlefield, they sought recognition of their worth as soldiers and men.

While affording them an opportunity to prove their manhood and become liberators of their people, the military experience nevertheless demoralized many men of color. Acceptance as soldiers in the Union army exposed them to excessive fatigue duty (nonmilitary labor such as well and trench digging, unloading vessels, erecting breastworks, and draining marshes), unserviceable equipment, and harassment from fellow soldiers and the civilian population. In addition, Confederate policy stipulated that captured black soldiers be treated as slaves in insurrection rather than as prisoners of war. As such, they could be shot on the spot or sold into slavery.

The Fort Pillow Massacre of April 1864 represents an especially egregious instance of the consequences of this policy. A Union post, Fort Pillow was garrisoned by black and white troops. Outnumbered by attacking Confederate soldiers, the Union forces surrendered. William J. Mays of Company B, Thirteenth Tennessee Cavalry, gave an eyewitness account of what happened next: "We all threw down our arms and gave tokens of surrender, asking for quarter . . . But no quarter was given. Voices were heard upon all sides, crying, 'Give them no quarter; kill them; kill them, it is General Forrest's orders.' I saw 4 white men and at least 25 negroes shot while begging for mercy . . . These were all soldiers."[158] Henceforward, black men engaged the Confederate troops with the battle cry "Remember Fort Pillow!" on their lips.

Pay inequities were particularly irritating to black men, especially those who had known freedom before the war and whose families' survival depended solely on that income. White enlisted men earned thirteen dollars and a clothing allowance each month; black soldiers received ten, three dollars of which could be deducted for clothing. The policy reflected payments made to military laborers, which had been authorized by Congress. In a September 1863 letter to Lincoln, Cpl. James Henry Gooding of the 54th Massachusetts expressed the frustrations of many of his comrades-in-arms over disparate treatment: "The patient, trusting descendant of Afric's Clime have dyed the ground with blood, in defence of the Union, and Democracy. Men, too, your Excellency, who know in a measure the cruelties of the iron heel of oppression, which in years gone by, the very power their blood is now being spilled to maintain, ever ground them in the dust."[159] The letter followed the assault of the 54th on Fort Wagner, where black soldiers had continued to advance on the enemy in the face of unrelenting firepower. Gooding reminded Lincoln of the patriotism shown by those and other black men, even as the nation declined to acknowledge their right to equal treatment: "But when the war trumpet sounded o'er the land, when men knew not the Friend from the Traitor, the Black man laid his life at the altar of the nation,—and he was refused . . . And now he is in the War, and how has he conducted himself? . . . Let the rich mound around Wagner's parapets be upturned, and there will be found an eloquent answer. Obedient and patient and solid as a wall are they. All we lack is a Paler hue and a better acquaintance with the alphabet . . . we have done A Soldier's duty. Why can't we have a Soldier's pay?"[160]

At that moment, a bill that addressed the pay inequity was before Congress, and Gooding and his comrades had hoped that the president's influence would help their cause. Frederick Douglass thought similarly. In a visit to the White House in August 1863, he laid before Lincoln the case of injustices done to the black soldier, including pay inequity. The president's response was familiarly conservative and cautious. He reminded Douglass that "popular prejudice" had been against the enlistment of black troops at all and that the inequity in pay was a "necessary concession" to public opinion. The black man's special purpose for entering the war, the president felt, should render him willing to serve under any conditions. In time, Lincoln promised, men of color would receive equal pay.[161]

While they waited for the president and the rest of America to treat them as soldiers, the men of the 54th and 55th Massachusetts decided that they would accept no pay until the nation prepared to grant them equal compensation. Even when Governor Andrew of Massachusetts intervened and convinced the state legislature to appropriate funds to supplement the pay of black soldiers, the men declined. So frustrating did the issue become that a few black men stacked their guns and refused to obey orders. The leaders of such demonstrations faced court-martial and paid with their lives. Finally, in June 1864, after much lobbying by progressive Republican leaders such as Thaddeus Stevens, Congress passed legislation ensuring equal pay for all Union soldiers and guaranteed as well that black men would receive the same clothing, equipment, arms, and rations as others in military service.[162]

African-American soldiers also pressed to be led by men of their own race. Although the exigencies of war demanded that black troops be used to save the Union, few whites seriously entertained the notion that black men were capable of serving as commissioned officers. During the course of the war, fewer than one hundred of them attained a rank above sergeant, and then primarily in the medical corps or as chaplains.[163] Enlisted men did not suffer this indignity in silence. "We want black commissioned officers," demanded one anonymous sergeant. "We want men we can understand, and who can understand us . . . We want to demonstrate our ability to rule, as we have demonstrated our willingness to obey."[164] Despite the passage of an act in early 1863 which stipulated that "No person of African descent shall be considered as an officer of the United States except company officers" (hence, excluding blacks from field grade ranks), Douglass counseled black men to challenge this "contemptible concession to the colour madness of the country" by entering military service. This was, he argued, "the speediest and best way to overcome the prejudice which has dictated unjust laws against us."[165]

As black men fought for freedom for the enslaved and the extension of full citizenship to all people of color, civilians pressed the cause at home. In the weeks and months following the pronouncement of emancipation, men and women of color expressed a new sense of empowerment. They faced challenges to their birthright forcefully and with assurance. One of the earliest examples of that new confidence came in July 1863, when rioting broke out in the city of New York. The immediate impetus for the violence was the opposition of poor whites, the Irish especially, to conscription. In March, Congress had passed an act that made it possible for men of means to avoid conscription by paying $300 or by securing a substitute. Poor men had no recourse but to serve or protest. Drafted to fight a war that would inure to the benefit of African Americans (since the issuance of the Emancipation Proclamation), they did not bear the burden without protest. Racial hatred inflamed by economic competition and an American culture that encouraged immigrants to denigrate blacks had resulted in long-standing antagonisms between the Irish and African Americans. During the four-day rampage, the protesters burned the draft building; murdered African Americans, attacking men, women and children indiscriminately; assaulted persons sympathetic to people of color; destroyed black-owned businesses and homes; and torched a facility that housed black orphaned children. When the rampage was finally quelled by Union troops, dozens of people lay dead.[166]

The riot elicited a strong response from members of the black community in New York and beyond. Asserting the rights of African Americans to an American patrimony, James W. C. Pennington, a black Presbyterian minister who resided in New York, blamed opposition to the draft on the foreign born. "Let the greedy foreigner know that a part of this country BELONGS TO US," he declared. "That in New York and other cities, we claim the right to buy, hire, occupy and use houses and tenements, for legal considerations; to pass and repass on the streets, lanes, avenues, and all public ways." Pennington reminded America that black men had fought to free the country from British tyranny and were now fighting to keep it free from southern treachery. He left no doubt about black men's expectations regarding their involvement in the war: "We are doing so with the distinct understanding that WE ARE

TO HAVE ALL OUR RIGHTS AS MEN AND AS CITIZENS, and that there are to be no side issues, no RESERVATIONS, either political, civil, or religious. In this struggle we know nothing but God, Manhood, and American Nationality, full and unimpaired."[167]

Throughout the North, African Americans demanded an adjustment to their legal status. In Lincoln's own Illinois they moved to overturn the state's black laws, which included a measure prohibiting the immigration of people of color. In California, local blacks challenged the law denying court testimony involving white men. And in Philadelphia, they challenged segregation in the operation of streetcars. Black petitioners complained that while young black men fought to exterminate slavery, their people were routinely excluded from or segregated on the rail lines. Protests eventually attracted the attention of the state legislature, and two years after the war ended, discrimination in public transportation was outlawed in the city.[168]

If the proclamation encouraged black men to assert their manhood and fight for citizenship, it held equal promise for black women. In addition to facing the same discrimination as men, free women of color in the North suffered from the added proscription of gender bias. The "cult of domesticity," which defined the ideal for middle class white women of the antebellum era, applied to few women of African descent. Most black women led lives sobered by economic realities. Like their men, they believed that slavery's demise and the elevation of the former bondsmen and women would inevitably enhance their own standing in the society.

Hence, free women in the North did what they could to ensure Union victory and ease the transition from slavery to freedom. The fund-raising efforts of women such as Elizabeth Keckley (Mary Todd Lincoln's dressmaker) provided black troops and contrabands relief from their suffering. Keckley, who had purchased her freedom before the war, founded the Contraband Relief Association, successfully solicited a significant contribution ($200) from Mrs. Lincoln, and inspired other groups to initiate relief efforts for the freed people. Harriet Jacobs, Sojourner Truth, and others dispensed aid and wisdom directly to the black refugees in the various camps that dotted the nation's capital. Members of the tiny black elite, such as Charlotte Forten, traveled to Union-occupied territory in the South and facilitated the freed people's transition from ignorance by teaching them to read. Harriet Tubman, the intrepid deliverer of enslaved people out of bondage in the decades before the war, returned to the South as a guide, scout, and spy for the Union forces. Not content to rest on her past exploits in ferrying fugitives via the underground railroad, her wartime actions facilitated the liberation of hundreds more along coastal South Carolina.

Enslaved women welcomed Lincoln's proclamation of freedom for reasons unique to their circumstances. Exposed to a labor regimen that tested their endurance, forced to suffer the separation of their families through sale, subjected to the sexual abuse of white men (and labeled as licentious because of it), African-American women held a particularly aggrieved position under slavery. As the course of the war made flight available to them, they seized the opportunity to abscond. A desire to bequeath to their children the freedom heretofore denied to themselves doubtless motivated many to seek asylum with the Union. Invariably, when women fugitives sought refuge within Union lines, they came with children and infants in arms, tied to backs, and keeping pace at their sides.[169] Once they reached the Union camps they experienced a mixed reception, but in some instances they were permitted to work for wages and were afforded opportunities unknown to them in bondage.

The women who remained behind on the plantations and farms saw their lives altered by the proclamation as well. If few exhibited the bravery and audacity of one woman who purportedly pulled up her dress and invited her owner to "Kiss my ass,"[170] others enjoyed the simple pleasure of being treated with dignity and respect. When Eliza Sparks recounted her wartime experiences, she remembered an encounter with a Union soldier who honored her by adding the title "Mrs." to her name.[171]

African Americans such as "Mrs." Sparks saw their newfound freedom as the impetus for moral uplift of a race debased by slavery. While in bondage they had been stripped of the ability to choose and remain faithful to mates, endured separation from loved ones, and suffered the abrogation of their rights as parents. Freedom would enable husbands and wives to enjoy the sanctity of marriage, black feminine virtue would be protected, and fathers and mothers would be able to exercise authority over their children.[172] Free blacks expected to benefit from this moral uplift as well, since slavery had tarnished the image of all people of color.

LINCOLN BECOMES THE "GREAT EMANCIPATOR"
I know that I am free, for I have seen Father Abraham and felt him.

—Anonymous Woman in Richmond, April 1865

Even before the war commenced, African Americans had, in Douglass's estimation, "given Mr. Lincoln credit for having intentions toward them far more benevolent and just than any he is known to cherish."[173] From the moment Lincoln issued the Emancipation Proclamation, African Americans were convinced that they had an ally in the White House. Expecting to be the beneficiaries of the president's special protection, they looked to him to shield them from the wrath of former masters and to facilitate their transition from bondage to freedom. Beyond this, they felt that a direct appeal to him would elicit a response.

Nowhere was that confidence in the president more emphatic than among the freed people of the South Carolina Sea Islands. In 1864, General Saxton, cataloguing the troubles of these people freed by the proclamation, observed that "amid all their griefs and disappointments they seem to have kept bright their faith in Mr. Lincoln. Their hope and confidence in him never wavers. They regard him as their great friend and deliverer, who, though often thwarted in his purposes of good by malign influences, will at last bring them to the promised land."[174] Instructions to the northern missionary who was tasked with delivering the freed people's request that Lincoln assist their efforts to acquire land, reveal the level of their faith in and esteem for him: "Speak to Linkum and tell him for we how we po'folks tank him and de Lord for we great privilege . . . De word cum from Massa Linkum's self, dat we take out claims and hold on ter um, an' plant um, and he will see dat we get um . . . but fore de time for plant, dese missionaries sells to white folks all de best land. [A]x Linkum for stretch out he hand an' make dese yer missionaries cut de land so dat we able for buy . . . ax Linkum for send us *his* word, and den we satisfy."[175]

While former slaves looked to Lincoln for protection of their interests, others worried that the proclamation would not survive legal challenge after the restoration of peace. In addition, despite flight and the granting of freedom as a consequence of service in the military, hundreds of thousands not touched by the document still remained enslaved in the border states. West Virginia, when it entered the Union in 1863, and Maryland and Missouri in 1864, finally brought satisfaction to the president by freeing their bondsmen and women. But proponents of freedom pressed vociferously for a constitutional amendment that would ensure a universal and uncontestable emancipation. Lincoln initially remained silent as senators debated the issue, and he declined to intervene in support of the amendment during the early House deliberations on the matter.[176] But at the national presidential convention, which met in Baltimore in June 1864, Lincoln publicly supported the idea of a constitutional amendment prohibiting slavery by encouraging its inclusion in the Republican platform. Moreover, he personally lobbied Democrats and others either undecided or opposed to it. In his message to Congress in December 1864, he reiterated his belief that it was "only a question of *time* as to when the proposed amendment will go to the States for their action" but suggested that the quicker Congress acted, the better.[177] At the end of January 1865, Congress obliged by passing the Thirteenth Amendment, which won ratification by the requisite number of states on December 18.

The Thirteenth Amendment never captured the imagination of black men and women as had the Emancipation Proclamation. Since Lincoln's election, the enslaved had overheard their owners expressing fear that the new president would end slavery. When he issued the proclamation, expectations that had been building from the beginning of the war were realized. In the two years after the decree appeared, Lincoln's reputation as emancipator solidified among African Americans; by war's end, his celebrity among them had reached a near godlike level. Many believed that he, with God's guidance, had "set all us slaves free."[178] That belief found expression when on April 4, 1865, Lincoln visited the fallen Confederate capital at Richmond. As he passed through the streets, a multitude of freedmen and women, still exuberant over their liberation, surrounded him. Thomas Morris Chester, a black Civil War correspondent attached to the Army of the James, witnessed the event and dispatched the following report to his newspaper, the Philadelphia *Press:* "The colored population was wild with enthusiasm. Old men thanked God in a very boisterous manner, and old women shouted upon the pavement as high as they had ever done at a religious revival . . . There were many whites in the crowd, but they were lost in the great concourse of American citizens of African descent . . . One enthusiastic old negro woman exclaimed: "I know that I am free, for I have seen Father Abraham and felt him."[179]

J. J. Hill, an orderly attached to the 29th Connecticut Colored Infantry, offered similar observations of black Richmond's reactions to Lincoln: "As the President passed along the street the colored people waved their handkerchiefs, hats and bonnets, and expressed their gratitude by shouting repeatedly, 'Thank God for his goodness; we have seen his salvation . . . ' It was a great deliverer among the delivered . . . They were earnest and heartfelt expressions of gratitude to Almighty God . . . thousands of colored men in Richmond would have laid down their lives for President Lincoln."[180] Less than two weeks later, Booth's bullet ended the president's life and threatened African Americans' newfound sense of security. Black people lamented Lincoln's passing, sensing in it perhaps the decline, if not death, of their own prospects for full inclusion in American society. Across the North, men and women of color donned mourning clothes and displayed black ribbons over their doors. Wherever Lincoln's funeral train stopped in its twelve-day journey to Springfield, African Americans gathered with the crowds paying their respects. Both former slaves and free men and women helped to raise money to erect monuments to the martyred president, the most significant contribution being made for the establishing of the Freedmen's Memorial, which stands in Lincoln Park, Washington, D.C., and was paid for almost exclusively by African Americans.[181] "The colored people have lost their best friend on earth," lamented Charlotte Scott. The former slave would pledge five dollars of her own meager earnings to the memorial fund.[182]

Concern over Lincoln's death, however, did not slow the African-American quest for equality. In fact, black reaction to the Freedmen's Memorial itself suggests that they saw for themselves a role in the reunited nation that clashed with white American assumptions. Despite their financing of the memorial, African Americans were allowed no voice in its design. Hence, when it was unveiled on April 14, 1876, some took issue with its image of a half-kneeling slave, beckoned by an emancipating president to rise up. Douglass, who delivered the oration at its unveiling, later declared that the memorial was too suggestive of subservience and dependency because "it showed the Negro on his knees when a more manly attitude would have been indicative of freedom."[183] African Americans were determined to achieve that "more manly attitude" in the coming years.

FREEDOM'S CHALLENGES IN THE POSTWAR ERA

The slave, having ceased to be the abject slave of a slave master, his enemies will endeavor to make him the slave of society at large.

—FREDERICK DOUGLASS, January 1863

In the months after Lincoln's assassination and the war's conclusion, African Americans sought to come to terms with the realities of their new lives. The passage of the Thirteenth Amendment solidified the statutory freedom that the Emancipation Proclamation had promised. But although legally released from the constraints of bondage, freed men and women continued to suffer from proscriptive measures. During the Johnson administration, defeated but impenitent former Confederates imposed black codes, which aimed to remove the sting of the lost cause and retain much of the old system of exploitation and discrimination. Destitute and uneducated former bondsmen and women stood little chance of success in this postwar environment, even with the help of federal troops of occupation and with the assistance rendered by the Freedmen's Bureau. Freedmen often were forced by necessity to occupy the same housing as they had when enslaved, and they worked in gang-labor arrangements for the very men and women who had held them in bondage. Corporal punishment continued as before, as southern whites (and northern men eager to exploit black labor) refused to concede to the freedmen's new status. Despite the protests of parents, freed children were returned to the quasi-slavery of apprenticeship. The newly emancipated were subjected to curfews and were denied the right to vote, hold office, and serve on juries. Economic independence proved virtually impossible because the freed people had little if any money to purchase land. Even when they were financially capable, whites often would not sell to them.

Lincoln anticipated such difficulties in the transition of the bondsman and woman from slavery to freedom. For most of his public life, he had argued that immediate emancipation would be detrimental to the freed people as well as the nation. Hence, in the final months of the war, he formulated a plan of Reconstruction that would allay the fears of whites, North and South, and provide what he considered to be a "reasonable" accommodation for the freed people. Lincoln's untimely demise before offering a full explanation of these adjustments has allowed historians to propose widely divergent interpretations of what the president wished for the former slaves in the aftermath of war. What is apparent from private letters and public addresses is that Lincoln favored a transition that, as usual, would be gradual, cautious, and acceptable to white Americans.

African Americans had a different view of their future. While enslaved, they had been denied control over their lives and their labor; the free men and women among them had suffered second-class citizenship. African Americans determined that a political voice and economic independence were essential to true freedom. Speaking before the annual meeting of the American Anti-Slavery Society in December 1863, Douglass warned that the work of the organization was not done. "A mightier work than the abolition of slavery now looms up before the Abolitionist," he reminded them. "When we have taken the chains off the slave, as I believe we shall do, we shall find a harder resistance to the second purpose of this great association." The work would be complete only when "the black men of the South, and the black men of the north, shall have been admitted, fully and completely, into the body politic of America."[184] Douglass countered the contention that ignorance and previous condition ill prepared blacks to exercise the rights accorded to other citizens: "In saying this, you lay down a rule for the black man that you apply to no other class of your citizens . . . If he knows enough to take up arms in defence of this Government, and bare his breast to the storm of rebel artillery, he knows enough to vote."[185] Douglass implored the nation to treat black men fairly, applying the same conditions of voting to them as to whites. In an appeal to the Republican Party's interest in building a solid political base in the South, he reminded them that they would need and benefit from the black man's vote.[186]

Black men pressed the cause of enfranchisement even more forcefully at a national convention held at Syracuse, New York, in October 1864. The delegation of 144 men from 18 states demanded an end to slavery and drew up a damning list of black people's grievances. "We have been denounced as incurably ignorant, and at the same time . . . debarred from taking even the first step toward self-enlightenment and personal and national elevation," they complained. "When the nation in her trial hour called her sable sons to arms, we gladly went to fight her battles, but were denied the pay accorded others, until public opinion demanded it; and then it was tardily granted."[187] In a message to their fellow Americans, the delegates exhibited their unease over "the weakness of our friends" who "fail to demand, from any reason, equal liberty in every respect!"[188] Had the Republican Party and the Lincoln administration acted in the beginning of the war to secure human equality, they charged, the abuse and injustices visited upon African Americans over the three years might have been allayed. The men at Syracuse appealed especially for the elective franchise, believing that "in the matter of government, the object of which is the protection and security of human rights, prejudice should be allowed no voice whatever."[189]

Other black men appealed directly to Lincoln in their quest for political equality. In May 1864 a group from North Carolina petitioned the president for a return "without detriment" of the political rights they had enjoyed in the state prior to 1835. They pledged to continue their aid to the country during the crisis and beseeched the president to "finish the noble work" he had begun by granting black men the right to vote.[190]

Louisiana's application for readmission to the Union in 1864 provided Lincoln with an opportunity to influence decision making regarding the franchise for black men. In the now-famous letter to Michael Hahn, who had been elected governor of the state in early 1864, the president broached the question of voting rights: "I barely suggest for your private consideration, whether some of the colored people may not be let in—as, for instance, the very intelligent, and especially those who have fought gallantly in our ranks. They would probably help, in some trying time to come, to keep the jewel of liberty within the family of freedom. But this is only a suggestion, not to the public, but to you alone."[191] The letter to Hahn was sent after representatives of New Orleans' free black (heavily mulatto) community presented a petition to Lincoln asking for his assistance in their fight for enfranchisement. In making their claim for full citizenship, the men boasted of their ownership of real and personal property, acquisition of education, gainful employment, and long-term service to the nation, including in the current war.[192] While Lincoln's message to Hahn clearly revealed his support of their cause, the tone of the letter indicated that the president was unwilling to chance a political backlash from those resistant to extending political rights to blacks. It came as a surprise to few that the state's new constitution failed to enfranchise black men.

In his last public address on April 11, 1865, Lincoln maintained that although the new government was not perfect, it was a first step. He desired to see some degree of enfranchisement of African Americans but argued that granting the state readmission into the Union would move black men more swiftly toward political participation.[193] Lincoln would not live to see the enfranchisement of black men, but his martyrdom gave African Americans an opportunity to press aggressively for political rights. On the July 4 following his death, thousands of blacks joined congressmen, members of the judiciary, and other government officials on the White House grounds. It was the first time that the vast majority of African Americans were able to celebrate as a free people the nation's birth. The gathering had been organized by a black association dedicated to preserving and celebrating Lincoln's memory. Seizing the moment, they took the occasion to voice their argument for full inclusion into American society. The opening prayer of Elder D. W. Anderson of the Nineteenth Street Baptist Church set the tone for the rest of the day. He beseeched God to give Andrew Johnson "light to see that there are constitutional rights for loyal men who are so by nature, as well as for those who are made so by the taking of an oath which they hate."[194] One of the principal speakers, New York attorney William Howard Day, reminded those assembled that "the Declaration of Independence is not yet fully carried out, nor will it be, until . . . the black man, as well as the white, is permitted to enjoy all the franchises pertaining to citizens of the United States of America." Letters of support from absent abolitionists such as Gerrit Smith, Charles Sumner, Salmon P. Chase, and Frederick Douglass were read aloud. Douglass's letter urged the group to remember that "justice and national honor" demanded the "immediate, complete, and universal enfranchisement of the colored people" throughout the entire nation.[195]

For the next few years, African Americans continued to agitate for enfranchisement. Foremost among their organizations in this regard was the National Equal Rights League, founded in 1865 and presided over by Ohio's John Mercer Langston. The league pledged to "encourage sound morality, education, temperance, frugality, industry, and promote every thing that pertains to a well-ordered and dignified life." Its primary aim, however, was to secure "a recognition of the rights of the colored people of the nation as American citizens," either by legal means or by appealing to the minds and conscience of whites.[196] National and state affiliates of the league met annually to formulate strategies for attaining their goal, including lobbying Congress and President Johnson. The latter showed his contempt for any effort to extend the franchise to black men when in February 1866 a delegation consisting of prominent black leaders called on him at the White House. Johnson rebuffed their argument that blacks bore the burdens of citizenship but none of the privileges. He declared that he had sacrificed much for black people and bristled at the idea of being "arraigned by some who can get up handsomely-rounded periods and deal in rhetoric, and talk about abstract ideas of liberty, who never periled life, liberty, or property."[197]

The franchise came not as a consequence of appeals to President Johnson, nor by working with the former Confederate states (as Lincoln had imagined), but rather it came at the hands of those in Lincoln's own party, many of whom had been guided by considerations of political advantage. Radical Republicans, concerned that an unrepentant South stood to regain its original power in Congress and politically challenge the victors, moved to secure citizenship for blacks through the Fourteenth Amendment to the Constitution and to enfranchise black men by means of the Fifteenth Amendment. African Americans in the South became the backbone of the Republican Party, sometimes nominating and voting for candidates of their own race but often supporting whites whom the party felt were best suited for governing. While a few black men captured high office, most won local elections. Once state governments returned to the hands of the former Confederates, the fate of the black voter and officeholder was sealed. Disfranchisement did not come immediately, but over the course of years, through violence, intimidation, and finally by legislation, African Americans were rendered politically voiceless.[198]

The extraordinary level of black agitation for political rights in the postemancipation era overshadows the degree to which the freed people desired and sought economic opportunity. If it appears, as some have suggested, that former slaves were more concerned with the ballot than equal access to the land, than perhaps it is because the franchise was promoted primarily by men who were burdened less by economic constraints than by lack of adequate political rights.[199] Their struggle found expression in the state and national convention movements and in public addresses, venues covered copiously by the press. Illiterate freed people's aspirations for land and economic independence were exhibited frequently in dictated and poorly worded appeals to local government officials and, of course, to Lincoln himself. Former slaves understood that their rights, even to the land, ultimately could only be protected by the franchise, but daily realities also impressed upon them the need to secure a livelihood that was worth protecting. While many freed people saw economic security and political rights as necessary components of full citizenship, the vote alone would not have held a great attraction for them absent the opportunity to earn a respectable and unencumbered living.

As enslaved people, African Americans had been defined by the value of their labor. As freedmen and women, they engendered doubt in the minds of whites that blacks would continue to work without the incentive provided by the lash. Lincoln had recognized the potential problems that a new economic order might create. His plan for circumventing them was as conservative as the one he proposed for securing political rights. Despite earlier doubts that the two races could coexist, he apparently surmised in early 1863 that former owners would treat freedmen and women fairly. In a letter to Maj. Gen. John McClernand just eight days after issuing the proclamation, Lincoln indicated that he could not retract the document. He did suggest, however, that even the states affected by the proclamation "need not to be hurt by it." He suggested that they "adopt systems of apprenticeship for the colored people, conforming substantially to the most approved plans of gradual emancipation." With aid from the government, he declared, "[the secessionists] may be nearly as well off . . .as if the present trouble had not occurred."[200] Seven months later, in a letter penned to Gen. Nathaniel P. Banks (commanding the Department of the Gulf) Lincoln intimated his wish to see a reconstructed Louisiana implement a "probationary period" in which contractual agreements between blacks and whites would characterize a "practical system by which the two races could gradually live themselves out of their old relation to each other."[201] In a second letter to Banks a few months later, Lincoln reiterated his willingness to accept "a reasonable temporary arrangement" for economically dependent blacks.[202] And on December 8 of the same year, in his annual message to Congress, the president justified this gradualist approach to economic independence by suggesting that such an arrangement would limit the "confusion and destitution which must, at best attend all classes by a total revolution of labor throughout whole States." Seeking to conciliate the South, he "hoped that the already deeply afflicted people in those States may be somewhat more ready to give up the cause of their affliction, if, to this extent, this vital matter be left to themselves.[203] Perhaps sensing possible trouble, Lincoln indicated that his reconstruction plan did not abridge the power of the president to prevent abuse.

In formulating this plan of reconstruction, Lincoln did not seek the counsel of the freed people themselves. Had he the opportunity (and inclination) to do so he would have been informed that a period of apprenticeship would not work for a people already impatient for economic independence. Neither did the president consider the varieties of ability and experiences that former bondsmen and women possessed. Instead, guided by nineteenth-century views of black ignorance and incompetence in regard to their own care and pursuing a conciliatory stance toward the South, he took a conservative approach to black economic development. It was not easily distinguishable from Judah P. Benjamin's plan to reward blacks who might be called on to serve the combative needs of the Confederacy.

African Americans did not share Lincoln's opinion of their abilities. For most of them, freedom without the opportunity to shape materially the terms and conditions of their labor hardly improved upon bondage. Their experiences with free labor during the war—gang units, fieldwork for women, corporal punishment, and other vestiges of slavery—had not reassured them that they might enjoy fair play with the return of peace.

Following their own desires, African Americans sought some degree of economic independence from former owners and whites in general. Realizing that this could be best accomplished by access to land, the freed people made every effort to acquire it. Unable to afford to purchase the entire estates offered by landowners, they attempted to pool their meager resources (often acquired from military bounties for reenlistment) or waited until a white man facing economic hardship decided to divide his acreage and consent to sell to blacks. Others entered the landholding class by purchasing the minuscule holdings of black men who had been free and had acquired property before the war. Most, however, waited for the government to reward their loyal service as soldiers with the sound economic foundation provided by landownership. Their aspirations met with bitter disappointment as lands the freed people thought would eventually be theirs were returned to their former Confederate owners.[204]

The return of most confiscated lands to their original owners increased the likelihood that freed people's access to cultivatable acreage would be limited primarily to what they could rent through the system of sharecropping. Sharecropping as a system of labor may have won a grudging acceptance from the majority of African Americans, but it satisfied neither their economic nor their psychological needs for land ownership. Despite the suggestion that blacks used labor shortages during the postwar era to pressure planters into acceptance of the system over a more restrictive, less independent form of labor, sharecropping was a negotiated settlement between people of unequal status, with the former slave occupying the lower position. Far from being a boon to freed people, it was merely an inferior alternative to land ownership.

The belief that they would be granted forty acres and a mule for years of uncompensated labor sustained some black people and kept them close to the lands that they had cultivated under slavery. Although a few purchased modest acreage and cultivated it on their own terms, the vast majority remained tenants or landless wage earners whose economic viability rested with the proclivities of former planters and northern whites who gained possession of marketable lands.[205] In an environment in which economic independence and social standing equated to landownership, most African Americans stood little chance of realizing the freedom that they felt the Emancipation Proclamation promised.

In his proclamation of amnesty and in his letter to General Banks in August 1863, Lincoln had also broached the possibility of education for the former slaves. Perhaps his own humble beginnings and limited education shaped his appreciation for the difficulty the newly emancipated would face as they moved from chattel to citizen. African Americans themselves also measured their freedom by the degree of access to education. Denial of literacy under slavery had left the freed people ignorant and dependent on the very persons who wished them the least success. If age and the necessities of earning a living precluded the adults from becoming literate, they determined to make learning essential in the lives of their children and grandchildren. In March 1865 Lincoln signed into law a bill that created the Freedmen's Bureau, the agency that, among other things, played a major role in establishing grammar schools and institutions of higher learning for the children of the freed people. Normal schools such as Hampton Institute and universities such as Howard and Fisk provided "training for life" and honed the leadership skills of generations of African Americans as a consequence of early support from the Freedmen's Bureau.

Education was held in such high regard in the African-American community that its leaders considered as a fitting tribute to Lincoln's memory a "Colored People's National Monument . . . a monument not of marble nor of brass merely, but a monument of Education . . . a seat of learning, dedicated to God, to Literature, and to the Arts and Sciences."[206] The monument—to be erected in the nation's capital and known as the National Lincoln Memorial Institute—was to be built for the education of the children of the freemen and freedmen, and their descendants. In the spring of 1865, prominent black leaders in the city, including the Rev. Henry Highland Garnet (at that time pastor of the Fifteenth Street Presbyterian Church), met and formed the Colored People's Educational Monument Association in Memory of Abraham Lincoln. Black leaders such as Frederick Douglass and George Downing of New York, and Robert Smalls of South Carolina, represented their states as vice presidents of the national organization.

In the committee's appeal for funds, it asserted that "in no other way can the people of color so well perpetuate the memory of Abraham Lincoln, as by carrying out, in this manner, the great aim he had in view—the elevation of their race throughout the land."[207] Apparently others agreed, for black newspapers such as the *Christian Recorder* periodically reported on donations that came into the organization. For several months, the committee ran weekly advertisements; such appeals stopped abruptly in the spring of 1866. In a letter to the editor of the *Christian Recorder* one suspicious reader wondered if perhaps a certain J. B. Smith of Boston had absconded with the funds. In any case, a National Lincoln Memorial Institute never materialized under the auspices of the Colored People's Educational Monument Association. Instead, an institution of higher learning was established a year later through the efforts of a group of men affiliated with the First Congregational Society of Washington, D.C. Prominent among them was Oliver Otis Howard, former Union general and at that time director of the Freedmen's Bureau. General Howard would lend his name to the new university and eventually would become its third president.

A PROMISE UNFULFILLED

It was once said by Abraham Lincoln that this republic could not long endure half slave and half free, and the same may be said with even more truth of the black citizens of this country. They cannot remain half slave and half free. They must be one thing or the other.

—FREDERICK DOUGLASS, 1889

As Reconstruction drew to a close, African Americans paused to reflect on their progress in the decade since emancipation. The hope and promise they had felt in 1865 had given way to a certain degree of pessimism. Correspondingly, the sentimentality that followed the president's assassination had been replaced by a more critical assessment of Lincoln's role in securing a just future for people of color. Although following Lincoln's death Douglass had declared him "emphatically the black man's President," conditions had altered his opinion over the following decade. In his address at the dedication of the Freedmen's Memorial to the martyred president on April 14, 1876, he praised Lincoln for ultimately embracing liberty as well as Union but pointed out that the president had initially been "more zealous in his efforts to protect slavery than to suppress rebellion." The president had been willing to "deny, postpone, and sacrifice the rights and humanity of the colored people to promote the welfare of the white people of this country."[208]

Douglass expressed even greater frustration a dozen years later on the twenty-sixth anniversary of emancipation in the District of Columbia. Citing the abuses endured and the constraints under which African Americans suffered throughout the nation, he contended that the former slave had made little progress: "He is the victim of a cunningly devised swindle, one which paralyzes his energies, suppresses his ambition, and blasts all his hopes; and though he is nominally free he is actually a slave. I here and now denounce his so-called emancipation as a stupendous fraud—a fraud upon him, a fraud upon the world. It was not so meant by Abraham Lincoln; it was not so meant by the Republican Party; but whether so meant or not, it is practically a lie, keeping the word of promise to the ear and breaking it to the heart."[209] Douglass's severe assessment of the condition of black people in the late nineteenth century followed his tour of two southern states where the operation of the new economic system reduced the former bondsmen and women to quasi-slavery. Low wages that made even subsistence difficult to achieve; the use of scrip that was honored only at one store, for a limited period of time; an accounting system that cheated the ignorant and illiterate; and the operation of crop-lien, imperiled the economic independence of the farmer who rented the lands he cultivated. Douglass appealed to the Republican Party to address the plight of the aggrieved black man and to place men in office who were committed to protecting the rights of all Americans.[210]

Douglass died a few years later, having failed to see his dream of a just America, a land of true equality, realized. The men and women who followed him continued the struggle in their own way. They understood that the America of the late nineteenth century would have to be coaxed into living up to the perceived promise of 1863. The most powerful of these leaders—Booker T. Washington—encouraged whites in their belief that black men and women were willing to occupy a place of social and political inferiority for the privilege of enjoying economic opportunity.[211] In a desperate effort to arrest the suffering of his people at the hands of the children of the vanquished, he adopted the plan Lincoln himself had pursued during the first several months of the war: he attempted to appease southern white men. For two decades, the "great accommodationist" urged the children of the formerly enslaved to earn the respect of white Americans through hard work and thrift, and counseled them to forego demands for full citizenship.

For good measure, Washington invoked the name of Lincoln, less because he wanted to remind Americans of the unrealized promise than because he wanted to convince white southerners that black men wanted nothing more than to be able to earn a decent living while residing among them. "Like Lincoln, the Negro race should seek to be simple, without bigotry and without ostentation," Washington declared.[212]

As Washington attempted to shape African Americans into ebony Lincolns, blacks faced the stark reality of lynch law and the denial of their human rights. Race riots became nearly ubiquitous, occurring in places as far flung as Springfield, Illinois (the home of Lincoln), and Atlanta. Legislatively sanctioned discrimination stripped African Americans of any legal means to thwart the attack on their rights.[213] Hence, as the nation prepared to celebrate the centennial of Lincoln's birth in 1909, African Americans joined with prominent white proponents of black rights in calling for a Lincoln Emancipation Conference. Organizers proposed that the conference assess the extent to which the nation had "lived up to the obligations imposed upon it by the Emancipation Proclamation." Black participants such as Ida B. Wells-Barnett (leading antilynching advocate), W. E. B. DuBois (scholar and chief critic of the Tuskegee machine headed by Booker T. Washington), and clergy (including the Rev. Francis Grimké and Bishop Alexander Walters), hoped for a "discussion of present evils, the voicing of protests, and renewal of the struggle for civil and political liberty."[214] The two-day conference—eventually renamed the National Negro Conference—met in New York on May 31. Out of it evolved the white-dominated National Association for the Advancement of Colored People, an organization that would provide the leadership for the fight against discrimination for the next half-century. Choosing to maintain his accommodationist stance, Booker T. Washington stayed away.

Four years later, on the fiftieth anniversary of the issuance of the Emancipation Proclamation, African Americans again seized the opportunity to remind the nation of the unfulfilled promise. Speaking before the Massachusetts legislature on the occasion of Lincoln's birthday, William H. Lewis, assistant attorney general of the United States, presented a message that was both disparaging and hope-filled. Lewis recounted the disabilities under which black men and women suffered on account of the color of their skin: popular sentiment ran counter to the Constitution and the principles of democracy, the right of black men to vote on the same basis as white men failed to gain acceptance in many areas of the nation, and the African American remained segregated, either by law or custom.[215] He argued that black people had fulfilled their obligations; they had justified Lincoln's faith in them. It was now left to the American people, Lewis believed, to grow more like Lincoln "in charity, justice, and righteousness." In so doing, they would "complete Emancipation of the Negro from the disabilities of color."[216]

But America did not heed Lewis's charge, and the disabilities black men and women faced mounted as the century progressed. Those who engaged in the great exodus out of the South in the early decades of the twentieth century (flight fueled by physical abuse and the absence of social justice, a political voice, and economic opportunity) found disappointment and a host of new challenges in the North. Unemployment and underemployment, *de facto* segregation, and brazen discrimination pushed African Americans further to the periphery of society and left them to solve problems of mammoth proportions. Group violence, especially as evidenced by the spate of race riots that threatened to engulf the nation at the end of World War I, hindered African Americans from seeing themselves as anything other than America's unwanted stepchildren. Disillusionment replaced faith in the proclamation and its author, especially as the party of Lincoln increasingly adopted the racial attitudes of southern (and northern) segregationists. *Pittsburgh Courier* editor Robert Vann's 1932 admonition to African Americans that they should "go turn Lincoln's picture to the wall" because the debt had been paid, signaled not only the black community's shift toward the Democratic Party but also reflected the decline of black infatuation with the "Great Emancipator."[217]

As Merrill Peterson has suggested in his seminal work on Lincoln's place in American memory, the modern Civil Rights Movement doubtless influenced the changing black perception of the icon by giving people of color the opportunity to embrace heroes within their own community.[218] Perhaps equally as important, disaffection with and indifference to Lincoln reflected black people's unwillingness to continue to occupy a position as probationary Americans. During a century of proving themselves "worthy" candidates for induction in the national family, they finally lost patience with gradualism and considerations of public opinion. They came to understand, as perhaps Lincoln himself did in 1865, that the nation would not willingly and unreservedly concede to unabridged freedom for those whose humanity had to be pronounced by decree and legalized by legislation. In their indifference to Lincoln and his proclamation, African Americans took responsibility for their own liberation, seizing it as their forebears had when the Civil War first began.

The centennial observance of the Emancipation Proclamation coincided with a pivotal period in the history of African Americans. A decade of sustained protest had led to some gains in civil rights, and the next few years would witness even more. This progress had been accomplished at great sacrifice and suffering; the year of the centennial was especially grim. It saw the murder by white supremacists of Mississippi's NAACP leader Medgar Evers; the bombing of the Sixteenth Street Baptist Church in Birmingham, which claimed the lives of four young girls; and the police abuse of black youth who had been recruited as soldiers in a children's crusade for freedom. In August, Civil

Rights activists took their concerns to the capital, organizing more than 200,000 people in a "March on Washington" that converged on the Lincoln Memorial. Martin L. King Jr's "I Have A Dream" speech—the defining moment of the event—captured the sentiment of African Americans who still lacked full inclusion in American society but who hoped that their fellow countrymen could appreciate the symbolism of standing in Lincoln's shadow.

In commemoration of the centennial of the declaration of freedom, the eminent historian John Hope Franklin published a book-length study of what he called "one of America's truly important documents." Franklin argued that, despite the proclamation's shortcomings, "in a very real sense it was another step toward the extension of the ideal of equality" championed by the Declaration of Independence. The proclamation's significance in the first one hundred years was that it reinforced the democratic and egalitarian foundation upon which the nation was supposedly established. Franklin hoped that the next one hundred years would witness the proclamation giving "real meaning and purpose to the Declaration of Independence.[219]

Beyond these occurrences, the centennial fostered no great national celebration of freedom. Overshadowed by the Civil War Centennial celebration, activities in commemoration of the Emancipation Proclamation occurred primarily at local levels and were carried out with minimal federal support. A program in front of the Lincoln Memorial on September 22, 1962, to commemorate the centennial of Lincoln's Preliminary Emancipation Proclamation failed to attract the level of support from the Kennedy administration for which organizers had hoped. Doubtless wishing to avoid antagonizing the South during a particularly tense time in race relations, the president declined an invitation to speak. Clearly, it seemed, America was still unwilling to concede to black people a place at the nation's table.

Shortly thereafter, however, Congress passed important legislation that was meant to guarantee to African Americans the social equality and political rights they had expected since Lincoln's decree. Equal enjoyment of public accommodations and unmolested access to the polls were made possible through the Civil Rights Act of 1964 and the Voting Rights Act of the following year. These measures, combined with school desegregation as manifested in *Brown v. Board of Education* of the previous decade, moved toward fulfillment of what blacks had perceived to be the proclamation's promise. Serious issues remained, however, not the least of which was the economic disparity that kept a significant portion of the African American community dependent and dejected, as it had in the days following slavery. Sharecropping no longer limited black economic opportunity but had been replaced by underemployment and joblessness. The house divided that Lincoln had feared in the 1850s had been realized in the form of two nations, one of which was populated disproportionately by impoverished African Americans.[220]

THE EMANCIPATION PROCLAMATION'S LEGACY

There will be some black men who can remember that, with silent tongue, and clenched teeth, and steady eye, and well poised bayonet, they have helped mankind on to this great consummation; while, I fear, there will be some white ones, unable to forget that, with malignant heart and deceitful speech, they have strove to hinder it.

—ABRAHAM LINCOLN TO JAMES C. CONKLING, August 26, 1863

How we view the Emancipation Proclamation is inextricably linked to our perceptions of who we are as a nation. Either the proclamation confirms our faith that the principles we hold dear are immutable or it suggests that we are disingenuous and never truly subscribed to the ideals of the Declaration of Independence. Perhaps more than any American, Lincoln embodies our national character, and in his decree we see the measure of the nation's commitment to inclusiveness and equality.

In issuing the Emancipation Proclamation, Lincoln set in motion events that facilitated freedom from bondage for the enslaved. Through the decree, he gave executive sanction to efforts African Americans had begun to take in the spring of 1861, and he inadvertently encouraged them to press more vigorously for recognition of their *own* definition of freedom—political rights, economic independence, and social justice. Black men and women understood its revolutionary implications; white Americans, just as resolutely, determined to ascribe to it no broader meaning than release from bondage.

Contrary to Lincoln's prediction in his letter to Conkling in the summer of 1863, the vast majority of white men (and women) did forget. As David Blight argues, North and South denied African Americans full inclusion in the society as whites sought to "bind up the nation's wounds" in the aftermath of war.[221] African-American service on the Civil War battlefield and loyalty beyond that era prompted neither gratitude nor a sense of obligation to extend to black men and women the same privileges that had been accorded to those who took up arms against the nation.

The Emancipation Proclamation initially fortified black people in their struggle to win recognition as Americans, and as its author, Lincoln became (in their eyes) the principal guarantor of the document's promise. African Americans came to realize, however, that the promise could not be realized without the nation's cooperation. Over the years, the legacy of slavery—racism, discrimination, and violence—often intervened to thwart sustained progress, and it continues to block certain segments of the African-American community from equal access to America's bounty. Although the black middle class has enjoyed a certain degree of progress as a consequence of the Civil Rights Movement, it falls short of what African Americans perceived the Emancipation Proclamation would bring. For now, Lincoln's pronouncement remains for many in the African-American community a document of historic interest, perhaps, but one that fails to engender the affection felt by the freed people who imagined and believed in its promise.

"DOING LESS" AND "DOING MORE"

The President and the Proclamation —Legally, Militarily, and Politically

FRANK J. WILLIAMS

To use a coarse, but an expressive figure, broken eggs cannot be mended. I have issued the Emancipation Proclamation, and I cannot retract it. After the commencement of hostilities, I struggled nearly a year and a half to get along without touching the "institution"; and when finally I conditionally determined to touch it, I gave a hundred days' fair notice of my purpose to all the states and people within which time they could have turned it wholly aside by simply again becoming citizens of the United States. They chose to disregard it, and I made the peremptory proclamation on what appeared to me to be a military necessity. It being made, it must stand.

—ABRAHAM LINCOLN TO JOHN A. MCCLERNARD, January 8, 1863

Abraham Lincoln's decision to emancipate slaves during the American Civil War provides the most convincing illustration of his extraordinary legal and political genius.

It is generally accepted—in public opinion polls and historians' surveys—that Lincoln was America's greatest president. But he was also one of its greatest lawyers. Because the Civil War was in many ways a conflict of jurisprudence, Lincoln was able, as president and commander-in-chief in a time of war, to demonstrate his touchstone talent in the law and politics. The unique circumstances were compounded by the fact that America's sixteenth president constantly evolved and thus his policy toward slavery and emancipation changed as he grew in office.

This is the story of Abraham Lincoln's great state paper and the initial conflict between Lincoln's constitutional obligations and his lifelong hatred of slavery.

For purposes of analysis, this chapter is divided into eight parts: (1) Lincoln's initial policy of refusing to accept the extension of slavery into the new territories but allowing it to remain in the states that had long permitted it; (2) his reaction to the First Confiscation Act of August 16, 1861; (3) his reaction to the Second Confiscation Act of July 17, 1862; (4) his preliminary Emancipation Proclamation, issued on September 22, 1862; (5) the interregnum between the proclamations; (6) the final Emancipation Proclamation of January 1, 1863; (7) the Thirteenth Amendment passed by Congress in January 1865 and ratified by the states in December of that year; and (8) a summary of Lincoln's jurisprudence—which encouraged a "right to rise," as historian Gabor S. Boritt has called it, in a nation that had made upward mobility possible for him, and ultimately led Lincoln to favor a transformed Constitution in tune with the natural rights jurisprudence of the Declaration of Independence, so that, at least theoretically, all men (and women), regardless of race, were equal.[1]

MAINTAINING THE STATUS QUO: *The First Conservative Step*

To the dismay of abolitionists during his own time and some revisionist historians since, America's sixteenth president at first seemed to be just another conservative Whig lawyer who belatedly joined the Republican party in the 1850s. Even if he personally disliked and generally opposed slavery, the political and philosophical line he drew in the vast American republic allowed for the continuation of slavery in the South. Lincoln's opposition to slavery came partly from a deep personal repugnance that tends to be overlooked, especially given his often-cited lawyerlike statements emphasizing his primary constitutional responsibility for preserving the Union. Thus, the extemporaneous remarks that he made in Philadelphia on his way to be inaugurated come as a surprise to some but serve to illustrate the depth of his feelings about slavery. A Union with slavery was not worth saving, he told his listeners:

> [There was] something in that Declaration giving liberty, not alone to the people of this coun- · try, but hope to the world for all future time. It was that which gave promise that in due time the weights should be lifted from the shoulders of all men, and that *all* should have an equal chance. This is the sentiment embodied in that Declaration of Independence.
>
> Now, my friends, can this country be saved upon that basis? If it can, I will consider myself one of the happiest men in the world if I can help to save it. If it can't be saved upon that prin- ciple, it will be truly awful. But, if this country cannot be saved without giving up that prin- ciple—I was about to say I would rather be assassinated on this spot than to surrender it.[2]

In the mysterious yet predictable manner of such things, Lincoln's recent critics have focused on what most historians mark as his greatest achievement: the beginning of the end of slavery. Lincoln, we have lately been told, was a racist, a defender of the status quo who did not really want to end slavery and who issued his Emancipation Proclamation in a cynical grab for political advantage, in order to win abolitionist votes without actually freeing any slaves. Scholars like Harry V. Jaffa disagree. In his milestone study *A New Birth of Freedom: Abraham Lincoln and the Coming of the Civil War,* Jaffa devotes considerable attention to demonstrating the growth and the sincerity of Lincoln's opposition to slav- ery. Answering the claim that Lincoln cared about slavery only for the political advantage it might yield, Jaffa offers a bit of reason: "Are we to say that Lincoln's reasons for thinking slavery morally wrong are to be discounted because he presented them in political campaigns? . . . There is reason to believe that Lincoln wrestled long and hard in private with the question of the morality of slavery, as he had with the question of free will and predestination. Having come to a conclusion, however, he could not let the matter rest there. Moral arguments point to moral obligations. Lincoln could advance the antislavery cause only by gaining political advantage for the antislavery argument."[3]

But his opposition to slavery and its extension was manifest, as ably demonstrated in his speech at Springfield, Illinois, on October 4, 1854. He objected to the Kansas-Nebraska Act, which introduced popular sovereignty, the policy that would have allowed slavery to spread into western territories if white settlers so voted: "What *natural* right requires Kansas and Nebraska to be opened to Slavery? Is not slavery universally granted to be, in the abstract, a gross outrage on the law of nature? Have not all civilized nations, our own among them, made the Slave trade capital, and classed it with piracy and murder? Is it not held to be the great wrong of the world? Do not the Southern people, the Slave- holders themselves, spurn the domestic slave dealer, refuse to associate with him, or let their families associate with his family, as long as the taint of his infamous calling is known?"[4]

In Peoria, Illinois, on October 16, 1854, Lincoln responded to Senator Douglas's efforts to repeal the Missouri Compromise with a statement that combined this sense of moral outrage and reverence for law

> I think, and shall try to show, that it is wrong; wrong in its direct effect, letting slavery into Kansas and Nebraska—and wrong in its prospective principle, allowing it to spread to every other part of the wide world, where men can be found inclined to take it.
>
> This *declared* indifference, but as I must think, covert *real* zeal for the spread of slavery, I can not but hate. I hate it because of the monstrous injustice of slavery itself. I hate it because it deprives our republican example of its just influence in the world—enables the enemies of free institutions, with plausibility, to taunt us as hypocrites—causes the real friends of freedom to doubt our sincerity, and especially because it forces so many really good men amongst ourselves into an open war with the very fundamental principles of civil liberty—criticizing the Declaration of Independence, and insisting that there is no right principle of action but *self-interest*.[5]

Moreover, Lincoln opposed slavery in public even when taking that position was risky. It is easy to forget that he lost the U.S. Senate seat he contested with Stephen A. Douglas in 1858. During their debates, Lincoln denounced southerners for holding slaves not because his only solution to the problem at that time—colonization, freeing slaves and keeping them in a lower status—was unacceptable to them, but rather because of his moral disgust with slavery. Lincoln repeated the position he had taken in earlier speeches: "There is no reason at all furnished why the Negro after all is not entitled to all that the Declaration of Independence holds out, which is 'life, liberty, and the pursuit of happiness' and I hold that he is as much entitled to that as the white man. I agree that the Negro may not be my equal and judge Douglas' equal in many respects certainly not in color, and in intellectual development, perhaps—but in the right to [eat] the bread which his own hand earns, he is my own equal and Judge Douglas' equal and the equal of every other man."[6]

Lincoln concluded his statement with a direct attack on Douglas's advocacy of "popular sovereignty":

> When [Judge Douglas] is saying that the Negro has no share in the Declaration of Independence, he is going back to the year of our revolution, and to the extent of his ability, he is muzzling the cannon that thunders its annual joyous return. When he is saying, as he often does, that if any people want slavery they have a right to have it, he is blowing out the moral lights around us. When he says that he don't care whether slavery is voted up or down, then, to my thinking, he is, so far as he is able to do so, perverting the human soul and eradicating the light of reason and the love of liberty on the American continent.[7]

With respect to the rights of people in the territory from which slavery had previously been excluded, Lincoln took a very hard line in opposition. In the last debate, as he attacked once again Douglas's solution of "popular sovereignty," he went so far as to argue that the people have no right to do wrong: "[Douglas] says that whatever community desires slavery has a right to it. He can say so logically, if it is not a wrong, but if he admits that it is a wrong, he cannot logically say that anybody has a right to do wrong." However, because he was so strongly committed to the democratic processes and the Constitution as it was, Lincoln could bring himself to limit the people's prerogative only in regard to the question of the extension of slavery in the territories. Lincoln denounced slavery as a "wrong" dozens of times in his final two debate appearances. In response to Douglas's popular sovereignty argument, Lincoln stated in the last debate: "[The extension of slavery] involves the two principles that are made the essential struggle between right and wrong. They are the two principles that have stood face-to-face, one of them asserting the Divine right of kings, the same principle that says you work, you toil, you earn bread, and I will eat it. It is the same old serpent whether it comes from the mouth of a king who seeks to bestride the people of his nation and to live upon the fat of his neighbor or whether it comes from one race of men as an apology for enslaving another race of men it is the same old policy."[8]

Near the end of his reply to Douglas's opening statement in the Alton debate, Lincoln suggested a way to reconcile the demands of competing values: the requirements of the Constitution on one side, and the end of slavery on the other:

> The real issue in this controversy, I think, springs from a sentiment in the mind, and that sentiment is this—on the one part it looks upon the institution of slavery as being wrong, and on the part of another class, it does not look upon it as wrong. The sentiment that contemplates the institution of slavery as being wrong, is the sentiment of the Republican party . . . They look upon slavery as a moral, social, and political wrong, and while they contemplate it as being such, they nevertheless have due regard for its actual existence among us and the difficulties of getting out of it in the States, and for all the constitutional obligations thrown around it; nevertheless, they desire to see a policy instituted that looks to the thing not growing any larger; they insist upon a policy that shall treat it as a wrong and as a mildest policy to that end they look to the prevention of its growing larger, and an end to it eventually. Now I have said, and I repeat it here, if there be any man among us who does not think that the institution of slavery is a wrong—that it is not a wrong in any one of the aspects in which I have spoken, he is misplaced, and ought not to be among us; and if there is a man who is so impatient of it as a wrong, as to disregard the difficulties of getting rid of it, or to disregard the constitutional obligations thrown around it, that man too is misplaced; we disclaim sympathy with him in political action; he is not placed properly with us.[9]

In the first half of the statement, Lincoln sounds like an abolitionist; in the second half, he in effect expiates the abolitionists out of the Republican party, demanding that those who stand with him take into account the requirements of the Constitution, the realities of the world, and the dire consequences of pursuing one's deeply held moral commitments without regard to those requirements and realities.

At first, Lincoln limited his antislavery fight to the battle against extending it into the new federal territories. Because the frontier lawyer had limited experience and contact with blacks, like most politicians his policy was to do the least he had to do. He wanted the problem of slavery to go away, and the fastest way to achieve that result was to favor colonization—a humane form of voluntary "ethnic cleansing"—an out-of-sight, out-of-mind solution. This program stuns many observers today, but it represents how the mainstream political world typically functioned, then and now.

In 1852, for example, in eulogizing his political hero Henry Clay, Lincoln took pains to quote the late statesman's belief that "there is a moral fitness in the idea of returning to Africa her children, whose ancestors have been torn from her by the ruthless hand of fraud and violence." To Lincoln, this made perfect sense, and he added: "May it indeed be realized!" Six years later, during the Lincoln-Douglas debates, Lincoln was still quoting Clay as a means of advocating colonization without quite making it his own major political priority.[10]

Lincoln took a long time before he lost interest in this scheme. A month before the final Emancipation Proclamation was to be issued, Lincoln was still advocating his plans for gradual emancipation and colonization of freed slaves. In his annual message to Congress on December 1, 1862, the president proposed a constitutional amendment that would compensate every state that freed its slaves before 1900. It would free forever all slaves who had been released from bondage during the war but would pay the slave owners who remained loyal to the Union. Congress would also provide money to colonize freed slaves in foreign countries. By this proposal, Lincoln sought to aid the border slave states and to offer the states of the Confederacy a way out of the war.

Congress, to Lincoln's dismay and frustration, paid scant attention to the president's proposals. Lincoln looked for a rational and quick way to deal with the problems caused by the existence of slavery in a free American society, and he believed he had found it in colonization. Like Henry Clay and Chief Justice John Marshall, who both belonged to the American Colonization Society, he became convinced that transporting African Americans from the United States would defuse several social problems. By relocating free blacks, those initially transported were to be freedmen. Colonization would remove those whom many white southerners considered the most potentially disruptive elements in their society. Consequently, Lincoln reasoned, southern whites would be more willing to free their slaves if they were going to be shipped off to Africa. At the same time, northerners would give more support for emancipation if freedmen were sent out of the country and kept from the free states where they would compete for jobs with white laborers. Moreover, colonization could elevate the status of the Negro race by proving that blacks, in a separate, self-governing community of their own, would be capable of making orderly progress in civilization. Lincoln insisted that this colonization be purely voluntary. Unlike some other colonizationists, he never favored forcible deportation. Thus, Lincoln thought, voluntary emigration of blacks would succeed "in freeing our land from the dangerous presence of slavery" and "in restoring a captive people to their long-lost father-land, with bright prospects for the future."[11]

In his 1862 message to Congress, Lincoln reiterated that he still strongly favored colonization: "And yet I wish to say there is an objection urged against free colored persons remaining in the country, which is largely imaginary, if not sometimes malicious. It is insisted that their presence would injure, and displace white [labor] . . . If there ever could be a proper time for mere catch arguments," he warned Congress, that time surely is not now. In times like the present, men should utter nothing for which they would not willingly be responsible through time and in eternity. Is it true, then, that colored people can displace any more white labor, by being free, than by remaining slaves? If they stay in their old places, they jostle no white laborers; if they leave their old places, they leave them open to white laborers. Logically, there is neither more nor less of it . . .

But it is dreaded that the freed people will swarm forth, and cover the whole land? Are they not already in the land? Will liberation make them any more numerous? Equally distributed among the whites of the whole country, and there would be but one colored to seven whites. Could the one, in any way, greatly disturb the seven?[12]

Yet by July 1, 1864, Lincoln's private secretary, John Hay, noted "that the President has sloughed off the idea of colonization."[13] Lincoln said nothing about it publicly after the issuance of the Emancipation Proclamation on January 1, 1863. One thing is certain: When Lincoln accepted freedmen as soldiers on January 1, 1863, he guaranteed a biracial future of the country because no president could ask a man to fight for his country and then tell him it was no longer his.

Often used to stir patriotic feelings, the passage in his annual message, "Fellow-citizens, we cannot escape history . . . The fiery trial through which we pass, will light us down, in honor or dishonor, to the latest generation,"[14] is actually a call to Congress to approve and understand his action of emancipation as opposed to patriotic or martial rhetoric. Lincoln's motives seem clear in the light of history. He was trying to calm people who feared the impact of the preliminary Emancipation Proclamation. It had been reported, for example, that white people in the southern Ohio counties along the Ohio River were in a panic over the order. They feared that when the final proclamation took effect, a flood of runaway slaves would be loosed upon them.

Like most politicians, Lincoln operated within a system of givens, and the most glaring justification for his position—focusing during the antebellum years on slavery where it might spread, not where it already existed—was that the U.S. Constitution protected slavery. It was protected by the three-fifths clause that gave more representation in Congress to those states where slave populations resided. Moreover, the *Dred Scott* Supreme Court decision of 1857 reinforced the status quo, at the very least.[15] It denied U.S. citizenship to African Americans, confirming the status of blacks in most parts of America. The United States Supreme Court stated that Congress could not prohibit the introduction of slavery into any territory of the United States. The Court also said that a black person could never be considered a citizen of the United States regardless of the laws set forth by any individual state.

This decision drew swift, intense, and heated opposition. It was also vital to the platform of the Republican Party, which nominated Abraham Lincoln for the presidency in 1860. But even before his nomination, Lincoln forcefully attacked the Court's ruling in this case. His first public statements denouncing the decision were made in a speech in Springfield, Illinois, on June 26, 1857. Lincoln was exceedingly clear about his displeasure with the Court's conclusions and was resolute in his conviction that the decision contradicted the basic tenets of the Declaration of Independence.

[We] think the Dred Scott Decision is erroneous. We know the court that made it, has often over-ruled its own decisions, and we shall do what we can to have it . . . over-rule this . . .

Judicial decisions are of greater or less authority as precedents, according to circumstances.

Chief Justice Taney, in his opinion in the Dred Scott case, admits that the language of the Declaration is broad enough to include the whole human family, but he and Judge Douglas argue that the authors of that instrument did not intend to include negroes, by the fact that they did not at once, actually place them on an equality with the whites. Now this grave argument comes to just nothing at all, by the other fact, that they did not at once, *or ever afterwards,* actually place all white people on equality with one or another. And this is the staple argument of both the Chief Justice and the Senator, for doing this obvious violence to the plain unmistakable language of the Declaration.[16]

If the activist decision was out of tune with American practice, Lincoln was not a demagogue or a revolutionary who thought that the president could overturn the Constitution, unlike the abolitionists who were willing to go to that exact extreme. He was a lawyer who valued the law.

But he remained antislavery in moral terms. "We all declare for liberty," Lincoln observed in 1864, "but in using the same *word* we do not all mean the same *thing*." For the North, freedom meant for "each man" to enjoy "the product of his labor"; to southern whites, it conveyed the power to do "as they pleased with other men, and the product of other men's labor."[17] And as Lincoln wrote that same year, in a letter to A. G. Hodges of Kentucky: "I am naturally anti-slavery. If slavery is not wrong, nothing is wrong. I can not remember when I did not so think, and feel . . . I claim not to have controlled events, but confess plainly that events have controlled me . . . If God now wills the removal of a great wrong, and wills also that we of the North as well as you of the South, shall pay fairly for our complicity in that wrong, impartial history will find therein new cause to attest and revere the justice and goodness of God."[18]

AND THE WAR CAME (CONFISCATION ACTS)

After the firebrands at Fort Sumter fired the first shot, triggering the outbreak of the Civil War, lawyer Lincoln—now President Lincoln—must have inwardly smiled, for as any lawyer knows, he who pulls the trigger is the guilty party. Initially Lincoln thought, as many did, that the war would be a short one and that with the overwhelming resources of the Union arrayed against them, the secessionists were doomed. He was terribly wrong in predicting the duration of the war and the extent of strong support for the Union in the South. Yet he was exactly right politically when he argued that his policy needed to aim at retaining the support of the border states—Kentucky, Delaware, Maryland, and Missouri. Even in the White House, he was still operating as the conservative lawyer in order to hold together what was left of the imperiled Union.

In the eighty days from his 1861 call for troops to the convening of Congress in special session on July 4, 1861, Lincoln performed a series of crucial acts by sheer assumption of presidential power—a foreshadowing of what was to come with his issuance of the Emancipation Proclamation as an executive order. He proclaimed not "civil war" in those words but the existence of "combinations too powerful to be suppressed by the ordinary course of judicial proceedings." He called forth the militia to "suppress said combinations," which he ordered "to disperse, and retire peaceably" to their homes. He proclaimed a blockade against the South, suspended habeas corpus rights, increased the size of the regular army, and authorized the expenditure of government money without congressional appropriation.[19] Congress is constitutionally empowered to declare war, but suppression of rebellion has been recognized as an executive function, for which the prerogative of setting aside civil procedures has been placed in the president's hands.[20]

Though he took surprising and stunning extraconstitutional steps while Congress was out of session to mobilize to confront the rebellion, he recognized from the first that these steps would eventually require ratification by Congress. This conscious recognition and acceptance separates his behavior from that of a dictator, though, of course, there remain critics who are unwilling to recognize the reality and needs of addressing a major civil war.

When Lincoln finally sent a message to the Congress in special session on July 4, 1861, he responded to his critics, especially Chief Justice Roger B. Taney, who had criticized the president for suspending the writ of habeas corpus in *Ex parte Merryman:*

> The whole of the laws which were required to be faithfully executed, were being resisted, and failing of execution, in nearly one-third of the States. Must they be allowed to finally fail of execution, even had it been perfectly clear, that by the use of the means necessary to their execution, some single law, made in such extreme tenderness of the citizen's liberty, that practically, it relieves more of the guilty, than of the innocent, should, to a very limited extent, be violated? To state the question more directly, are all the laws, *but one,* to go unexecuted, and the government itself go to pieces, lest that one be violated?[21]

Lincoln was willing to let first the military and then the Congress take the lead on most national issues—save the most important one: the overall conduct of the war, and the overarching goal of reconstituting and preserving the Union. Congress responded precisely as the president expected, and then Congress went further than the president. Confiscation Acts clearly aimed at undermining slavery were proposed by Republican senator Lyman Trumbull (Illinois) and passed by Congress. The bill empowered the government to confiscate property used to aid the rebellion (First Confiscation Act) as well as property of those who supported the Confederacy (Second Confiscation Act). Although Lincoln signed the new laws, neither the president nor Attorney Gen. Edward Bates vigorously implemented either of the two acts. While the acts did represent the wish of many northerners to attack slavery and no doubt eventually quickened Lincoln's resolve to embrace emancipation, they failed to have a major impact on wartime freedom.[22]

Congress passed the first act after Gen. Benjamin Butler in May 1861 began admitting fugitive slaves into Union lines as contrabands. The new law authorized the president to seize any property used to aid the insurrection and terminated the claims of masters over those persons (slaves) employed to assist the Confederate military. The act, however, failed to define the status of slaves whose owners forfeited their claims to them. The proceedings were to be adjudicated in federal district and circuit courts with pertinent jurisdiction, that is, where the property was located or had been seized. This meant, as of August 1861, that most property subject to confiscation remained within the

Confederacy. Congressional discussion over the first act was brief and partisan. Only Democrats and border-state Unionists in the House opposed the bill, while only one Republican voted with Senate Democrats against it. (See Appendix for full text of the law.)

Later, and without Lincoln's consent, Union general John C. Frémont initiated a more direct attack upon those slaveholders who supported the rebellion. In September 1861 he unilaterally proclaimed rebel property seized and slaves freed in Missouri, where he was operating as Union commanding general. When Frémont declined to change the proclamation to conform to the First Confiscation Act, Lincoln revoked Frémont's proclamation, in large part to avoid pushing Kentucky and other border states into joining the Confederacy. Many in the North protested the president's action and urged Congress to legislate further against the rebels' right to hold human property. Most Union generals, however, were reluctant to enforce even the first act or to encourage fugitive slaves to enter their lines. Nonetheless, contrabands continued to arrive, and some were put to work on behalf of the Union.

In 1862 radical Republicans, as part of their crusade to perfect the American Republic, initiated legislative activity designed to attack slavery more directly. Not only did they end slavery in Washington, D.C., through compensated emancipation, but also Congress passed on March 10, 1862, an Article of War forbidding military officers to return runaway slaves to their owners. They also crafted a Second Confiscation Act, which permitted the seizure of property of rebelling southerners and freed forever any slaves of rebellious owners who came into Union lines. Rules of law, however, complicated this measure. At some point, the government would have had to prove in a U.S. district court that a southerner was actually engaged in rebellion. Thus, the measure was not as radical as it appeared.

Lincoln's December 3, 1861, message to Congress noted the pressure for more vigorous measures against the South but urged that the war not degenerate "into a violent and remorseless struggle." Senator Trumbull nonetheless introduced his second act two days later on December 5. It called for the "absolute and complete forfeiture forever" of all property that belonged to those who supported the rebellion. Over the next seven months, Congress debated a variety of such confiscation proposals at considerable length. Supporters of sweeping confiscation argued that forfeiture could extend beyond the life of the offender because the property itself was made guilty by the owner's support of the rebellion. Confiscation was therefore not a bill of attainder and not unconstitutional. The use of in rem proceedings, supporters argued, would allow forfeiture of property without the owner's presence, as the action would be brought against the property itself—the slaves—and confiscation could be accomplished more expeditiously. Most Republicans supported the notion of moderate confiscation, to be executed by the president only for military purposes and only for the life of the rebel. They argued that property could not be guilty and that the in rem proceedings were unconstitutional. Confiscation could not extend beyond the offender's life and therefore could not be the basis for Reconstruction. Most Republicans agreed that slaves could be emancipated through confiscation, although almost no one expressed interest in their status after slavery other than to provide for their colonization outside the United States.

Moderates prevailed in the final confiscation bill. It provided confiscation and punishment for six classes of rebels, broad executive authority (including the power to pardon), the opportunity for rebels to swear allegiance and avoid confiscation, the liberation of slaves in Union-controlled areas, and the colonization of willing freed slaves. The bill did not explicitly allow for forfeiture beyond the offender's life. The act also did not free slaves unless courts found their owners to be rebels, and it gave the military no power to adjudicate the matter of ownership. Nor did the act affect slaves of nonrebels or those who swore allegiance to the North. Only two Republicans in the House and two in the Senate joined Democrats to oppose the second act. In an overwhelmingly Republican Congress, the bill passed handily. (See Appendix for full text of the law.)

Lincoln had indicated that he favored less severe measures against the South. In March 1862 he had urged gradual emancipation for the border states and reiterated this plea when Congress passed the second act. He had also revoked Gen. David Hunter's April proclamation freeing slaves in Georgia, Florida, and South Carolina. In response, worried Republican moderates dispatched Maine senator William Pitt Fessenden to ask the president how to avoid a veto of the second act. The result was a joint resolution, subsequently passed by Congress, which guaranteed that confiscation of rebels' slaves would only be prospective and that no forfeiture of real property would extend beyond the life of the offender. One result of the compromise was that it weakened an already drastically modified version of Trumbull's original bill and suggested that no land would be available for freed slaves or Northern soldiers and that eventual reconstruction of the Union would be limited. Like the first, the Second Confiscation Act was not very well crafted and would only be implemented on a case-by-case basis. Nor did Congress provide any funds for its implementation, thereby deterring local officials from enforcing it vigorously. Appropriations for colonization would come later to entice northerners to support emancipation or confiscation.[23]

Lincoln signed the law on July 17. But in an unusual move designed to communicate his lingering concerns, he also sent his draft veto message to Congress for their review. Although the president supported confiscation for military purposes, he worried that "a justly discriminating application of it, would be very difficult," if not impossible.[24] His chief concern was that confiscation should not extend beyond the life of the offender. Yet Lincoln did realize the importance of attacking slavery, which remained a central motivation for confiscation. Because of the president's constitutional doubts, the act was accompanied by the explanatory joint resolution, which stipulated that only a life estate terminating with the death of the offender could be sold and that at his death his children could take the fee simple by descent as his heirs without deriving any title from the United States. In applying this act, passed in pursuance of the war power rather than the power to punish treason, the Supreme Court in *Wallach v. Van Risweick* quoted with approval the English distinction between a disability absolute and perpetual and one personal or temporary.[25]

Only two weeks after forcing Congress to modify its latest attempt to legislate confiscation, Lincoln decided to move on his own. Examined as a political and legal decision, it should have surprised no one. Lincoln, the ever-resourceful politician-lawyer, was retaining the presidential prerogative to strike at slavery in order to win the war and save the Union—actions he believed to be within his exclusive power. By mid-summer 1862, Lincoln was discussing openly with several of his cabinet members his growing conviction that military law and government necessity now required the emancipation of slaves by an executive order. In the meantime, he began drafting a document, cutting and pasting clauses from the Confiscation Act. On July 22 Lincoln read a rough draft of an Emancipation Proclamation to his cabinet.

In pursuance of the sixth section of the act of congress entitled "An act to suppress insurrection and to punish treason and rebellion, to seize and confiscate property of rebels, and for other purposes" Approved July 17. 1862, and which act, and the Joint Resolution explanatory thereof, are herewith published, I, Abraham Lincoln, President of the United States, do hereby proclaim to, and warn all persons within the contemplation of said sixth section to cease participating in, aiding, countenancing, or abetting the existing rebellion, or any rebellion against the government of the United States, and to return to their proper allegiance to the United States, on pain of the forfeitures and seizures, as within and by said sixth section provided.

And I hereby make known that it is my purpose, upon the next meeting of congress, to again recommend the adoption of a practical measure for tendering pecuniary aid to the free choice or rejection, of any and all States which may then be recognizing and practically sustaining the authority of the United States, and which may then have voluntarily adopted, or thereafter may voluntarily adopt, gradual abolishment of slavery within such State or States—that the object is to practically restore, thenceforward to be maintain[ed], the constitutional relation between the general government, and each, and all the states, wherein that relation is now suspended, or disturbed; and that, for this object, the war, as it has been, will be, prosecuted. And, as a fit and necessary military measure for effecting this object, I, as Commander-in-Chief of the Army and Navy of the United States, do order and declare that on the first day of January in the year of Our Lord one thousand, eight hundred and sixtythree, all persons held as slaves within any state or states, wherein the constitutional authority of the United States shall not then be practically recognized, submitted to, and maintained, shall then, thenceforward, and forever, be free.[26]

This draft proclamation, in its very unfinished state, remained unpublished. Only two of Lincoln's advisors gave it their wholehearted assent, Attorney General Bates, the most conservative member of the cabinet, and Secretary of War Edwin M. Stanton, who showed no hesitation in supporting it. Ultimately, however, he agreed with Secretary of State William H. Seward that the president must wait for a military victory before announcing it to the public. "I do not want to issue a document that the whole world will see must necessarily be inoperative, like the Pope's bull against the comet!" Lincoln agreed. "Would my word free the slaves, when I cannot even enforce the Constitution in the rebel States?"[27] By September 17, however, Lincoln had his victory on the battlefield at Antietam.

July was a month filled with presidential initiatives on the issue of slavery. Recruiting of Negroes began under authorization of the Confiscation Act and was approved, along with an act to amend the Force Bill of 1795, by the president on July 17.[28] Negro recruitment was discussed in the cabinet meeting on July 22 when Lincoln submitted the first draft of the Emancipation Proclamation. He also authorized the recruitment of "free Negroes" and runaway slaves into the military and the seizure of any property for military purposes. In fact, the president wrote a little-known memorandum on recruiting Negroes:

> To recruiting free negroes, no objection.
>
> To recruiting slaves of disloyal owners, no objection.
>
> To recruiting slaves of loyal owners, *with their consent,* no objection.
>
> To recruiting slaves of loyal owners *without* consent, objection, *unless the necessity is urgent.*
>
> To conducting offensively, while recruiting, and to carrying away slaves not suitable for recruits, objection.[29]

On July 25, 1862, Lincoln issued another proclamation, invoking the sixth section of the second Confiscation Act, and warning all persons "to cease participating in, aiding, countenancing, or abetting the existing rebellion."

Administration of the First Confiscation Act by Virginia-born attorney general Bates, now a conservative from Missouri, was strict but limited, reflecting Lincoln's own nagging political and legal concerns. Not until January 1863 did the president actually authorize the attorney general to enforce the first act. Nor did Bates produce a policy on how to implement the act; instead he urged local officials to read the act themselves and carefully pursue only that property that had been used to assist the rebellion. The small amounts of property confiscated under the first act reflected the conservative influence of Bates and the very real difficulty of finding such property in the South.

Bates's enforcement of the second act was no more vigorous. This circumspection again followed the president's example. In late August 1862, Horace Greeley, editor of the influential *New York Tribune,* had expressed disappointment at the lax enforcement. Lincoln replied, in a letter to the editor, that he would "save" the Union "in the shortest way under the Constitution." As the president put it, "I shall do *less* whenever I shall believe what I am doing hurts the cause, and I shall do *more* whenever I shall believe" it will help restore the Union.[30] To Bates, this meant "doing less." He and Lincoln asked district attorneys to take few risks, keep expenses down, prevent injustice to property owners, and limit embarrassment to the government.

On November 13, 1862, Lincoln finally authorized Bates to seize, prosecute, and condemn property under the second act.[31] However, the president omitted any reference to slaves, thereby leaving the emancipation provisions to the military, which generally ignored them. Lincoln's orders also allowed Bates to control confiscation and deny local officials latitude in the execution of the second act. Bates expected them to execute the law vigilantly but with care to "avoid hasty and improvident seizures." District attorneys also proved reluctant to prosecute cases unless they were guaranteed expenses, which Bates rarely granted. Attorney General Bates's greatest contribution to the confiscation effort was passing along information about property liable to seizure. Although his administration of the second act was honest and careful, it lacked any conviction that the law was just or good.

Military officers, the first to encounter property of any sort in the South, were the best potential enforcers of the Confiscation Acts. Several commanders suggested that they would be vigorous in the prosecution of the second act, but not much confiscation occurred by the military. In occupied New Orleans, for example, Gen. Benjamin Butler threatened confiscation and thereby persuaded a majority of residents to pledge allegiance to the Union. In 1864, Gen. Lew Wallace issued two orders for the confiscation of property in Maryland, but Bates objected because they interfered with his authority. Ultimately, nothing—and no one—was confiscated. Although the emancipation clause was separate from the confiscation and treason clauses, the act prescribed absolutely no means of enforcement. It declared "forever free" slaves taking refuge in the lines of the army from "persons . . . in rebellion," but there was no way to determine who the owners were and what their loyalties might be. Lincoln claimed that no slave was ever freed by the Second Confiscation Act. In contrast, the Emancipation Proclamation involved no cumbersome and impractical judicial proceedings. The army became the means of enforcement. Where the army succeeded in vanquishing Confederates, slaves were freed. In the end, few commanders showed much interest in confiscation, despite some prodding by Secretary of War Stanton, and that suited Bates, who wished to control administration of the acts, however tepid his support for them.

Treasury department officials, who followed in the military's path, also could have been effective agents of confiscation. They saw confiscable property before marshals or district attorneys appeared in most areas and could have prevented property title transfers, which often protected slaves from confiscation. But their primary responsibilities lay in collecting captured and abandoned property. Moreover, the two Union treasury secretaries during the war, Salmon P. Chase and William Pitt Fessenden, encouraged officials to cooperate with the attorney general. The inability to profit from handling confiscable property also deterred the treasury officials from expanding their opportunities. As a result, except in New Orleans, little confiscation took place in concert with treasury officers.

New Orleans realized the second largest amount of money from confiscated property, largely because it remained under Union control for such a long period and was the wealthiest city in the South. Even so, only $60,000 from the sale of confiscated property was collected there, which represented almost one-fifth of the final total.[32] Virginia proved to be the most vulnerable area for confiscation, but it occurred there mostly after the war.

On December 8, 1863, in his annual message to Congress, Lincoln offered a pardon to most participants in the rebellion if they would take an oath of allegiance to the United States. This exercise to accelerate reunification seriously undercut confiscation for the remainder of the war. Proponents of confiscation failed to object to the pardoning process provided for in the second act, but by early 1864 some moved to repeal the joint resolution to allow confiscation beyond the life of the offender. It was even argued that Lincoln, having carefully studied the views of legal expert William Whiting, solicitor for the War Department, now believed that forfeiture could extend beyond the life of the guilty party because confiscation did not rest upon treasonous behavior.[33] Nevertheless, the various efforts over the following year to revoke the resolution failed.

By January 1865, Lincoln favored confiscation for only the most prominent rebels. According to Confederate vice president Alexander H. Stephens, who met Lincoln that February for an aborted peace conference at Hampton Roads, Virginia, the president even assured the South that he would be lenient in his use of confiscation. His successor Andrew Johnson also wanted to spare the South a harsh reconstruction based on widespread confiscation. Unlike Lincoln, however, Johnson used confiscation to punish more classes of rebels, as his May 1865 pardon proclamation indicated. He focused particularly on owners with property valued at over $20,000, many of whom resided in Virginia. Those excluded from pardons had to request them personally from the president. In the end, most rebels were able to escape confiscation, but not before the new attorney general, James Speed, enjoyed four months in which to implement the second act with some vigor. By that September, however, Johnson suspended enforcement of the second act and directed the Freedmen's Bureau to return property that was to have been rented to freedmen. The irony is that the second act was forcefully executed only after the war ended and only for four months. Oliver Otis Howard, director of the Freedmen's Bureau, tried but failed to circumvent Johnson's wish to restore land to former rebels.

Therefore, as historian Harold Hyman has put it, "the 1861 and 1862 Confiscation Acts specify that penalties were to come into play only after Federal courts brought in guilty verdicts in individual litigation. In short, Lincoln, Bates, the Cabinet and the Republican majority in Congress did not tear themselves away from Constitutional and Criminal Law Guidelines long antedating the Civil War. So far as procedures to determine accused disloyalists, 'guilt where concerned, whatever the novelty of the subject matter, except temporarily in military occupation zones, the Congress held' . . . disloyalty laws were to be enforced by national courts." Hyman concludes, "in almost all respects the new statutes proved to be duds."[34] Bates concurred with Lincoln that they were legal, but limited.

Contrary to predictions from both opponents and supporters of confiscation, the courts went on to liberally interpret the first and second acts. They granted Congress the benefit of the doubt on most procedural questions and accepted the constitutional argument for confiscation. In *Miller v. United States*,[35] the Supreme Court upheld the Confiscation Acts by observing that confiscation "is an instrument of coercion, which, by depriving an enemy of property within reach of his power, whether within his territory or without it, impairs his ability to resist the confiscating government, while at the same time it furnishes to that government means for carrying on the war." The court believed the issue had been settled in the *Prize* cases, which made clear that the right to confiscation involving other nations "exists in full force when the war is domestic or civil."[36]

His approval of the Confiscation Acts notwithstanding, Lincoln had come more slowly than some of his fellow Republicans to the idea of an executive order to end slavery. This was not because he supported the peculiar institution. The protection of the territories from the cancer of slavery had been his bedrock position throughout the 1850s, but he had always insisted that slavery, as it existed in the southern states, was sanctioned by the U.S. Constitution, and that liberating the slaves could only be accomplished voluntarily by those states. During the war his efforts at ending slavery included proposing compensation for border states like Maryland and Delaware if they would free their slaves. His annual message of 1862 even suggested a constitutional amendment that would end slavery gradually, voluntarily, with compensation—and only by 1900.

Barely ten days before he read aloud to his cabinet the first draft of his proposed executive order emancipating slaves in Confederate-held states, Lincoln made certain to issue another public plea to border states for orderly compensated emancipation. Always cautious and ever lawyerly, the president continued to hope that the slavery cancer could be contained without convulsing the country. And he continued to offer colonization as bait to his reluctant contemporaries. In his July 12 statement on compensation, he urged:

Can you, for your states, do better than to take the course I urge? . . .

I do not speak of emancipation *at once*, but of a *decision* at once to emancipate *gradually*. Room in South America for colonization, can be obtained cheaply, and in abundance; and when numbers shall be large enough to be company and encouragement for one another, the freed people will not be so reluctant to go . . .

You are patriots and statesmen; and, as such, I pray you, consider this proposition . . . Our common country is in great peril, demanding the loftiest views, and boldest action to bring it speedy relief. Once relieved, it's [*sic*] form of government is saved to the world; it's [*sic*] beloved history, and cherished memories, are vindicated; and it's [*sic*] happy future fully assured, and rendered inconceivably grand.[37]

Ever alert to the importance of public opinion, Lincoln remained restrained in his approach to emancipation because of the need to maintain the allegiance of the border states, whose support he believed crucial to the winning of the war. The U.S. Constitution embedded slavery in the legal apparatus of the government. Justification for emancipation rested solely on the war power. Lincoln's reply to Horace Greeley asserted that "I would save the Union . . . If there be those who would not save the Union, unless they could at the same time *save* slavery, I do not agree with them. If there be those who would not save the Union unless they could at the same time *destroy* slavery, I do not agree with them. My paramount object in this struggle *is* to save the Union, and is *not* either to save or destroy slavery." He was quick to add that he was presenting his "view of *official* duty; and I intend no modification of my oft-expressed *personal* wish that all men every where could be free."[38]

Historian Don E. Fehrenbacher has characterized Lincoln's reply to Greeley as disingenuous, "a brilliant piece of propaganda."[39] Biographer Benjamin P. Thomas believed Lincoln "used Greeley's outburst to prepare the people for what was coming."[40] Indeed, when he wrote to Greeley, Lincoln had already decided to issue the proclamation. Sensitive to the extent of his use of constitutional authority following an era of weak executive power, Lincoln hesitated. But just as he moved toward an understanding of the necessity of an uncompromising military effort that would shake the morale of southern civilians, so he too could understand that as a commander of the armed forces he had the constitutional power to emancipate the enemy's slaves. There were significant signs of this change in his attitude by 1862. After all, the president ultimately did *not* veto the Second Confiscation Act, which included slaves in its provision that the Union could confiscate the property of those who supported the Confederacy.

THE PRELIMINARY EMANCIPATION PROCLAMATION

The Battle of Antietam, however inconclusive and disappointing to the president, was the long-awaited first major Eastern military success for the Union. Gen. Robert E. Lee, tired of fighting defensively on his own state's ground and by nature aggressive, had boldly decided to take the war north. The battle in Sharpsburg, Maryland, was a dangerous gambit because it stretched the southern army's supply line. The battle was intense, the field littered with dead and wounded within moments of the opening gunshot. After the battle, a Pennsylvania soldier walking on the battlefield lamented, "No tongue can tell, no mind conceive, no pen portray the horrible sights I witnessed this morning. God grant these things may soon end and peace be restored. Of this war I am heartily sick and tired." A soldier from Wisconsin called the battle "a great tumbling of all heaven and earth."[41] The two giant armies fought to a virtual standstill, until Lee finally turned back south—an uplifting sight for Union soldiers unused to seeing the backs of retreating Confederates.

With a Union victory, albeit a costly one with total casualties exceeding 26,000 in one horrifying day, Lincoln felt emboldened enough finally to issue, on September 22, the preliminary version of the Emancipation Proclamation—"preliminary" because the final one was to be issued on January 1. Already expecting heavy criticism from some quarters for leaning toward abolition, Lincoln knew that if the Union army's fortunes took another turn for the worse, he could easily miss the opportunity to act. With something resembling a victory, he could push ahead. The cries of radical Republicans and governors who wanted an end to slavery had risen to a fever pitch, and more and more, sentiment was turning their way. The political numbers were with Lincoln, and even with congressional midterm elections looming, he felt he could act.

The Emancipation Proclamation had two incarnations. The preliminary proclamation declared that the slaves in areas still in rebellion against the United States on January 1, 1863, one hundred days hence, would be then and forever free. The president also promised to recommend to Congress a program of gradual and compensated liberation of slaves for concurring states. The military was not to enforce the fugitive slave laws that required their return.

The proclamation was brief and free of Lincoln's usual rhetorical flourishes. Yet few who read it doubted its revolutionary potential.

BY THE PRESIDENT OF THE UNITED STATES OF AMERICA:

A PROCLAMATION.

I, ABRAHAM LINCOLN, President of the United States of America, and Commander-in-Chief of the Army and Navy thereof, do hereby proclaim and declare that hereafter, as heretofore, the war will be prosecuted for the object of practically restoring the constitutional relation between the United States, and each of the States, and the people thereof, in which states that relation is, or may be suspended, or disturbed.

That it is my purpose, upon the next meeting of Congress to again recommend the adoption of a practical measure tendering pecuniary aid to the free acceptance or rejection of all slave states, so called, the people whereof may not then be in rebellion against the United States, and which states, may then have voluntarily adopted, or thereafter may voluntarily adopt, immediate, or gradual abolishment of slavery within their respective limits; and that the effort to colonize persons of African descent, with their consent, upon this continent, or elsewhere, with the previously obtained consent of the governments existing there, will be continued.

That on the first day of January in the year of our Lord, one thousand eight hundred and sixty-three, all persons held as slaves within any state, or designated part of a state, the people whereof shall then be in rebellion against the United States shall be then, thenceforward, and forever free; and the executive government of the United States, including the military and naval authority thereof, will recognise and maintain the freedom of such persons, and will do no act or acts to repress such persons, or any of them, in any efforts they may make for their actual freedom.

That the executive will, on the first day of January aforesaid, by proclamation, designate the States, and parts of states, if any, in which the people thereof respectively, shall then be in rebellion against the Untied States; and the fact that any state, or the people thereof, shall on that day be, in good faith represented in the Congress of the United States, by members chosen thereto at elections wherein a majority of the qualified voters of such state shall have participated, shall, in the absence of strong countervailing testimony, be deemed conclusive evidence that such state and the people thereof, are not then in rebellion against the United States.

That attention is hereby called to an act of Congress entitled "An act to make an additional Article of War" approval March 13, 1862, and which act is in the words and figure following:

"*Be it enacted by the Senate and House of Representatives of the United States of America in Congress assembled.* That hereafter the following shall be promulgated as an additional article of war for the government of the Army of the United States, and shall be obeyed and observed as such:

"ARTICLE—. All officers or persons in the military or naval service of the United States are prohibited from employing any of the forces under their respective commands for the purpose of returning fugitives from service or labor, who may have escaped from any persons to whom such service or labor is claimed to be due, and any officer who shall be found guilty by a court-martial of violating this article shall be dismissed from the service."

"Sec. 2. *And be it further enacted* That this act shall take effect from and after its passage."

Also, to the ninth and tenth sections of an act entitled "An act to suppress Insurrection, to punish Treason and Rebellion, to seize and confiscate the property of rebels, and for other purposes," approved July 17, 1862, and which sections are in the words and figures following:

"Sec. 9. *And be it further enacted* That all slaves of persons who shall hereafter be engaged in rebellion against the government of the United States, or who shall in any way give aid or comfort thereto, escaping from such persons and taking refuge within the lines of the army; and all slaves captured from such persons or deserted by them and coming under the control of the government of the United States; and all slaves of such persons found *on* (or) being within any place occupied by rebel forces and afterwards occupied by the forces of the United States, shall be deemed captives of war, and shall be forever free of their servitude, and not again held as slaves.

"Sec. 10. *And be it further enacted.* That no slave escaping into any State, Territory, or the District of Columbia, from any other State, shall be delivered up, or in any way impeded or hindered of his liberty, except for crime, or some offence against the laws, unless the person claiming said fugitive shall first make oath that the person to whom the labor or service of such fugitive is alleged to be due is his lawful owner, and has not borne arms against the United States in the present rebellion, nor in any way given aid and comfort thereto; and no person engaged in the military or naval service of the United States shall, under any pretence whatever, assume to decide on the validity of the claim of any person to the service or labor of any other person, or surrender up any such person to the claimant, on pain of being dismissed from the service."

And I do hereby enjoin upon and order all persons engaged in the military and naval service of the United States to observe, obey, and enforce, within their respective spheres of service, the act, and sections above recited.

And the Executive will in due time recommend that all citizens of the United States who shall have remained loyal thereto throughout the rebellion, shall (upon the restoration of the constitutional relation between the United States, and their respective states, and people, if that relation shall have been suspended or disturbed) be compensated for all losses by acts of the United States, including the loss of slaves.

In witness whereof, I have hereunto set my hand, and caused the seal of the United States to be affixed.

Done at the City of Washington, this twenty second day of September, in the year of our Lord, one thousand eight hundred and sixty two, and of the Independence of the United States, the eighty seventh.

By the President: ABRAHAM LINCOLN
WILLIAM H. SEWARD, Secretary of State.[42]

Lincoln issued his proclamation in general orders format, meaning that it was an order from Commander-in-Chief Lincoln to his armed forces. The president had complete control over the army, making it unnecessary to go to Congress to make the proclamation effective; thousands of other orders similar to it were issued, though none so controversial or pivotal to United States history.

Lincoln's handling of emancipation demonstrates his concentric legal and political grasp of issues. The problem was prodigious. Nothing in the Constitution authorized the Congress or the president to confiscate property without compensation. When the preliminary Emancipation Proclamation was issued on September 22, 1862, the legal basis of the action seemed obscure. Lincoln cited the two Confiscation Acts of Congress for justification. Occupying a large part of the proclamation, they had little to do with the subject, indicating that Lincoln had not really settled in his own mind the issue of his power to act. When the time came for the final Emancipation Proclamation on January 1, 1863, Lincoln determined that his act was a war measure taken as Commander-in-Chief to weaken the enemy. Thus, justification for emancipation rested on the war power. His interpretation of the law of war was correct. A contemporary treatise on international law stated, a "belligerent has, strictly speaking, a right to use every means necessary to accomplish the end for which he has taken up arms . . . From the moment one State is at war with another, it has, on general principles, a right to seize on all the enemy's property, of whatsoever kind and wheresoever found, and to appropriate the property thus taken to its own use, or to that of the captors." Seizing enemy property is confirmed by the Constitution which empowers Congress to "make Rules concerning Captures on Land and Water."[43]

A major conceptual change occurred between the preliminary and final versions. The first indicated that the intent of the proclamation was to preserve the Union; the final, justified as a war measure, made clear that the purpose was to free slaves in rebellious areas—a new goal of the war. In the preliminary version, "restoring the constitutional relation" between the United States and the states in secession was cited. This version, published in various newspapers, broadsides, and pamphlets, also offered the possibility of the federal government's compensating southerners in rebelling states for the loss of what they considered their property—in this case, slaves. The idea of such payment was appalling to abolitionists and various other Union supporters, because it went right to the core issue of whether human beings could be owned in a free society. When the final Emancipation Proclamation was issued, it was justified "as a fit and necessary war measure for suppressing said *rebellion*," not just as an effort for reunion. "Now, therefore, I, Abraham Lincoln, President of the United States by virtue of the power in me vested as Commander-in-Chief of the army and navy of the United States, in time of actual armed rebellion against the authority and government of the United States, and as a fit and necessary war measure for suppressing said rebellion . . . do order and declare that all persons held as slaves within said designated States and parts of States are, and hence forward shall be free."[44] Thus, in the middle of the war, doing his utmost to preserve the Union and at the same time extending rights to a large portion of slaves was no longer a conflict. Lincoln, without Congress's acting, felt liberated to pursue both goals simultaneously even though he went out of his way to make clear that saving the Union took precedence over the other.

Lincoln's boldness—and considerable political risk taking—cannot be taken for granted. As much as abolitionists criticized Lincoln for not moving quickly enough on emancipation, others who feared its impact condemned him just as vigorously. Press reaction was far from universally congratulatory, and for a time, the evidence suggests, Lincoln worried that his decision might prove the downfall of his administration. For issuing the proclamation, he was called "Abraham Africanus I" by one northern newspaper editor.[45]

Not too many days after the preliminary proclamation was issued, Vice President Hannibal Hamlin wrote a letter to the president to express his "undissembled and sincere thanks for your Emancipation Proclamation," which he predicted would "stand as the great act of the age . . . wise in Statesmanship as it is Patriotic"[46] But Lincoln was not so sure. In a reply he labeled "strictly private," the president poured out his fears and frustrations over the early public response to his document. The fascinating letter reveals a chief executive who knows he will be judged not just by history but by his political constituency—and is clearly not at all sure he will emerge a winner. Modern Americans who doubt the revolutionary impetus and grand daring behind Lincoln's most famous act will understand from the Hamlin letter how unpredictable its author believed its impact would be.

> My Dear Sir: Your kind letter of the 25th is just received. It is known to some that while I hope something from the proclamation, my expectations are not as sanguine as are those of some friends. The time for its effect southward has not come; but northward the effect should be instantaneous.
>
> It is six days old, and while commendation in newspapers and by distinguished individuals is all that a vain man could wish, the stocks have declined, and troops come forward more slowly than ever. This, looked soberly in the face, is not very satisfactory. We have fewer troops in the field at the end of six days than we had at the beginning—the attrition among the old outnumbering the addition by the new. The North responds to the proclamation sufficiently in breath; but breath alone kills no rebels.
>
> I wish I could write more cheerfully; nor do I thank you the less for the kindness of your letter.[47]

THE INTERREGNUM

During the one hundred days between proclamations, the president's gloom was justified. Historian William B. Hesseltine has convincingly argued that "in Lincoln's desk the Emancipation Proclamation would probably have remained had it not been for the increased activities of the radicals and a new move from the governors."[48] Two days after the issuance of the preliminary Emancipation Proclamation, a group of northern governors discontented with the Lincoln administration met in Altoona, Pennsylvania, to discuss war policy. President Lincoln had answered Horace Greeley's "Prayer of Twenty Millions" by saying on August 22 that his policy on slavery was subordinate to saving the Union. The Union had lost the second battle of Bull Run on August 30, Lincoln had restored George B. McClellan to the command of the Army of the Potomac on September 2, and Robert E. Lee had invaded Maryland on September 4.   Pennsylvania governor Andrew G. Curtin and Massachusetts governor John A. Andrew organized a conference of loyal governors to meet on September 24. Some governors wanted Seward out of the cabinet, others disliked McClellan, and still others wanted slavery abolished. Seven days before the meeting, McClellan stopped Lee at Antietam, and newspapers reported the day before the conference that Lincoln had issued the preliminary Emancipation Proclamation. It turned the governors around, and their final action, described as an "address," commended the proclamation and recommended a "reserve" of 100,000 men to repel invasions. Lincoln cordially invited the governors to the White House, where, on September 26, he heard their address and defended McClellan.

But Lincoln knew that the governors' endorsement would not fill the armies. The preliminary Emancipation Proclamation strengthened Democratic appeal to the war-weary, antiblack population. The proclamation made it more necessary than ever that the president find new methods for obtaining soldiers and combating the opposition. It made victory on the battlefield more urgently required than ever.

Criticism of the Emancipation Proclamation was much subdued after the president issued on September 24 another proclamation suspending the privilege of the writ of habeas corpus throughout the country and authorizing the arbitrary arrest of any person "guilty of any disloyal practice, affording aid and comfort to Rebels against the authority of the United States."[49]

Mark E. Neely Jr., in *The Fate of Liberty: Abraham Lincoln and Civil Liberties*, has suggested that the first-time suspension of habeas corpus for the whole country grew out of Stanton's August 8 orders to enforce the Militia Act of July 17, 1862, which empowered the secretary of war to draft militia men for nine months in states that failed to make their quota.[50] Stanton aimed at enforcing the first national conscription in U.S. history. Whatever the reason for the suspension of the writ, Democrats like Senator James Bayard of Delaware read it to mean that the president was "declaring himself a dictator, (for that and nothing less it does)."[51] Whatever Lincoln's intent, the new proclamation had a chilling effect on public dissent and press criticism as well, as editors feared they might be locked up in a military prison if they objected to administration policies.

Proclamations notwithstanding, President Lincoln continued to have problems with General McClellan. On July 8, Lincoln had visited him at Harrison's Landing to see the condition of the Army of the Potomac after the Seven Days battles. McClellan had handed Lincoln a presumptuous letter outlining his views on the conduct of the war. "It should not be a war looking to the subjugation of the people of any state," he wrote. "Neither confiscation of property, political execution of persons, territorial organization of States, or forcible abolition of slavery should be contemplated for a moment . . . A declaration of radical views, especially upon slavery, will rapidly disintegrate our present armies."⁵² Clearly the general's views were not shared by the president, who had already decided to draft an Emancipation Proclamation. McClellan's war aims only underscored Republican suspicions that the general's heart was not in waging war. Worse, McClellan's ideas seemed to some an only slightly veiled opening bid for the Democratic presidential nomination two years later. In fact, some New York Democrats had already approached the general to be their candidate.

As it happened, McClellan's failure to follow up his Antietam triumph in September and October 1862 was destined to end his military career. Dispatch after dispatch from Washington urged him to give the Confederates a knockout punch. McClellan responded with excuses for delay—he was outnumbered, must train new recruits, and could not march until his men had new clothing and shoes—all this despite the tattered condition of Lee's defeated army. The president visited the army at the beginning of October and personally urged McClellan to get moving. Upon his return to the capital, Lincoln had Gen. Henry Halleck order McClellan to advance. Several days later, McClellan explained that his advance must be delayed until he could replace fatigued horses. Lincoln replied with a sarcastic telegram: "Will you pardon me for asking what the horses of your army have done since the Battle of Antietam that fatigues anything?"⁵³ Lincoln's patience finally ran out, and on November 7 he relieved McClellan from command, appointing a reluctant Ambrose E. Burnside his successor. While the soldiers gave McClellan an emotional farewell, talk about marching on Washington and their own government came to nothing. Lincoln justified his decision to his secretary John Hay: "I peremptorily ordered him to advance . . . [he kept] delaying on little pretext of wanting this and that. I began to fear he was playing false—that he did not want to hurt the enemy. I saw how he could intercept the enemy on the way to Richmond. I determined to make that the test. If he let them get away I would remove him. He did so & I relieved him."⁵⁴

American voters, in turn, "relieved" some of their elected officials. Most congressional and gubernatorial nominations for the 1862 elections were made before Lincoln issued the preliminary Emancipation Proclamation, but emancipation inevitably became a key issue in all northern elections. While the proclamation strengthened the Republican party in New England and the upper Northwest by attracting support from abolitionists, elsewhere the result was decidedly negative. Lincoln expected to lose Republican votes because of emancipation. Democrats compounded his weaknesses by effectively using the suspension of the writ of habeas corpus to their further political advantage, arguing that, together, the suspension and the preliminary proclamation offered indisputable evidence that Lincoln aspired to become a dictator. At least the president's political acumen, if not his policies, was vindicated when he learned the election results. He and the Republican party suffered a severe setback. Democrats made huge gains in New York, Pennsylvania, Ohio, Indiana, and Illinois. While the Republican party retained control of the new House of Representatives, which would not meet until December 1863, its majority was drastically reduced. Democrats increased their membership in the next Congress by thirty-one seats. Indisputably bad news for the Republicans, it was not a fatal defeat.⁵⁵

When the lame-duck Congress convened in December 1862, the Republicans reaffirmed emancipation. First, they rejected a Democratic-sponsored House resolution that declared that anyone in the government who proposed to wage war "for the overthrowing or interfering with the rights or established institutions of any of the States" was guilty of "a high crime against the Constitution." Then, by a straight party vote, the House adopted a resolution endorsing Lincoln's Emancipation Proclamation.[56] Although Congress may arguably have led the way with its toothless but symbolic Confiscation Acts, now it was following Lincoln on the road to true freedom.

Following their success in the 1862 election, Democrats hoped the president would withdraw the Emancipation Proclamation. Their hopes grew when they read Lincoln's annual message to Congress on December 1. The president proposed a constitutional amendment to provide for the compensated, gradual—not until 1900—emancipation in every state "wherein slavery now exists." Many asked why Lincoln would recommend this measure if he planned to issue the Emancipation Proclamation on January 1. But those who interpreted the message as a substitute for the proclamation missed the point. The president also said that no proceedings under the September 22 preliminary proclamation would be delayed by his proposal, and that all slaves freed "by the chances of war" would remain "forever free." As he memorably concluded, in one of his greatest perorations (which, unfortunately, tradition forbade him from delivering personally):

> The dogmas of the quiet past, are inadequate to the stormy present . . . As our case is new, so we must think anew, and act anew. We must disenthrall ourselves, and then we shall save our country. Fellow citizens, we cannot escape history . . . The fiery trial through which we pass, will light us down, in honor or dishonor, to the latest generations. In *giving* freedom to the *slave*, we *assure* freedom to the *free*.[57]

For weeks, General Burnside, encamped in Virginia, had seemed ready to respond to Lincoln's desire for hard marching and hard fighting by giving the North the victory the president desired to support his policies, including emancipation. The entire army was opposite the town of Fredericksburg by November 19. However, pontoons that Burnside had ordered for crossing the Rappahannock River were lost and did not arrive until the end of November. This delay allowed Lee to concentrate his army on the heights behind Fredericksburg before Burnside's army could bridge the river. On December 11, Union engineers encountered sniper fire as they began to place the pontoons. Finally, the army crossed the river for an attack on December 13. But Burnside's aggressiveness would yield no victories. Lee had 74,000 men along a seven-mile front. The 113,000 Union troops were organized in "grand divisions" of two corps each. Confederate general James Longstreet had riflemen posted along a sunken road behind a stone wall at the base of Marye's Heights on the Union right. Artillery commanded the half-mile stretch of open ground over which the Union troops had to advance. The Union troops showed great courage as they launched seven futile assaults against Marye's Heights. When dark fell, the ground in front of the stone wall was covered for acres with dead and dying men. By the time the shooting stopped, the Union army had suffered 12,600 casualties—the Confederates fewer than 5,000. Nothing had been gained, and Burnside was beside himself with grief for his bleeding army. His subordinates talked him out of personally leading a charge the next day. The Army of the Potomac pulled back over the river during the night of December 15.[58]

Lincoln's desire for military success required an unprecedented winter campaign in a season when armies normally rested and refitted during the months of bad weather. Burnside's failure at Fredericksburg became Lincoln's hell and brought to a head a political crisis that had been simmering throughout the fall months. Many Republicans, dissatisfied with the administration's conduct, focused on Secretary of State Seward. Distrusted by radicals since his efforts at compromise during 1860–61, Seward was believed to be the "unseen hand" whose conservative influence over Lincoln had undermined vigorous presidential leadership—especially on the issue of slavery. On December 16 and 17, all but one Republican senator voted to request a reorganization of the cabinet. The resolution, clearly aimed at Seward, was inspired by Secretary of the Treasury Chase, Seward's main rival in the cabinet and a close associate of the radical senators. The constitutional crisis that followed would test Lincoln's leadership. If Lincoln gave in to the senatorial demand, he would lose control of his administration. Apoplectic, the president told a friend, "What do these men want? . . . they wish to get rid of me, and I am sometimes half disposed to gratify them . . . Since I heard last night of the proceedings of the caucus I have been more distressed than by any event of my life . . . We are now on the brink of destruction. It appears to me the Almighty is against us, and I can hardly see a ray of hope."[59]

Lincoln met with a delegation of eight senators on December 19 but did not reveal that Seward had already submitted his resignation. He calmly listened to the senators' speeches attacking his secretary of state. To his credit, the president invited the delegation back the next day for further discussion, exhibiting his usual political skills when they returned. The president had arranged for all members of the cabinet, except Seward, to be present. Lincoln told the senators in a tactful but forceful speech that whenever possible, he consulted the cabinet about important questions, but he alone made the decisions; that members of the cabinet sometimes disagreed but that all supported a policy once it had been decided upon; and that Seward remained a valued member of the administration. The president then asked each cabinet member for confirmation, and all had little choice but to agree—even Chase, who had earlier told the senators that Seward was responsible for the dysfunction in the cabinet. If he now denied it, he would lose face with his Senate allies, but if he reaffirmed it, he would lose the confidence of the president. Chase endorsed Lincoln's statement but tried to extricate himself by saying that major decisions should have been more fully discussed by the cabinet. But the senators knew that Lincoln had won the day. Embarrassed, Chase offered his resignation the next day. "Where is it?" demanded Lincoln. Chase handed it over, and Lincoln scanned the letter. "This," he said, "cuts the Gordian knot. I can dispose of this subject now without difficulty." Thus, the Republican senators could not have Seward's resignation without losing Chase as well. Lincoln used a characteristic metaphor to describe his triumph. "Now I can ride; I have a pumpkin in each end of my bag." In the end, the president refused both resignations, the cabinet remained unchanged, and another crisis passed.[60]

As the year 1862 came to a close, Lincoln yet again proved himself a master politician—and did so without making enemies. On January 1, Lincoln signed the document proclaiming freedom for all slaves in the portions of the Confederate states not then occupied by Union troops. Few Americans, white or black, knew how many roadblocks and detours their president had avoided and conquered en route to his most historic act.

THE FINAL EMANCIPATION PROCLAMATION

On December 30, copies of the preliminary draft of the final Emancipation Proclamation were prepared and distributed to members of the cabinet.

[December 30, 1862]

Whereas, on the twenty second day of September, in the year of our Lord one thousand, eight hundred and sixty-two, a proclamation was issued by the President of the United States, containing among other things the following, to wit:

[Blank space for insertion]

Now therefore I, Abraham Lincoln, President of the United States, by virtue of the power in me vested, as Commander-in-Chief, of the Army, and Navy of the United States in time of actual armed rebellion against the authority and government of the United States, and as a proper and necessary war measure for suppressing said rebellion, do, on this first day of January in the year of our Lord one thousand eight hundred and sixty three, and in accordance with my intention so to do, publicly proclaimed for one hundred days as aforesaid, order and designate as the States and parts of States in which the people thereof respectively are this day in rebellion against the United States, the following to wit:

Arkansas, Texas, Louisiana, except the Parishes of

[Blank space for insertion]

Mississippi, Alabama, Florida, Georgia, South Carolina, North Carolina, and Virginia, except the forty-eight counties designated as West Virginia, and also the counties of

[Blank space for insertion]

And by virtue of the power, and for the purpose aforesaid, I do order, and declare, that all persons held as slaves within said designated States, and parts of States, are, and henceforward forever shall be free; and that the Executive government of the United States, including the military and naval authorities thereof, will recognize and maintain the freedom of said persons and will do no act, or acts to repress said persons, or any of them, in any suitable efforts they may make for their actual freedom. And I hereby appeal to the people so declared to be free, to abstain from all disorder, tumult, and violence, unless in necessary self defence; and in all cases, when allowed, to labor faithfully, for wages.

And I further declare, and make known, that such persons of suitable condition will be received into the armed service of the United States to garrison and defend forts, positions, stations, and other places, and to man vessels of all sorts in said service.[61]

Each cabinet member was requested to make suggestions. Most of the suggested revisions dealt with only two issues: (1) specific identification of states and parts of states exempt from the proclamation—now under Union control because any territory within Union lines could insist that federal civil law was now applicable there and that the use of the president's war powers, like suspension of the writ of habeas corpus and martial law, no longer applied in those areas occupied by Union forces;[62] and (2) the concern by Bates, Seward, Postmaster Gen. Montgomery Blair, and Chase over the language that the government "will recognize and maintain the freedom of said persons and will do no act, or acts to repress said persons, or any of them, in any suitable efforts they may make for their actual freedom," and Lincoln's "appeal to the people so declared to be free, to abstain from all disorder, tumult, and violence, unless in necessary self defence." Believing this language to be too provocative, the president finally acquiesced so that the final Emancipation Proclamation read "that the Executive government of the United States, including the military and naval authorities thereof, will recognize and maintain the freedom of said persons." The proclamation would "enjoin upon the people so declared to be free to abstain from all violence, unless in necessary self defence; and I recommend to them that, in all cases when allowed, they labor faithfully for reasonable wages." Otherwise, the final draft delivered the promise made in the preliminary Emancipation Proclamation.

On January 1, 1863, with fingers still aching from shaking hands at a New Year's reception, Abraham Lincoln signed the final Emancipation Proclamation. It freed "henceforth and forever" slaves "within any state or designated part of a State whose people . . . shall then be in rebellion against the United States." It directed that the military protect the freedom of slaves and accept blacks, who were already serving in the armed service of the United States. (This latter provision was the most significant change between the preliminary and the final proclamations.) Lincoln again based the authority of his proclamation on his power as the commander-in-chief and specifically termed the measure "a fit and necessary war measure for suppressing [the] rebellion."

By the President of the United States of America:

A PROCLAMATION.

Whereas, on the twenty second day of September, in the year of our Lord one thousand eight hundred and sixty two, a proclamation was issued by the President of the United States, containing, among other things, the following, to wit:

"That on the first day of January, in the year of our Lord one thousand eight hundred and sixty-three, all persons held as slaves within any State or designated part of a State, the people whereof shall then be in rebellion against the United States, shall be then, thenceforward, and forever free; and the Executive Government of the United States, including the military and naval authority thereof, will recognize and maintain the freedom of such persons, and will do no act or acts to repress such persons, or any of them, in any efforts they may make for their actual freedom.

"That the Executive will, on the first day of January aforesaid, by proclamation, designate the States, and parts of States, if any, in which the people thereof, respectively shall then be in rebellion against the United States; and the fact that any State, or the people thereof, shall on that day be, in good faith, represented in the Congress of the United States by members chosen thereto at elections wherein a majority of the qualified voters of such State shall have participated, shall, in the absence of strong countervailing testimony, be deemed conclusive evidence that such State, and the people thereof, are not then in rebellion against the United States."

Now, therefore I, Abraham Lincoln, President of the United States, by virtue of the power in me vested as Commander-in-Chief of the Army and Navy of the United States in time of actual armed rebellion against the authority and government of the United States, and as a fit and necessary war measure for suppressing said rebellion, do, on this first day of January, in the year of our Lord one thousand eight hundred and sixty three, and in accordance with my purpose so to do publicly proclaimed for the full period of one hundred days from the day first above mentioned, order and designate as the States and parts of States wherein the people thereof respectively, are this day in rebellion against the United States, the following, to wit:

Arkansas, Texas, Louisiana (except the parishes of St. Bernard, Plaquemines, Jefferson, St. John's, St. Charles, St. James[,] Ascension, Assumption, Terrebonne, Lafourche, St. Mary, St. Martin, and Orleans, including the (city of New Orleans) Mississippi, Alabama, Florida, Georgia, South-Carolina, North-Carolina, and Virginia, (except the forty eight counties designated as West Virginia, and also the counties of Berkley, Accomac, Northampton, Elizabeth-City, York, Princess Ann, and Norfolk, including the cities of Norfolk & Portsmouth,[ )]; and which excepted parts are for the present, left precisely as if this proclamation were not issued.

And by virtue of the power, and for the purpose aforesaid, I do order and declare that all persons held as slaves within said designated States, and parts of States, are, and henceforward shall be free; and that the Executive government of the United States, including the military and naval authorities thereof, will recognize and maintain the freedom of said persons.

And I do hereby enjoin upon the people so declared to be free to abstain from all violence, unless in necessary self-defence; and I recommend to them that, in all cases when allowed, they labor faithfully for reasonable wages.

And I further declare and make known, that such persons of suitable condition, will be received into the armed service of the United States to garrison forts, positions, stations, and other places, and to man vessels of all sorts in said service.

And upon this act, sincerely believed to be an act of justice, warranted by the Constitution, upon military necessity, I invoke the considerate judgment of mankind and the gracious favor of Almighty God.

In witness whereof, I have hereunto set my hand and caused the seal of the United States to be affixed.

Done at the City of Washington, this first day of January, in the year of our Lord one thousand eight hundred and [L.S.] sixty three, and of the Independence of the United States of America the eighty-seventh.

By the President:
ABRAHAM LINCOLN.
William H. Seward,
        Secretary of State.[63]

In his final Emancipation Proclamation, Lincoln specifically exempted the Union border states as well as various parts of the former Confederacy, mentioning particular states and parts of states that were already under the control of the Union army. Hence some critics complained, and some have argued since, that he had in effect freed no one. Suspicious abolitionists agreed with Seward that "We show our sympathy with slavery by emancipating the slaves where we cannot reach them and holding them in bondage where we can set them free."[64] In truth, always conscientious about exercising his power judiciously—even sparingly—Lincoln believed his military prerogatives did not extend into regions of the former Confederacy that were already in the process of returning to the Union, and accordingly, under the civilian authority of state and local officials. Hearing of the emancipation order through the slave grapevine, thousands of slaves, even in territory still controlled by the Confederacy, fled to the protection of the Union lines. Their numbers gave the lie to the view that the proclamation did not immediately free the slaves in the South. Later, Seward expressed his belief that the Emancipation Proclamation freed at least 200,000 slaves by February 1865.[65] With support of the administration, the slaves walked, ran, or rowed to freedom.

A former Alabama slave, Wallace Turnage, who in the late nineteenth century wrote an account of his years in slavery, recalled that in 1864 he escaped in a rowboat on Mobile Bay, where he was rescued in rough weather by a Union gunboat: "I Now dread the gun and handcuffs and pistols no more. Nor the blewing of horns and running of hounds; nor the threats of death from the rebel's authority. I can now speak my opinion to men of all grades and colors, and no one to question my right to speak."[66]

No matter how many slaves were actually freed under the specific auspices of the Emancipation Proclamation, what proved essential to the war was that Lincoln, by issuing it, had made the liberation of slaves a goal of the Union government. Not only did emancipation begin removing the useful labor of blacks from the home front of the Confederacy, but it added their labor power to the Union cause. Even though the president described emancipation as a "necessary war measure," he also showed political shrewdness by making it a goal of his administration. Despite objections from some soldiers, they quickly came to realize that emancipation had become just as important as defeating the Confederacy and preserving the Union. Emancipation no longer meant destroying slavery by defeating southerners who were defending the institution and relying on it to wage war, threatening the Union.[67]

Henry V. Jaffa has answered revisionist scholarship insisting that the Emancipation Proclamation was a cynical document of little actual effect: "The Emancipation Proclamation progressively deprived the Confederacy of a vast reservoir of slave labor, which had enabled many more Southern whites to serve in the Confederate ranks than would otherwise have been possible. It also added great numbers of emancipated slaves to the ranks of the Union armies, as well as giving them the greatest of all incentives to fight. Notwithstanding the Proclamation's exceptions and exemptions, which proved temporary, it destroyed the viability of the institution of chattel slavery in the whole Union."[68]

What about the charge that the proclamation, because justified on the ground of "military necessity," should not be taken seriously as an assertion of moral authority? Jaffa writes: "In issuing the Proclamation, Lincoln acted from military necessity. In the Gettysburg Address, Lincoln called upon the nation to ratify what had been done, not simply because it was necessary, but because it was good."[69]

Historian James M. McPherson has convincingly pointed out that it was the horrific war that led Lincoln to support a revolutionary transformation of the American republic. This required adopting not only more aggressive military tactics but also a more radical position on slavery than he had previously embraced.[70] The status quo was no longer tenable. Ultimately, Lincoln adopted the position that slavery should be ended entirely by the war. This required him to move away from a careful bipartisan strategy used early in the war, which was designed not to alienate border state moderates and Democrats. While Lincoln may have hesitated, his determination was clear by the time he delivered the Gettysburg Address on November 19, 1863. As Garry Wills notes in *Lincoln at Gettysburg,* the 272 words of this speech deliberately attached the hope of universal rights contained in the Declaration of Independence to the war effort.[71] No longer was the North fighting to restore the Union and no longer was the extension of freedom a happenstance of war tactics. Rather, "a new birth of freedom" was the very reason that the war was being fought. In an earlier phrase, Lincoln had said that "we here highly resolve that these dead shall not have died in vain." This is a statement that Lincoln would not have made at the beginning of the war, when he was trying to reunite the country without regard to what was done about slavery. Three weeks after delivery of the Gettysburg Address, in his annual message to Congress, Lincoln pledged that he would "not attempt to retract or modify the Emancipation Proclamation." He added teeth to the measure by making acceptance of the proclamation a condition of the loyalty oath that would be administered to individuals repatriated in what had been rebel territory.

As Gen. Ulysses S. Grant pointed out with some indignation after the war: "The South had 4,000,000 of negroes. These negroes kept the farms, protected the families, supported the armies, and were really a reserve force, a most important reserve force in a fighting nation. Those 4,000,000 of negroes did a work that white men would have been compelled to do. Yet they are never counted in any summary of the forces of the South. They are forgotten as if they never had existed."[72] Lincoln did not forget that the black labor force existed, and he was determined to use his proclamation to remove that advantage from the rebels.

Now, as the northern armies moved deeper into the Confederacy, more and more slaves were freed. The end of slavery thus became a national war goal of the U.S. government and for many white northerners and all black ones, the moral justification of a brutal conflict.

The Emancipation Proclamation also encouraged the use of blacks ("suitable persons") to "garrison forts, positions, stations, and . . . man vessels." Some African Americans had already fought in battles in Louisiana, Tennessee, and Kansas. But Lincoln—who had never before called for blacks as infantry—now, as he did on many important issues, changed his mind and became a fervent advocate of enlisting black troops. The president spoke to the importance of "inducing the colored people to come bodily over from the rebel side to ours."[73] When they did, as he proudly noted in a letter to Gov. Andrew Johnson in March 1863, they represented "the great *available* and yet *unavailed* of, force for restoring the Union," adding, "The bare sight of fifty thousand armed, and drilled black soldiers on the banks of the Mississippi, would end the rebellion at once."[74] Lincoln realized that arming southern blacks, "to whatever extent it weakened the enemy," aided reunion and made emancipation an acceptable national goal. "I thought that whatever negroes can be got to do as soldiers, leaves just so much less for white soldiers to do, in saving the Union . . . But Negroes, like other people, act upon motives. Why should they do anything for us, if we will do nothing for them? If they stake their lives for us, they must be prompted by the strongest motive—even the promise of freedom. And the promise being made, must be kept."[75]

Lincoln was solicitous of the situation of blacks, especially when they were at risk. The widow of Maj. Lionel Booth, commander of black soldiers killed in the Fort Pillow massacre in 1864, requested that the widows and children of black soldiers ought to receive the same benefits as those received by the widows and children of white soldiers. Lincoln agreed, and a pending bill was amended so that blacks as well as whites would receive benefits.[76] Lincoln also signed an order on July 30, 1863, that would put Confederate prisoners to death in retaliation for black prisoners being executed.[77]

Proclamation notwithstanding, Lincoln did still need the continued support of the slaveholding border states. He remained fearful that the border states would bolt the Union if he emancipated their slaves. Maryland did not outlaw slavery until 1864, and Tennessee and Missouri waited until early 1865. Delaware and Kentucky—the latter of which had 60,000 slaves—retained slavery until it was outlawed by the Thirteenth Amendment to the Constitution in December 1865—many months after the war was over and Lincoln assassinated. Lincoln eloquently summarized his position on emancipation in an 1864 letter reviewing what he had said at a March 1864 meeting with the governor of Kentucky, a former senator from that state, and a Kentucky newspaper editor, to discuss the enlistment of slaves as soldiers. He stated that he believed in 1862 that the "indispensable necessity for military emancipation, and arming the blacks would come" unless the border states accepted his proposal for compensated emancipation. When the border states declined his offer, "I was driven to the alternative of either surrendering the Union, and with it, the Constitution, or of laying strong hand upon the colored element, I choose the latter." Lincoln carefully set forth a distinction between his own values and his obligations under the Constitution:

> I am naturally anti-slavery. If slavery is not wrong, nothing is wrong. I can not remember when I did not so think, and feel. And yet I have never understood that the Presidency conferred upon me an unrestricted right to act officially upon this judgment and feeling. It was in the oath I took that I would, to the best of my ability, preserve, protect, and defend the Constitution of the United States. I could not take the office without taking the oath. Nor was it my view that I might take an oath to get power, and break the oath in using the power. I understood, too, that in ordinary civil administration this oath even forbade me to practically indulge my primary abstract judgment on the moral question of slavery.[78]

Lincoln consistently believed he had no constitutional authority to declare a broader emancipation. Instead, he felt that the war powers granted to him as president would make legal, and the courts would sustain him if he issued, a narrower emancipation with a specific military purpose— hastening the end of rebellion.[79] But make no mistake: The proclamation was still a "great American document of freedom," as John Hope Franklin wrote in 1963.[80]

Technical, legal, political, and military issues aside, the proclamation was clearly of larger moral significance. It recognized that the war was fundamentally about the injustice of slavery. Many northerners had tried to avoid acknowledging that the war was inextricably linked to the bondsman's plight. The emancipation changed that. "The war became more than a war to save the integrity and independence of the Union. It became also a war to promote the freedom of mankind,"[81] Franklin has written. The abolitionist Henry Ward Beecher, upon hearing Lincoln's preliminary Emancipation Proclamation on September 22, 1862, said, "That Proclamation may not free a single slave, but it gives liberty a moral recognition."[82]

Some abolitionists did remain upset at the emancipation's exceptions. But throughout the North and South, Lincoln's proclamation was greeted by slaves and freedmen as a broad emancipation. Slaves were spurred to flee to freedom and take up arms in the Union cause because they now knew that there was an administration in Washington that had adopted a policy of liberty for them if they escaped. By April 1865, approximately 186,000 black soldiers and sailors had joined the struggle.[83]

Perhaps the Emancipation Proclamation was greater than the sum of its parts. It is properly remembered as a great document; the exact wording is arguably not that important. Its wording is definitely not inspiring, except the closing phrase: "And upon this Act, sincerely believed to be an act of justice, warranted by the Constitution upon military necessity, I invoke the considerate judgment of mankind and the gracious favor of Almighty God." Its mundane specificity is almost mind-numbing, but it was, in fact, the work of the Great Emancipator.

On January 1, 1863, after nearly two years of armed rebellion by eleven slaveholding states, President Abraham Lincoln proclaimed that the slaves in eight of those states and in large portions of two others were freed forever and that their freedom would be recognized and protected by the U.S. government and its armed forces. Apart from the Declaration of Independence, this proclamation may be the single most significant statement of policy issued by a governing authority in the history of the country. It marked the end of governmental support for slavery, reversing a pattern of the national government to treat slavery as a domestic practice of individual states, the operation of which existed outside the scope of federal power. It gave legal standing to the freedom already claimed by African Americans who were throwing off the shackles of bondage and moving to Union lines. And it shifted the moral tenor of the Civil War from a quest to restore the Union and its governing authority to an armed struggle for Union that would also result in freedom for slaves. Despite its moral significance, the actual proclamation reads like the legal document it was intended to be. Yet its legalese, written as a war measure by the commander-in-chief to survive challenges in court, could not hide the true meaning and purpose of the Emancipation Proclamation—the end of American slavery.

At the war's outbreak, the Union government had adopted as its policy the suppression of the rebellion. The Lincoln administration, out of conviction and legal interest, defined the rebellion as the work of a minority of southern insurrectionists. The Union would achieve success by restoring control of the eleven seceded state governments to people loyal to the Union. Under such a scenario, slaves and slavery did not play a part. Loyal southerners had a right to their property, and Lincoln feared driving them into the ranks of the secessionists if his government appeared to use the incident of rebellion to emancipate slaves. Practically, if Lincoln's government moved precipitously against slavery, the four slaveholding border states might be induced to secede as well. For this reason Lincoln himself had refused to endorse efforts by generals John Frémont and David Hunter to free slaves in sectors under their command early in the war.

This reluctance angered black and white abolitionists, who pointed out that the white southerner's resolve to uphold slavery had caused the Civil War, and that slave labor made Confederate resistance more formidable by freeing more white southerners to serve in the military. Further, as Confederate resistance continued, the insurrection by an armed minority looked more and more like a war. Because the Lincoln government determined to treat captured Confederate soldiers according to the laws of war, it seemed to follow that the laws of war could be extended to justify the seizure of enemy property.

Not everyone in the North agreed with emancipation. Even the Union army was filled with rumors of mutiny over the proclamation. The legislature of Illinois condemned the proclamation so virulently with fears of black immigration that it was shut down by Gov. Richard Yates. In Indiana, Gov. Oliver P. Morton could not garner a quorum in the senate to approve the state's budget.[84] Even New York City erupted in a riot over the draft in July 1863, which quickly turned into a bloody anti-emancipation revolt. To one critic, James Conkling, the president made clear the resolve behind his order—as he wrote on August 26, 1863: "You dislike the emancipation proclamation; and, perhaps, would have it retracted. You say it is unconstitutional—I think differently. I think the constitution invests its commander-in-chief, with the law of war, in time of war. The most that can be said, if so much, is, that slaves are property. Is there—has there ever been—any question that by the law of war, property, both of enemies and friends, may be taken when needed? And is it not needed whenever taking it, helps us, or hurts the enemy?"[85]

The letter exemplified the Lincoln who consistently took the shortest distance between two legal points. The proposition as a matter of law may be argued, but this analysis focuses on Lincoln's political and legal approach to the law rather than the law itself. Lincoln saw the slavery problem with the same logical directness with which he saw most problems. A commander-in-chief may, under military necessity, take property. Slaves are property. There is a military necessity, so the commander-in-chief proclaims that the property is taken.

Lincoln's legal logic is also evident in his letter to Conkling: "You say you will not fight to free negroes. Some of them seem willing to fight for you; but, no matter. Fight you, then, exclusively to save the Union . . . Whenever you shall have conquered all resistance to the Union, if I shall urge you to continue fighting, it will be an apt time, then, for you to declare you will not fight to free negroes."[86]

THE THIRTEENTH AMENDMENT

After 1863, Lincoln sought additional ways to advance emancipation in the slaveholding border states of Maryland, Delaware, Kentucky, and Missouri, where he did not have military authority to end slavery. He insisted on a plank in the 1864 Republican platform supporting a Thirteenth Amendment to the Constitution that would abolish slavery throughout the United States.[87]

Ironically, this proposed Thirteenth Amendment was significantly different from a proposed amendment that was transmitted to the states by Abraham Lincoln ten days after his inauguration. That Thirteenth Amendment would have forbidden the federal government from interfering with slavery in those states where the institution was already established: "No amendment shall be made to the Constitution which will authorize or give to Congress the power to abolish or interfere, within any State, with the domestic institutions thereof, including that of persons held to labor or service by the laws of said State."

The permanent abolition of slavery in the United States offered greater authority but required far more political effort and authority than an executive order. The first resolutions for a constitutional amendment abolishing slavery came before the House and Senate in December 1863. The final form of the resolution embodied in the Thirteenth Amendment was reported to the Senate by Lyman

Trumbull, chairman of the chamber's judicial committee. Its wording closely mirrored those passages in Thomas Jefferson's 1787 Northwest Ordinance that barred slavery from the nation's first frontier territories.

Lincoln lobbied personally for the new Thirteenth Amendment.[88] Politically, its fate rode on the 1864 presidential election. The platform of the Democratic party pledged recognition of state rights, which was understood to refer to the right of states to authorize and maintain slavery if they so chose. Lincoln's Republican party platform called for the "utter and complete extirpation" of slavery, which was understood to include the passage of the Thirteenth Amendment. Although documentary evidence is lacking, Lincoln truly authorized this plank himself. Just six weeks after the Gettysburg Address, Missouri senator John Henderson, introduced an emancipation amendment. Congress debated this amendment and other versions introduced afterward in the first half of 1864. In June 1864, Lincoln publicly endorsed the amendment, even though the required number of representatives was not yet ready to give it their approval. In any event, Lincoln had come out unequivocally in favor of immediate, uncompensated emancipation.

Northern Democrats portrayed emancipation as prolonging the war, but, as Michael Vorenberg makes clear, rescinding the proclamation alone would not have ended the war. Nothing short of Confederate surrender would have led to peace.[89] Lincoln himself required conditions such as "restoration of the Union and the abandonment of slavery," which he insisted Horace Greeley present at the informal negotiations with Confederate emissaries in Niagara Falls during the summer of 1864, knowing they would be unacceptable to the Confederate government. At this stage in the war, Lincoln insisted on both freedom and Union, which was tantamount to a Confederate capitulation.

Although the resolution calling for submission of the amendment to the states easily won its required two-thirds assent in the Senate on April 8, 1864, by a thirty-eight to six vote, passage by the House proved more difficult. In fact, the resolution failed to achieve a two-thirds majority when first submitted in June 1864. But that summer brought a presidential campaign, and Lincoln made "such amendment to the Constitution . . . as shall terminate and forever prohibit the existence of slavery within . . . the United States" part of the Republican platform on which he ran.[90] Reelected by a wide margin in 1864, Lincoln lent his personal prestige and employed his vast patronage and political powers to prod the House of Representatives into passing the amendment when it reconvened. Lincoln believed in the morality of the proposed amendment and as a bonus thought its passage by the Congress would further erode the Confederate war effort. Although the 1864 election gave his party a sufficient majority to break the deadlock in the House, he wanted the sitting Congress to approve the proposal, as the new Congress would not convene until December 1865. Should Democrats generally, and especially those from the border states, reverse their votes, it would dash the Confederacy's hopes that the border states might come to its rescue.

To that end, Lincoln authorized and supported Secretary of State Seward's massive lobbying effort in New York, whose large congressional delegation was critical to the fate of the amendment and whose borders contained many Democrats. With Lincoln's reelection in November, anti-emancipation forces in the House recognized the new order. The joint resolution embodying the Thirteenth Amendment, with Lincoln's influence, was finally adopted in the lower house on January 31, 1865, by a vote of 119 to 56, with eight Democratic congressmen abstaining to allow a two-thirds majority.

Several copies of the Thirteenth Amendment resolution were quickly published, most likely created as fund-raisers for events like the great Sanitary Commission Fairs in Philadelphia and Boston. The urge to create these souvenirs reflected the tremendous significance of the amendment's passage. Almost four years after the firing on Fort Sumter—and two years after the executive Emancipation Proclamation—the Congress of the United States had recognized that the Civil War was against slavery and that the Union would insist that "neither slavery nor involuntary servitude, except as punishment for crime, whereof the party shall have been duly convicted, shall exist within the United States, or any place subject to their jurisdiction."

Thirteen of these congressional souvenir copies of the Thirteenth Amendment were signed by Abraham Lincoln. Ironically, given his pivotal role in making the Civil War a conflict about emancipation and his dedication to the principle embodied in the amendment, Lincoln's signature on—or endorsement of—the resolution submitting the Thirteenth Amendment for ratification was entirely unnecessary. Lincoln customarily signed copies of acts and resolutions of Congress, but the Supreme Court had ruled in 1798 that the president "has nothing to do with the proposition or adoption of amendments to the Constitution."[91] Indeed, the Senate was so offended by Lincoln's signature on the official copy of the resolution, now in the National Archives, that on February 7, 1865, that chamber adopted another resolution condemning Lincoln's signing of the document as unconstitutional.

Ratification of the Thirteenth Amendment was swift. To his immense satisfaction, Lincoln's own Illinois ratified it the day after the resolution was sent to the states for approval. President Andrew Johnson required ratification of the amendment by former confederate states as part of his policy of reconstruction, and the confirmation by eight of these formerly seceded states helped the Thirteenth Amendment to gain the assent of the required three-fourths of the states and to become, on December 18, 1865, "valid as part of the Constitution of the United States."[92]

The wording of the Thirteenth Amendment to the U.S. Constitution is simple and straightforward: "Neither slavery nor involuntary servitude . . . shall exist within the United States, or any place subject to their jurisdiction." Its passage ended debate about the status of the American institution that, as Lincoln had said, "all knew . . . was, somehow, the cause of the [civil] war."[93] Because it lacked the symbolism and military force of President Lincoln's Emancipation Proclamation and because it was ratified after Lincoln's assassination, the Thirteenth Amendment often receives short shrift. But Lincoln recognized its importance from the first. The validity of his Emancipation Proclamation rested on his powers as commander-in-chief. Whether his wartime measure could survive challenges in courts or would have permanence after the war remained an open question. Second, his Emancipation Proclamation excluded portions of the seceding states that were already in Union hands. Although these states, taking advantage of Lincoln's proclamation of amnesty and reconstruction, had crafted state constitutions that abolished slavery, nothing prevented these states from resurrecting the "peculiar institution" in the future. Finally, the border slave states had not acted on proposals for compensated emancipation, and their domestic institutions lay wholly outside the scope of Lincoln's executive authority. Without a constitutional amendment, the guarantee of slavery's demise at war's end remained uncertain.

This conundrum was further illustrated in President Lincoln's disagreement with Secretary of the Treasury Chase over exempting parts of two states from the Emancipation Proclamation. Chase implored Lincoln to include parts of Virginia and Louisiana that were made exempt on January 1, 1863. On September 2, 1863, Lincoln replied to Chase:

The original proclamation has no constitutional or legal justification, except as a military measure . . . If I take the step [of removing the exemptions] must I not do so, without the argument of military necessity, and so, without any argument, except that the one that I think the measure politically expedient, and morally right? Would I not thus give up all footing upon constitution or law? Would I not thus be in the boundless field of absolutism? Could this pass unnoticed, or unresisted? Could it fail to be perceived that without any further stretch, I might do the same in Delaware, Maryland, Kentucky, Tennessee, and Missouri; and even change any law in any state?[94]

Although the president was dead before its final ratification in 1865, his jurisprudence had permanently altered the course of the nation. The mere fact that he pushed for the ratification of the Thirteenth Amendment signifies that America's sixteenth president was indeed the Great Emancipator who transformed the republic forever. His commitment to equal opportunity was now extended to all, regardless of race.

In recent years, it has become fashionable to denigrate the Thirteenth Amendment because it did not give former slaves equality before the law and it did not compensate them for the travail of slavery. It simply freed them from chattel bondage, but left former slaves captives of the emerging condition of enforced segregation. This present-minded view misses the point of how radical the Thirteenth Amendment was in its time. If the Constitution was, as William Lloyd Garrison insisted, "a covenant with death and an agreement with Hell" because it explicitly protected slavery, reversing that recognition was earth shattering.[95]

CONCLUSIONS

More than any other thing he did during the Civil War, Lincoln's act of emancipation demonstrated his political courage.[96]

First, he was clear and self-confident in his belief that issuing the proclamations was the correct thing to do at the time. As he thought about emancipation early in the war, he learned to trust his own judgment. For this first prerequisite of political courage he had to be steady amid a barrage of criticism. And criticism is what he received—from Army of the Potomac commanding general George B. McClellan, along with soldiers and sailors who believed that they did not enlist to free blacks but only to restore the Union, and from the northern public and newspapers editors who called him the "wooden head in Washington." On Sundays, if he had time, he would read editorials about his administration and then ask himself, "Is Abraham Lincoln a man or a dog?"[97]

Second, he knew his own mind. One gets the impression that he would have sacrificed everything before retreating from this act. As Lincoln said afterward, "The promise being made, must be kept."

Third, Lincoln was obsessed with character. When he spoke of character he spoke of selflessness and honor. To a critic of emancipation, Lincoln wrote, "Why should they [the black soldier and sailor] do any thing for us, if we do nothing for them?"[98] In the end, over 186,000 black soldiers and sailors served in the Union army and navy.

Finally, Lincoln was most alive in the midst of the fray. Lincoln's metamorphosis from espousing a war aim of reunion to demanding reunion and emancipation demonstrates this.

Nearly 500 years ago, Niccoló Machiavelli wrote in *The Prince* that the hardest thing in government was to create a new system of organization. Machiavelli hoped that if a unified Italian Republic could somehow be founded, it would maintain itself over time. Abraham Lincoln's method of pragmatism is reminiscent of Machiavelli's. Although Lincoln's overarching goal during the Civil War was to insure the continued existence of a unified American republic, his pragmatism allowed him to create the basis for a "new birth of freedom."[99] Abraham Lincoln's method allowed for the great experiment in self-government to permanently endure. Machiavelli would have applauded Lincoln's performance.

Lincoln's jurisprudence on Civil War issues evolved over time and was predicated on his work as a lawyer and Illinois politician, maturing when he entered the White House and changing further throughout his presidency. The outbreak of the war gave him the opportunity to reconcile the contradiction in the natural law jurisprudence of the Declaration of Independence and the positive (man-made) law jurisprudence of the U.S. Constitution, which was the result of a compromise between the North and the South in 1787.

Initially, Abraham Lincoln was willing for the South to retain slavery while banning it from the federal territories. Until the firebrands at Fort Sumter pulled the trigger, Lincoln acted as a traditional Whiggish lawyer, content for the status quo to endure. As the military situation grew worse and lasted longer than anyone imagined, he faced the new situation by belatedly recognizing the wishes of blacks themselves and the opportunity to use them to fight for the Union. Taking lawyerly and political care as his policy evolved—and radicalized—he assumed genuine leadership over the military and Congress. By issuing the Emancipation Proclamation, Lincoln changed America. He deserves credit for taking the steps that would amend the Constitution to insure that his jurisprudence for people would transform the basis of the Union.

PICTURING FREEDOM

The Emancipation Proclamation in Art, Iconography, and Memory

HAROLD HOLZER

> O symbol of God's will on earth
> As it is done above!
> Bear Witness to the cost and worth
> Of justice and of love.
> —POEM BY JOHN GREENLEAF WHITTIER, composed
> for the dedication of Thomas Ball's
> Emancipation statue, Boston, 1876

On March 4, 1865, Abraham Lincoln stood on the portico of the U.S. Capitol to take the oath of presidential office for a second time and deliver what he quickly came to regard as the greatest speech of his career.

For the most part, his second inaugural address sounded more like a sermon than an oration. Slavery, the president gravely told the throng gathered in the plaza, had been one of those "offences" deserving of the wrath of God. The "terrible war" was the "woe due to those by whom the offence came." And it might yet come to pass, he warned, that "every drop of blood drawn with the lash, shall be paid by another drawn with the sword." Until his concluding call for "malice toward none," it was not a speech designed to comfort its listeners. Indeed, Lincoln himself conceded that the address "was not immediately popular."[1]

To the secretary of the National Soldiers Historical Association, however, "no such Anti-Slavery words have elsewhere been so forcibly used as those in your Second Inaugural." John D. Caldwell quickly wrote to the president, asking for his original manuscript so he could reproduce facsimile copies to raise funds for his charity. Lincoln politely declined but concluded that the speech would "wear as well as—perhaps better than—any thing I have produced." He could not have doubted that the reason was its overt, and frank, focus on slavery, the issue Lincoln believed was "somehow, the cause of the war."[2]

Ever since 1863, moreover, Lincoln had realized that the Emancipation Proclamation was the crowning achievement of his presidency—that it had put his name "into history," as he noted on the day he signed the document. Two years later, at the second inaugural, he had publicly invoked the name of God to consecrate both the proclamation and the human sacrifice required since to enforce it. By the time he began a second term that he surely thought would be devoted to overseeing the full extinction of slavery, the president seemed at peace with the judgments of God and posterity alike.[3] By then, America's artists were also beginning to echo this twinned sense of reverence and celebration.

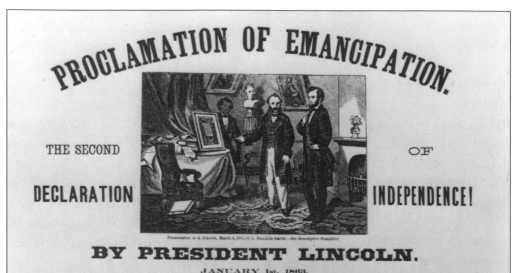

PROCLAMATION OF EMANCIPATION.

THE SECOND

OF

DECLARATION

INDEPENDENCE!

Presentation to A. Lincoln, March 6, 1865, by L. Franklin Smith.—See Descriptive Pamphlet.

BY PRESIDENT LINCOLN.

JANUARY 1st, 1863.

In presenting to the public, the Liberty-loving people of the United States, this elegant historical memorial, we feel that no comment is needed upon its great and noble subject, the undying parchment that sealed to Fame the name of our beloved Martyr-President, that made Abraham Lincoln the great liberator of a race, that made 1863 a great era in the history of the Republic, and wiped away the great stain that for eighty years had darkened its glorious annals. It is undying and immortal, beloved and revered, and further comment is unnecessary.

A suitable copy or memento of this great document should be and will be in the house of every lover of his country. One finer or better adapted to the demands of the public than this, we hesitate not to say, has not yet been produced. In beauty of design, artistic finish, and yet within the means of all, it is unsurpassed.

SUN, LIBERTY, EAGLE, NATIONAL BANNERS.

GEORGE WASHINGTON,

Benjamin Franklin,	Thomas Jefferson.
Chief Justice Story.	John Quincy Adams,
John Wesley,	William Penn.
Lucretia Mott,	L. Maria Child.

ABRAHAM LINCOLN,

William H. Seward,	Horace Greely,
Salmon P. Chase,	Charles Sumner,
James H. Lane,	Cassius M. Clay,
John S C. Abbott,	Wm. H. Burleigh.

JOHN C. FREMONT,

Wendell Phillips,	Owen Lovejoy,
Rev. Nathan Brown,	H. Ward Beecher,
Benjamin F. Butler,	Gerrit Smith,

Ten Vignettes,
Representing the Curse of Slavery and Blessings of Liberty.

Fury, Satan, Calhoun and Jeff Davis.
Plantation Scene.
Slave, Auction, Separation.
Branding Slaves, C. S. on forehead. Barbarism.
Goddess of Liberty, Upas Tree, Slave, Hounds.
Purity, Dove, Olive Branch.
School.
Happy Family, Restoration.
Church, House, Plowing, Civilization.
Justice, Man, Railroad, Steamboat, Ship.

The Proclamation is on fine plate paper, 20 by 26 inches, appropriately and beautifully colored, 32 portraits; in all, over 120 figures, with descriptive pamphlets sent to any address by mail; postage paid on receipt of $2.00.

The Greatest Novelty of the Age! The Proclamation of Emancipation Illustrated!!

Card Photograph containing 721 words, 10 vignettes, 38 Portraits, and over 124 figures, should adorn every loyal lady's Album. *Price 20 Cents.*

LITHOGRAPHED BY ROSENTHAL, AND PUBLISHED BY L. FRANKLIN SMITH,

No. 327 Walnut Street, P. O. Box 2423 Philadelphia, Pa.

FIG. 1

L. Franklin Smith, *Proclamation of Emancipation./ The Second Declaration of Independence! By President Lincoln. January 1ˢᵗ, 1863.* Engraved advertising broadside, Philadelphia, 1865.

(Stern Collection, Library of Congress)

Just two days after delivering his extraordinary inaugural speech, in fact, Lincoln welcomed to the White House a visitor bearing a gift that surely confirmed the president's sense of his own emergence "into history." L. Franklin Smith was a print publisher from Philadelphia who came to Washington on March 6, 1865, to present personally to the president his latest lithograph: a tribute to the nation-changing document and its author (Fig. 1).[4]

Smith set up the framed print on a table for Lincoln's inspection. What followed can be considered a precursor to the contemporary White House "photo opportunity." When he entered the room, the president saw an elaborate, hand-tinted, twenty-by-twenty-six-inch reproduction of the engrossed text of the Emancipation Proclamation—the final copy, as written out by a penmanship specialist. Reproduced in the shape of a shield, the proclamation was surrounded by cameo portraits of the nation's founders, along with the nineteenth-century's principal antislavery leaders. Surmounting Smith's design were images of George Washington (beneath an American eagle), Benjamin Franklin, John Quincy Adams, and the outspoken women leaders Lucretia Mott and Lydia Maria Child.

Pictured below was a veritable gallery depicting fourteen modern leaders, with Lincoln occupying the central place, alongside such contemporaries as abolitionists Wendell Phillips, Geritt Smith, Owen Lovejoy, Charles Sumner, and Rev. Henry Ward Beecher; newspaper editor Horace Greeley; and Gen. Benjamin F. Butler. All, significantly, shared a hatred of slavery. Included in the picture, too, was an assortment of vignettes by lithographer Max Rosenthal, designed on one hand to represent the "curse of slavery" (brutal punishment and degrading auctions), and on the other the "blessings of liberty" (education, religion, family life, and economic opportunity).

The resulting composition, its publisher boasted with a spirited hyperbole typical of the age, constituted nothing less than "The Greatest Novelty of the Age! The Proclamation of Emancipation Illustrated!!" Smith no doubt knew that a few other printmakers had tackled the same theme with similar commemorations, but he argued that his picture "should be and will be in the house of every lover of his country. One finer or better adapted to the demands of the public than this, we hesitate not to say, has not yet been produced. In beauty of design, artistic finish, and yet within the means of all, it is unsurpassed." Its price was two dollars.[5]

The publisher proved to be an inspired promoter. Shortly after Lincoln's death a few weeks after Smith's White House visit, he published an advertising broadside to promote his "novelty" (Fig. 2), describing the Emancipation Proclamation as "the second Declaration of Independence," and featuring a small lithograph that depicted the publisher presenting his print to the president at the White House on March 6. In the annals of Civil War–era iconography, it remains the only known print of Abraham Lincoln *examining* a print. Appropriately enough, the subject of both the image, and the image of its ceremonial presentation, was emancipation.

Smith left no doubt why the subject deserved such lavish attention and publicity. As his advertising broadside explained, "In presenting to the public, the Liberty-loving people of the United States, this elegant historical memorial, we feel that no comment is needed upon its great and noble subject, the undying parchment that sealed to Fame, the name of our beloved Martyr-President, that made Abraham Lincoln the great liberator of a race, that made 1863 a great era in the history of the Republic, and wiped away the great stain that for eighty years had darkened its glorious annals. It is undying and immortal, beloved and revered, and further comment is unnecessary."

FIG. 2

Max Rosenthal, *Proclamation of Emancipation*. Hand-colored lithograph, published by L. Franklin Smith, Philadelphia, 1865. (Courtesy of the Lincoln Museum, Fort Wayne, IN, Ref. #2216)

As it turned out, other printmakers quickly would provide "further comment." The emancipation, later than one might suspect, but more emphatically than one might imagine, became the dominant theme of Lincoln art and iconography for the rest of the nineteenth century. In the graphic arts, Lincoln would be celebrated as a great emancipator in a huge variety of imagery: pictures that showed him signing and reading the proclamation, personally unshackling slaves, or symbolically providing the biblical "blessings of liberty" to which Smith's picture had alluded. Not only would the dry words of his legalistic document be celebrated as if they were poetry but so would its author—eventually in far more vivid pictorial terms than Smith was willing to attempt in early 1865.

Prints were not the only medium to celebrate the Emancipation Proclamation. Painters and sculptors soon did so evocatively, and, to the extent it could, photography did likewise. Genuine "photo opportunities" were uncommon in Lincoln's era, and no effort was made to stage a formal photograph of the actual signing of the final emancipation document at the White House on New Year's Day, 1863. This was a tragically lost opportunity, as the technology already existed to rally the principals and make a group picture—although it would probably have required restaging outdoors or in a studio, where light was more ample.[6]

Photographers could at least copy the work of artists who invented such scenes, and could issue the results in small-sized versions designed for carte-de-visite albums. This kind of adaptation, made necessary because the photographers never thought to invite Lincoln to immortalize his historic proclamation before the cameras, thus ironically reversed the process by which most political prints of the day had been created—slavishly copied from period photographs. In the case of emancipation iconography, it became common for photography to reproduce art, and not the other way around. However they were manufactured, such photographs effectively added to the growing stock of commemorative images. White House visitor L. Franklin Smith, for example, quickly managed to publish a "Card Photograph" version of his own *Proclamation of Emancipation* print. Somehow, it crammed together 721 words, 38 portraits, and over 124 separate figures—more than in his larger original lithograph—ready to "adorn ever loyal lady's Album" at only twenty cents apiece.

Painters and sculptors also labored on the emancipation subject—their work crafted occasionally from precious life sittings—and often their efforts, too, were in turn adapted in other media. Paintings thus inspired prints, which inspired photographs. Sculptures might in turn be photographed or engraved. This emerging tradition of interlocking, interdependent art and commerce produced an avalanche of reverential portraiture that fixed in history the image of Lincoln as the Great Emancipator. Journalists, biographers, historians, and preachers offered tributes of their own, but in art, perhaps most vividly and indelibly of all, Lincoln and his Emancipation Proclamation lived on in family albums, on parlor walls, in public spaces, and in public memory.

Lincoln, who in 1860 described himself as "a very indifferent judge" of his own portraits, nonetheless proved a very willing participant in their creation, given the opportunities. He had first sat for artists following his nomination to the presidency in May. Always reasonably cooperative when asked thereafter to pose, he became all but complicit in the forging of his own celebratory portraiture after 1863, particularly when the portrayals focused on the subject of freeing the slaves.[7]

From the time he emerged as a candidate for national office, Lincoln was portrayed to the public

FIG. 3

[Nathaniel] Currier and [James Merritt] Ives, *The "Nigger" in the Woodpile.* Lithograph, New York, 1860. (Courtesy of the Lincoln Museum, Fort Wayne, IN, Ref. #537)

in some pictures as a revolutionary who threatened to change the relationships between black and white people in the United States. In political cartoon sheets and in newspaper caricatures designed to appeal to Democrats—but often published by the same profit-motivated printmakers simultaneously issuing straightforward portraits as well as anti-Democratic lampoons—Lincoln was often depicted as a dangerous abolitionist. A typical example was Currier and Ives's campaign print *An Heir to the Throne, Or the Next Republican Candidate,* showing Lincoln introducing as his potential successor a human curiosity then on exhibit at Barnum's Museum in New York: a pathetic African dwarf cruelly dubbed the "What Is It?" An even cruder Currier and Ives lampoon, *The "Nigger" in the Woodpile* (Fig. 3), further stripped the long-suffering slaves of their humanity by portraying a prototypical slave only as a political problem for Lincoln and his party. The message of such prints was clear: the election of Lincoln, carrying his log rail, would lead to the empowerment of half-human creatures like the "What is It," seen in the print carrying a parallel symbol, his spear.

The slavery issue indeed made Lincoln's a "perilous voyage to the White House," the title of yet another caricature—in all likelihood "borrowed" from another Currier and Ives composition—showing Lincoln attempting to cross "Salt River" and reach the White House, encumbered by an African American who clings to his back. As frequently ridiculed as he was on the abolition issue, however, it is worth noting that Lincoln became acquiescent when it came to posing for formal artistic treatments of the theme. In fact, he was particularly amenable to posing when it came to the subject of emancipation.[8] On at least two such occasions, he invited artists to work inside the White House, where they functioned in the manner of European court artists, enjoying broad access to the president during particularly trying periods for the administration. It surely helped convince Lincoln to devote time to their projects that both of the works they proposed were designed to portray him as an emancipator. In the end, both paintings enjoyed critically acclaimed display, and both were adapted into wildly popular engravings. Lincoln's well-placed cooperation helped cement his nineteenth-century image as Great Emancipator.

What remains the single most curious aspect of Emancipation Proclamation iconography, however, is not the plethora of images produced after 1865 but the relative scarcity of such pictorial tributes before Lincoln's death. More than two years elapsed between Lincoln's final proclamation on January 1, 1863, and Smith's visit to the White House to unveil his lithographic tribute on March 6, 1865. Between 1862 and 1864, however, one can count on one's fingers the number of pictures produced to commemorate what was arguably the most newsworthy nonmilitary event of the entire Civil War. And newsworthy events were the special province of the fast-working printmakers.

It is, of course, difficult to argue the importance of the *absence* of evidence. Yet the political culture of the Civil War era so typically encouraged the manufacture, distribution, and patronage of the graphic arts that it must be viewed as remarkable that so few emancipation images rolled off the presses between 1863 and 1865. Beginning with his nomination to the presidency in May 1860, printmakers had made Lincoln one of their principal subjects. Engravers and lithographers in New York, Hartford, Boston, Philadelphia, and Chicago churned out dozens of campaign portraits, broadsides, and cartoon sheets that year to satisfy the demonstrable public hunger for Lincoln pictures. Among the campaign prints issued that year were hostile cartoons, many identifying Lincoln as a secret abolitionist whose election would result in emancipation and racial equality, unpalatable to most Americans at the time.

Then, in 1861, once Lincoln unexpectedly altered his appearance by growing whiskers, the printmakers issued another body of work designed to reintroduce the new president with his new beard. For the rest of that year, and on into 1862, engravers and lithographers produced additional pictures of Lincoln with his new military and civilian families—his cabinet ministers and field commanders. (In several studies I wrote in the 1980s with Mark E. Neely Jr. and Gabor S. Boritt, we traced the emergence of this body of work. We described the pictures as commercial phenomena produced by publishers in anticipation of public demand, unlike the campaign pictures commissioned in the twentieth century by political parties. In Lincoln's time, prints were eagerly embraced by customers who testified to their allegiances and patriotism by displaying such pictures in the sacred confines of their private homes.)[9]

Yet such attention from printmakers was conspicuously absent when it came to the most momentous act of Lincoln's presidency. True, the journalist Noah Brooks reported a "grand rush" for copies of the preliminary document when it was first announced on September 22, 1862. Charles Eberstadt, in his still-consulted 1950 bibliography of emancipation printings, noted that separately printed copies of the text began appearing in 1862. "Framed and displayed in thousands of homes and prominent places," Eberstadt argued, "emancipation became a watchword of almost hysterical power and incalculable effect . . . an ever-present reminder of the war's true justification . . . important as a propaganda and morale factor."[10]

But Eberstadt's claims were wildly inflated. No explosion of Great Emancipator graphics greeted the announcement of either the preliminary or final proclamation. Eberstadt's own compilation of known proclamation reprints counted only eighteen editions published in 1862 and 1863, including those issued officially by the federal government. Only one of them—A. Kidder's three-by-two-inch miniaturized version—featured an image of the emancipator.[11] In no way could such a dribble of pictorial response be described as "hysterical." In fact, it was astonishingly muted.

The documented explanation for this scarcity, if it was ever recorded, has vanished forever. Few business records of any kind survive from the golden age of American political printmaking. But since we know that the printmakers themselves made the publishing decisions—not the political organizations, to whom prints were often marketed—it can be reasonably surmised that engravers and lithographers simply did not immediately believe that pictorial representations of the proclamation would attract buyers.

Why? For one thing, the document may have seemed too controversial at first to suggest flattering pictorial representations that would appeal to large numbers of the print-purchasing public. Notwithstanding the widely held twentieth-century judgment of Lincoln as the beloved Great Emancipator, his proclamation, when first issued, was bitterly controversial and widely condemned, not only in the Confederacy but also among northerners, large numbers of whom were willing to fight a war to save the Union but not to free blacks. The president himself lamented six days after announcing the proclamation that "stocks have declined, and troops come forward more slowly than ever," admitting, "this, looked soberly in the face, is not very satisfactory." The political firestorm whipped up by emancipation may have seemed too toxic at first to suggest that heroic "Moses" imagery of its chief architect would be palatable to mass audiences. Printmakers were in the business of making money, not history.[12]

Moreover, at its most basic—and perhaps, to white customers, most threatening—level, the proclamation promised to change the status of black people. From all that we know, white people did not then display pictures of black people in their homes. African Americans themselves would later constitute what modern publishers might term a "niche market" for such pictures. Warning his people against "national forgetfulness," Frederick Douglass would eventually urge his people to embrace recollections of history, calling the past "the mirror in which we may discern the dim outlines of the future and by which we may make them more symmetrical." But precious few African Americans had the resources to purchase commemorative prints as early as 1863.[13]

Furthermore, the preliminary proclamation's immediate effect on southern slavery was negligible. It took the January 1 proclamation as well as the steady subsequent march of Union armies into the Confederacy to transform Lincoln's promise into a reality. As far as printmakers were concerned, the proclamation's bold words perhaps seemed, at first, as William H. Seward had feared when he first heard them in the summer of 1862, like a "last *shriek,* on the retreat."[14]

Then there were the words themselves. However handsomely they might be engrossed or rendered in fancy calligraphy, the text of the proclamation was hardly the stuff to inspire great art. All these factors probably conspired to inhibit the immediate production of emancipation prints, widespread public interest (and concern) notwithstanding. It was controversial, and except for caricature, printmakers typically steered clear of controversial subjects. Its effect was still unknown. It called for portrayals of black people, and its language did not easily suggest graphic interpretation, much

FIG. 4

"Potomac," *Grand Sweepstakes for 1862. Won by the Celebrated Horse "Emancipation."* Lithograph, ca. 1862.
(Print Collection, Miriam and Ira D. Wallach Division of Art, Prints and Photographs, the New York Public
Library, Astor, Lenox and Tilden Foundations)

less inspiration. The absence of prints celebrating emancipation in the year it took effect strongly
suggests that Lincoln's policy was not universally or warmly greeted by a sizable portion of northerners, for had the reverse been true, printmakers would have eagerly and quickly produced engravings
and lithographs to meet popular demand. In such ways graphic media—or their absence—can testify
eloquently to public opinion during the Civil War.

The earliest surviving pictorial acknowledgments of emancipation should serve to remind modern
viewers that the document was deeply controversial when it was first issued. It hardly inspired reverential portraiture at the outset. The proclamation had its supporters but many critics as well.

Evidence can be found as early as 1862, when the Emancipation Proclamation emerged as a key
issue in the congressional elections destined to result in Democratic gains in the House and the Senate. That fall, an unknown printmaker known only as "Potomac" issued a cartoon sheet showing Lincoln in jockey's silks, whipping toward the finish line a white horse with a human-shaped black face,
labeled "Emancipation." The unusual print, *Grand Sweepstakes for 1862. Won by the Celebrated Horse
"Emancipation"* (Fig. 4), showed in the foreground a number of delighted African-American spectators
viewing the race, but the white spectators nearby seem thoroughly displeased by Lincoln's imminent
victory. Although the lampoon praised Lincoln for winning the decisive "race," it also conveyed the
unflattering idea that he had mounted his emancipation steed for purely political purposes.

In the Confederacy, meanwhile, where critical works might have proliferated had not wartime

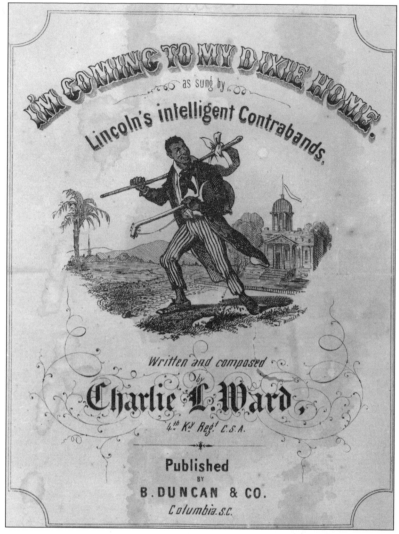

FIG. 5

Printmaker unknown, *I'm Coming to My Dixie Home. As sung by Lincoln's intelligent Contrabands.* Lithographed sheet music cover, published by B. Duncan and Co., Columbia, South Carolina, ca. 1862. (The Museum of the Confederacy, Richmond, Virginia)

deprivation all but gutted the region's printmaking industry, B. Duncan of Columbia, South Carolina, managed to issue *I'm Coming to My Dixie Home, as sung by Lincoln's intelligent Contrabands* (Fig. 5). This illustrated sheet music cover showed a slave fleeing the Palmetto state, banjo in his arms, to join the Union army. The print may suggest to modern viewers an idea rather the opposite of what was originally intended. Southern print buyers may have mocked such contrabands, but northerners—in a view vindicated by history—celebrated their courage in fleeing and fighting for their own freedom.[15]

For a variety of reasons, the Confederate print industry died in its infancy, severely limiting the

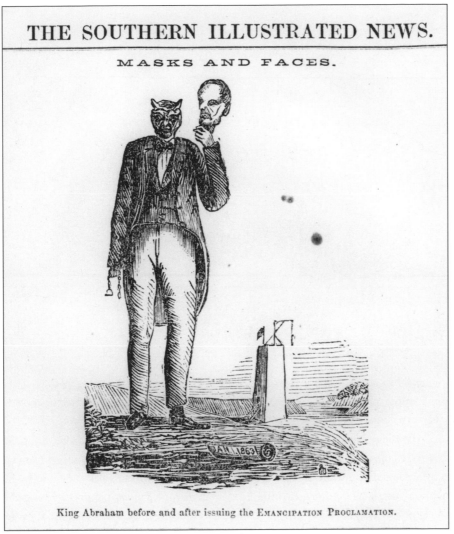

FIG. 6

Printmaker unknown, *Masks and Faces. King Abraham before and after issuing the Emancipation Proclamation.*
Wood engraving, published in the *Southern Illustrated News,* Richmond, November 8, 1862.
(Collections of the New York Public Library, Astor, Lenox and Tilden Foundations)

pictorial outcry against emancipation. One major factor, the chronic shortage of paper, ink, and wood for engraving, conspired to curtail picture production as early as 1861. Artists grew scarce, too. They were either recruited for military service or assigned to official government work, the engraving of stamps and currency. Finally, the two principal southern printmaking centers, Baltimore and New Orleans, either remained under Union control or fell into federal hands within a year, after which Union censors prevented any pictorial expressions of pro-Confederate nationalistic sentiment, for which a market almost certainly would have thrived, despite economic hardship.[16]

One source of virulent anti-Lincoln, anti-emancipation graphics struggled on, however, until at

FIG. 7

Currier and Ives, *"Your Plan and Mine"* [Showing George B. McClellan, Jefferson Davis (twice) and Abraham Lincoln]. Lithograph, New York, 1864. (Courtesy of the Lincoln Museum, Fort Wayne, IN, Ref. #2071)

least 1864—the Confederate counterpart to the New York pictorial *Harper's Weekly,* the *Southern Illustrated News.* In most editions, the paper extolled Confederate military heroes, but every so often, its artists lampooned Lincoln in a crudely drawn cartoon. On November 8, 1862—only six weeks after the president issued the Emancipation Proclamation—the *Southern Illustrated News* published a scathing attack. *Masks and Faces* (Fig. 6) showed Lincoln, the despised document at his feet, unmasking his familiar, bearded face to reveal himself to be Satan in disguise. In the background, the half-finished Washington Monument has been refitted as a gallows, where a noose (dangling from a split-rail gallows) awaits this political prince of darkness.[17]

The early appearance of this print proved an exception, in the North as well as in the South. Not until the start of the 1864 presidential campaign did publishers unleash the first significant wave of Lincoln imagery focused on emancipation. With the industry motivated by profits, not politics, the 1864 market was served with pro-Lincoln cartoons praising the Proclamation and anti-Lincoln caricature designed to appeal to Democrats who opposed it.

A typical pro-Lincoln campaign cartoon, Currier and Ives's *"Your Plan and Mine"* (Fig. 7), compared Lincoln's policy of enlisting freedmen to the peace plan of his opponent, George B. McClellan, which the cartoon warned would reenslave them. Anti-Lincoln prints predicted, in turn, that the emancipation would turn white America upside down by introducing such controversial social reforms as race-mixing and racial equality. In some of these prints, Lincoln himself was portrayed as

FIG. 8

"CAL," *Behind the Scenes* [Showing Lincoln as Othello]. Lithograph, New York, 1864.
(Library of Congress)

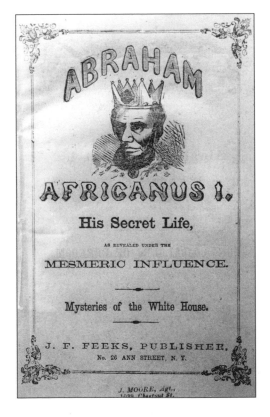

FIG. 9

Printmaker unknown, *Abraham Africanus I.*
Lithographed title page for a campaign pamphlet, published by J. F. Feeks, New York, 1864.
(Frank and Virginia Williams Collection of
Lincolniana)

African American. One cartoon showed him in crude blackface starring in a stage performance of *Othello* (Fig. 8), and he again appeared as an ostentatiously crowned king in the illustrated title page to an anti-Lincoln screed, *Abraham Africanus I: His Secret Life* (Fig. 9).

Still, the output of decidedly pro-emancipation graphics remained surprisingly low. With sympathetic publishers reluctant to focus on the explosive emancipation issue during the first few years after the proclamation's issuance, the path to celebration of Lincoln as an emancipator was neither sure nor swift.[18]

The commercial and psychological logjam that inhibited pictorial commemoration of the Emancipation Proclamation was initially broken in March 1863—by a journeyman painter from Philadelphia and his pro-Republican, antislavery patrons. Veteran artist Edward Dalton Marchant (1806–87), born in Massachusetts, had earned his professional reputation in New York in the 1840s, exhibiting widely and traveling throughout the country before relocating in 1854 to Philadelphia, where he worked for the next thirty years. For two decades, he enjoyed professional involvement there with the Pennsylvania Colonization Society, painting a number of portraits of the leaders of the group, which advocated the abolition of slavery and relocation of slaves to Africa.[19]

In November 1862, two months after Lincoln issued his preliminary Emancipation Proclamation, his supporters in Philadelphia formed a Union Club—later to be absorbed into the city's Union League—pledged to support of the president, suppression of the rebellion, and emancipation. Within weeks, its members decided to commission Marchant to paint a portrait of Lincoln that the club intended to donate to the city's reigning shrine to liberty, Independence Hall.[20]

In December, Marchant and his patrons obtained a crucial endorsement—a much-needed letter of introduction to the president—from John Wein Forney, a Philadelphia native who published the pro-Lincoln *Washington Chronicle* and served as secretary of the U.S. Senate. Forney wrote: "My dear Mr. President—the bearer, Mr. E. D. Marchant, the eminent Artist, has been empowered by a large body of your personal and political friends to paint your picture for the Hall of American Independence. A generous subscription is made—and he visits you to ask your acquiescence, and to exhibit his testimonials. He will need little of your time. There is no likeness of you at Independence Hall. It should be there; and as Mr. Marchant is a most distinguished Artist, and is commanded by the most powerful influences, I trust you will give him a favorable reception."[21]

The letter persuaded Lincoln to pose. No doubt he was flattered by the prospect of having his portrait hanging alongside those of the nation's founders in a historic building that he regarded with such "deep emotion" that he had declared there in 1861: "I would rather be assassinated on this spot than to surrender it." Preoccupied as he was in early 1863 by the grueling demands of managing the war, Lincoln afforded Marchant a considerable amount of his valuable time so the artist could complete his picture.[22]

Determining at the outset to portray Lincoln as an emancipator, Marchant began work on his composition in March 1863. "My studio was for several months in the White House," he later recalled with pride, "where I was in daily communication with the remarkable man whose features I sought to portray." Marchant "sought—and, I am told, with some success—to symbolize, on canvas, the great, crowning act of our distinguished President." Marchant depicted Lincoln in formal attire, signing the

FIG. 10

John Sartain, after a painting by Edward Dalton Marchant, *Abraham Lincoln, Sixteenth President of the United States* [with facsimile signature]. Engraving, published by Bradley and Co., Philadelphia, 1864. (Courtesy of the Lincoln Museum, Fort Wayne, IN, Ref. #3326)

document and symbolically breaking the shackles binding the feet of a statue representing liberty in the background. The finished work, Marchant happily recalled, elicited a "rather enthusiastic" response from those who saw it.[23]

If it was exhibited at Independence Hall at all, the painting was shown there only briefly, and by 1864 it was installed permanently at Philadelphia's Union League headquarters, no small honor. Its real fame, however, was generated by a handsome print adaptation produced in Philadelphia that same year, just in time to meet a resurgent interest in Lincoln portraiture during his campaign for reelection. Engraved by John Sartain and published by Bradley and Co., the print (Fig. 10) proved an enormous success, despite that, like the painting on which it was based, it depicted Lincoln as rather stiff and barrel-chested, and dressed in an outlandish wraparound white tie that had gone out of style the generation before. Nonetheless, according to Marchant, "the demand for it on my publisher has been of late, and for some time, fully up to a thousand a day; and the press which prints it is never idle during any of the twenty-four hours, except those which include the Sabbath; and I fear, at times, even that has been entrenched on, despite my positive injunction against it." As proof of its popularity, the print was quickly copied without authorization and published in a smeary, cheap, lithographed edition. Marchant himself later reissued a vignetted engraved edition under his own copyright.[24]

The triumph of the Marchant effort, on canvas and in print, seemed at last to unleash the long-delayed flurry of interest in emancipation imagery. The year 1864 proved the watershed for such iconography—with public interest in the subject perhaps stirred more by the approaching presidential election campaign than by the proclamation itself. Lincoln's order, after all, was already more than a year old, akin to ancient history to printmakers who typically created best-sellers out of newsworthy events. Pro-emancipation prints also served to respond pictorially to anti-Lincoln campaign cartoons that year, many of which took emancipation to the next, illogical step, suggesting that Lincoln favored race mixing.

In January of that year, Chicago publisher Thomas B. Bryan sent the president proof copies of "the lithographed Fac-Similes of your Proclamation of Freedom" by local printmaker Edward Mendel. The design featured a handsome portrait of Lincoln surmounted by a figure representing the goddess of Liberty clutching an American flag. Aware that Lincoln had donated his original handwritten copy of the Proclamation to the Chicago Sanitary Fair to raise funds for wounded soldiers, Bryan now proposed to earmark the "net proceeds" from the sale of the prints to the same cause.[25]

Lincoln replied that the print "impresses me favorably as being a faithful and correct copy," and true to his word, Bryan directed that the revenues it produced—at least a "liberal share of the profits"—go to the U.S. Sanitary Commission. In a tense reelection year in which soldiers, so many of whom had opposed the proclamation, were to be encouraged to vote, Lincoln must have been pleased to see a tangible example of the benefits of emancipation accruing to the troops.[26]

That same month, the Chicago lithographer A. Kidder seemed to be speaking for many of the printmakers who would soon enter the emancipation marketplace when he sent Lincoln his new, larger illustrated reproduction of the proclamation, along with a request for a favor. Describing himself as a "humble Artist," he wrote: "I have this day sent you 50 copies of your great Proclamation of Freedom, which has been engraved and Lithographed from designs gotten up by me the taste and ingenuity of which have received the highest commendations of all artists who have seen it. The form in which I have now placed it will enable every American citizen to place it among his household Gods & teach their children how you delivered from bondage a nation in a day." Kidder asked "no higher recognition" on the president's part than to have a letter of acknowledgment "under your own hand & signature which I will then regard higher than any honor or emoluments or any earthly favor." No reply has surfaced, but under most circumstances, Lincoln characteristically obliged such requests. He may well have done so for Kidder, whose later editions of *Emancipation* boasted a bold facsimile of the president's signature.[27]

Emancipation went on to become a central issue in the election campaign of 1864, and thus the focus of much attention in graphics that were published to illustrate and influence the race. Just as Lincoln likely recognized the political and historical benefits of posing for Edward Dalton Marchant, professional politicians now recognized the vital role that emancipation graphics could play in the election race. When Lewis Dodge of Buffalo wrote to Lincoln in August 1864 to ask for an autograph "to be attached to your Emancipation Proclamation now being lithographed for publication with an acrostical Poem embracing your name and portrait," one such political operative recommended that the president provide the signature. "I think it will be a very good document and have a Lively influence this fall," he argued.[28]

Once again, Lincoln failed to reply—at least, no autograph sent to Dodge has ever been uncovered. However, by mid-1864 he had demonstrated an extraordinary willingness to cooperate patiently and enthusiastically with an artistic effort to commemorate emancipation. For six months that year, Lincoln gave free run of the White House to New York painter Francis Bicknell Carpenter (1830–1900), who conceived the idea of creating a heroic group portrait showing Lincoln reading his earliest proclamation draft to his cabinet in the summer of 1862.

As Carpenter later explained,

I conceived of that band of men, upon whom the eyes of the world centered as never before upon ministers of state, gathered in council, depressed, perhaps disheartened at the vain efforts of many months to restore the supremacy of the government. I saw . . . the head of the nation, bowed down with his weight of care and responsibility, solemnly announcing, as he unfolded the prepared draft of the Proclamation, that the time for the inauguration of this policy had arrived; I endeavored to imagine the conflicting emotions of satisfaction, doubt, and distrust with which such an announcement would be received by men of the varied characteristics of the assembled councillors [sic].[29]

"I wish to paint this picture *now*, while all the actors in the scene are living and while they are still in the discharge of the duties of their several high offices," the artist wrote to Illinois congressman Owen Lovejoy in an effort to win his endorsement and introduction to the president. "I wish to make it the *standard* authority for the portrait of . . . *Mr. Lincoln* as it is the great act of his life by which he will be remembered and honored through all generations." Carpenter promised at once to have "a small engraving in the highest style . . . made . . . from a small copy I shall make of the large picture."[30]

Lovejoy was impressed by Carpenter's proposal and recommended the artist to Lincoln. Gaining access to the White House, Carpenter remembered the "electric thrill" he felt when he first glimpsed the president at a reception there. The homely Lincoln broke the ice by joking: "Do you think, Mr. Carpenter, that you can make a handsome picture of *me*?" Understandably flustered, the painter, whose first impression of his subject was that he was "haggard-looking," mumbled something reassuring in reply, then immediately asked if he could meet Lincoln after the soiree and describe his project in detail. "I reckon," came the response. Later that evening, after Carpenter got the opportunity to discuss his conception of the painting, Lincoln promised, "Well, Mr. Carpenter, we will turn you in loose here [sic], and try to give you a good chance to work out your idea."[31]

In fact, Lincoln did more than merely turn Carpenter loose. He obligingly sat for a series of life sketches, both standing beside and sitting at the cabinet table at which he had first read the Emancipation Proclamation to his ministers in July 1862. He allowed Carpenter access to his office to make a number of drawings of the room's architectural and decorative details, sometimes permitting the artist to sketch him during private meetings, often to the surprise and annoyance of inhibited visitors.

Lincoln also permitted Carpenter to bring one of Mathew Brady's photographers to the office to make a series of flawed but unique camera studies inside the White House—marking the first time a president of the United States sat for a photographer inside the executive mansion. Earlier, in response to the artist's insatiable craving for models and studies to aid his work, Lincoln went with Carpenter to Brady's Washington gallery. There, on February 9, 1864, the president sat for the most famous series of photographs ever made of him, including the poses later engraved for the copper penny and the five-dollar bill. It is likely that Carpenter himself helped compose the photographs.[32]

Such cooperation demonstrated that Lincoln understood the difference between ephemeral, commercial ventures like L. Franklin Smith's 1865 lithograph, for which he spared a few moments of his time, and epochal projects like Carpenter's 1864 history painting, to which he devoted much energy, access, and enthusiasm. But even to minor emancipation-related iconography, it seems, he occasionally provided remarkable cooperation and sympathy, largely unnoted by historians, as if Lincoln sensed that one sort of production appealed to voters, and the other to posterity. Carpenter himself helped arrange for a fellow "artist" to present one such emancipation print to Lincoln in 1864, which he remembered as "an elaborate pen-and-ink 'allegorical, symbolic' representation" of the proclamation. Carpenter recalled the print and the reaction of the man it was designed to honor.

> The composition contained a tree, representing Liberty; a portrait of Mr. Lincoln; soldiers, monitors, broken fetters, etc.; together with the text of the proclamation, all executed with a pen. Artistically speaking, such works have no value,—they are simply interesting, as curiosities. Mr. Lincoln kindly accorded the desired opportunity to make the presentation, which occupied but a few moments, and was in the usual form. He accepted the testimonial, he said, not for himself, but in behalf of "the cause in which all were engaged." When the group dispersed, I remained with the President. He returned to his desk; while I examined curiously the pen work, which was exceedingly minute in detail. "This is quite wonderful!" I said, at length. Mr. Lincoln looked up from his papers. "Yes," he rejoined; "it is what I call *ingenious nonsense!*"[33]

When it came to his own project, Carpenter was a meticulous worker, showing no inclination to rush his work to the public like the anonymous calligrapher who produced "ingenious nonsense." Carpenter proceeded methodically from sketches and studies to photographic models to individual oil studies (of Lincoln and his entire cabinet[34]) before he ever stretched his nine-foot-by-fourteen-and-a-half-foot canvas inside the State Dining Room to begin his formal work. His final design was anything but haphazard. A realist who eschewed "imaginary curtain or column, gorgeous furniture or allegorical statue," Carpenter nevertheless found himself creating a symbolic composition for his ambitious work, demonstrating a canny understanding of political nuance in the process.

> There was a curious mingling of fact and allegory in my mind, as I assigned to each his place on the canvas. There were two elements in the Cabinet, the radical and the conservative. Mr. Lincoln was placed at the head of the official table, between two groups, nearest that representing the radical [portrayed, appropriately, at left, with the Conservatives at right];

but the uniting point of both . . . The chief officers of the government were thus brought, in accordance with their relations to the Administration, nearest the person of the President, who, with the manuscript proclamation in hand, which he had just read, was represented leaning forward, listening to, and intently considering the views presented by the Secretary of State.[35]

Here, Carpenter revealed something of a regional bias that perhaps flawed his artistic conception. In choosing to portray Lincoln listening to Seward, instead of the other way around, the artist may have been paying sympathetic tribute, whether conscious or unconscious, to a Secretary of State who hailed from Auburn, only a few miles from Carpenter's home town of Homer. Or so other jealous cabinet members seemed to think when he viewed the finished work.

Secretary of the Treasury Salmon P. Chase, for example, was heard to complain that the picture had been made "subsidiary to Seward who is talking while everyone else either listens or stares into vacancy." Chase insisted that it would have been more appropriate to show "the 22nd of September when the Proclamation was really read to the Cabinet." If the picture was designed as a tribute to Seward, Carpenter's upstate New York neighbor ironically proved less than grateful. The Secretary of State remembered that the Emancipation Proclamation had not been, as Carpenter contended, "the crowning act of the Administration" at all. It was "merely incidental" to the work of "the saving of popular government for the world." Carpenter would have been better advised, Seward thought, to portray the decisive cabinet meetings that led to the reenforcement of Fort Sumter in 1861.[36]

Such interpretive quibbling was not Lincoln's style. As the president told the artist, "the portraiture is the main thing, and that seems to me absolutely perfect." Gazing at the picture before it went on public display in the East Room, he declared to Carpenter: "In my judgment, it is as good a piece of work as the subject will admit of . . . and I am right glad you have done it." For "as affairs have turned," Lincoln noted with one eye turned to posterity, "it [the proclamation] is the central act of my Administration, and the great event of the nineteenth century." Although the finished canvas appears static and artificial to modern eyes—with its principal characters seated along one side of a long table in the manner of a stage set—in its day it proved enormously fresh and appealing. Earlier than almost anyone, Lincoln seemed to appreciate the painting and sense its potential effect on his reputation.[37]

It proved considerable. The canvas itself went on a national tour and was viewed by crowds of visitors and hailed enthusiastically by art critics. The *New York Evening Post* gushed that Carpenter had "achieved a success which time will go on ripening to the latest day that Americans honor the nobility of their ancestors." The *New York Times* added: "The production well deserves to rank with the most notable of the paintings commemorative of important events in American history." Like Lincoln, Attorney Gen. James Speed perceived the source of the painting's appeal: "The naturalness of the picture makes it . . . one of the grandest and most beautiful achievements of art that I have ever seen."[38]

But Carpenter's influence on Lincoln's reputation and the public memory of emancipation was not fully exerted until Alexander H. Ritchie produced a best-selling engraved adaptation (Fig. 11). Although Lincoln subscribed to a fifty-dollar artist's proof, the first of many celebrities to add their names to the publisher's ceremonial order book, the president did not live to see the picture appear.

FIG. 11

A[lexander]. H[ay]. Ritchie, after a painting by Francis Bicknell Carpenter, *The First Reading of the Emancipation Proclamation Before the Cabinet*. Cabinet photo, published for the "Lincoln Union," 1870; copy of the engraving published by Derby and Miller, New York, 1866. (Collection of Harold Holzer)

(His personal copy, delivered to his son after the assassination, today hangs on the library wall at Robert T. Lincoln's Vermont estate, Hildene.) Its publication in 1866 represented, and no doubt helped achieve, the apex of national interest in celebratory emancipation prints designed for display in private homes. A thousand orders for the Carpenter picture poured into the offices of New York publishers Derby and Miller in the first month after its appearance. By the 1880s the company would claim that some 30,000 prints had been pulled from the original plate before it wore out.[39]

To market the engraving, Carpenter elicited and published laudatory comments from the *Post* and the *Times*, as well as from the composition's subjects, even those who had expressed doubts when they first glimpsed the original canvas in the White House. Potential buyers were surely touched when they read that when he saw the print, Lincoln's secretary of the navy Gideon Welles had been overcome by "a feeling of sadness . . . for the great and good man . . . whom we all love." Secretary of War Edwin M. Stanton added, "The work is, in every respect that I am capable of judging, entirely satisfactory, and worthy of national admiration, as a fitting commemoration of Mr. Lincoln's great deed." As for Secretary of State Seward, who had earlier criticized the picture privately, he now declared publicly that the print was "a vivid presentation of the scene, with portraits of rare fidelity to nature."[40]

Among newspapers, the *New York Evening Post*, more than others, immediately sensed the picture's potential impact within the sacred setting of the American home. Despite its large size, it reported, "The engraving . . . will no doubt take its place among the pictures which the people hang upon their walls to commemorate one of the great and most notable acts in the nation's history." It did precisely that.[41]

Typically sold preframed in gleaming maple, with gold-leaf highlighting, the print remained a best-seller for nearly as long as the fashion for popular prints endured in America—until the days when kitchen wall calendars ultimately replaced parlor pictures as home decorations. At some point, the *New York Independent,* which had praised the picture as "eminently successful," purchased the Ritchie plate for $8,000 and offered freshly made ten-dollar engravings as a bonus for new subscriptions to the newspaper. Photographic copies appeared for sale as well, and some editions of the print eventually appeared engraved along with reproductions of the handwritten text of the Proclamation—the result not unlike the kind of "ingenious nonsense" the artist and subject had once seen together in the White House. Late in the century, prints were still being advertised in an "extraordinary limited offer" for only one-dollar apiece, by the International Portrait Company on New York's Fifth Avenue. Noted an advertising flyer for the reprint, "It is a fitting memorial of the famous 'War President's' great life work, and should be found on the walls of every 'patriotic American home.'"[42]

Ever enterprising, Carpenter lived off his triumph, creating a number of additional Lincoln paintings over the years (and always dating them 1864—the year of his personal experience with the president). In 1877, after a long and frustrating effort, he sold his original emancipation canvas for $25,000 to a generous private patron, who in turn donated it to Congress in 1878. Although Carpenter harbored hopes that the picture would take its place in the Capitol Rotunda alongside paintings of the nation's founders, he, like Edward Dalton Marchant before him, was disappointed. Although Carpenter's *First Reading of the Emancipation Proclamation* became and remains the only verifiable nineteenth-century painting of Abraham Lincoln housed in the Capitol collection, it was long ago relegated to a seldom-visited stairway leading to the Senate gallery. Its modern-day banishment belies the popularity and influence it exerted in the years after Lincoln's assassination.[43]

Carpenter had determined to impose no "imaginary curtain" into a scene he believed suggestive enough on its own terms. Unbeknownst to the artist, he shared this belief with none other than the father of Communism, Karl Marx. Writing of the Emancipation Proclamation, Marx commented disparagingly of its "mean pettifogging" literary style, which to his ears sounded like the arguments "one lawyer puts to his opposing lawyer." But, as Marx hastened to add, "this does not alter their historic content, and indeed it amuses me when I compare them with the drapery in which the Frenchman envelops even the most unimportant point."[44] Lincoln's act required no drapery to insure its immortality, either in history or iconography.

As for Lincoln, even during Carpenter's prolonged White House stay, he could remain perplexingly indifferent to the power of Emancipation Proclamation iconography—at least when it did not overtly celebrate the emancipator. In June of that year, a number of New England admirers including abolitionist William Lloyd Garrison sent Lincoln a painting entitled *Watch Meeting, December 31st, 1862. Waiting for the Hour,* by William Tolman Carlton (1816–88). The dramatic, torch-lit scene depicting slaves anxiously waiting with what Garrison described as "heartfelt emotion and thrilling delight for the midnight hour of December 31, 1862, to pass, and the introduction of that new year which was to make them free" under the Emancipation Proclamation.[45]

Six months later, Lincoln had not bothered to acknowledge its receipt, although widely circulated photographic copies had made the painting rather famous. Garrison was compelled to write to the president again and ask if some thank-you letter could yet be written to relieve its donors "of much embarrassment." Lincoln took almost three more weeks to reply to Garrison, apologizing for "the seeming neglect occasioned by my constant engagements." He had enjoyed the "flattering and generous gift" of the "spirited and admirable painting," but after telling his secretaries not to draft an acknowledgment so that he might write one himself, had somehow "committed the discourtesy of not replying at all." Of course, Abraham Lincoln was never particularly interested in emancipation portrayals—unless they portrayed Abraham Lincoln.[46]

Not all artists enjoyed critical acclaim, popular success, or even widespread contemporary recognition for their original emancipation works. Marchant and Carpenter wisely shared the same sort of popular approach to their efforts: simple, uncluttered, lifelike portraiture and minimal use of easy-to-parse symbolism (Marchant's unshackled Liberty statue, Carpenter's left-and-right grouping of cabinet radicals and conservatives). Both probably knew that American audiences seldom understood, much less embraced, more complex messages. Of equal importance, both these artists' works were quickly adapted by superb engravers and distributed by robust publishing houses.

Two important works of emancipation art that have been widely reproduced since in textbooks and magazine articles, gaining no small degree of fame among Civil War and Lincoln students, enjoyed scant circulation during the Lincoln-emancipation era. The first was a peculiar but arresting canvas by the Irish-Scottish painter David Gilmour Blythe (1815–65). While still a teenaged immigrant in the Pittsburgh area, Blythe learned art and sculpture as an apprentice interior designer. In his subsequent travels, he was exposed to the work of Boston artist David Claypoole Johnston (whose own son later painted Abraham Lincoln from life) and may have embraced his humorous, complex, often grotesque style—half portrait, half caricature. Through the 1840s and 1850s, Blythe himself slowly evolved into a peripatetic, if not terribly successful, portrait painter.[47]

Like many artists of his time, Blythe was enthralled by the drama of the Civil War, although he seemed unable to develop a consistent way of approaching it. For example, he produced an accomplished panoramic landscape of *General Doubleday Crossing the Potomac* en route to Gettysburg with his army in June 1863, and a hellish scene of human suffering in *Libby Prison*.[48] Adapting a totally different style, he portrayed the president for the first time in *Lincoln Crushing the Dragon of Rebellion* (1862). In a symbol-laden, cartoonlike composition, Blythe depicted his subject in an almost slapdash manner, casually dressed in homespun, literally beating back a Copperhead monster with a club shaped like a Lincolnian log rail.[49]

Blythe reached the pinnacle of this new, expressionistic style with his *President Lincoln Writing the Proclamation of Freedom, January 1, 1863*. Here was the polar opposite of Edward Dalton Marchant's image of a formally clad Great Emancipator. Blythe's Lincoln, his face downcast, his hair rumpled, is shown sitting in a cluttered office, wearing an open shirt and slippers, one of which has fallen off. He balances the proclamation-in-progress on his lap atop a pile of books and documents that includes the Bible and the Constitution. The room is in disorder, suggesting the chaotic state of national war and the pressures facing the beleaguered Union leader.

Every detail and decoration in the office symbolizes either Lincoln's determination or challenges:

FIG. 12

[Peter E.] Ehrgott, [Adolphus] Forbriger and Co., after a painting by David Gilmour Blythe, *President Lincoln Writing the Proclamation of Freedom, January 1, 1863*. Chromolithograph, published by M. Dupuy, Pittsburgh, 1864. (Courtesy of the Lincoln Museum, Fort Wayne, IN, Ref. #2051)

a map of the rebel states covered by a heavy railsplitter's maul; a map of Europe (representing the dangerous potential for foreign intervention) hanging in the background; a bust of Lincoln's ineffective predecessor James Buchanan, hanging hauntingly from a bookcase by its neck; and scales of justice to remind Lincoln that he must balance his quest to restore the Union with a determination to respect the Constitution. American flags serve as drapes; a copy of the presidential oath reminds Lincoln of his pledge to preserve, protect, and defend the Constitution; an American flag window shade keeps bad news from reaching him from outside; and various religious and military tracts scattered about the floor suggest inspiration and authority. Visible in the foreground is a battered old trunk bearing Lincoln's name and hometown, representing not only Lincoln's humble origins but also the real political danger of his imminent return to private life in Illinois should the emancipation policy backfire.

Records of the Blythe painting's public exhibition, if it was ever displayed, have never been discovered. The canvas might have been lost to history altogether had it not been adapted by a Cincinnati lithographer, Ehrgott, Forbriger and Co., and published in 1864 by M. Dupuy in Blythe's hometown of Pittsburgh (Fig. 12). Yet even this attempt to broaden its appeal failed—judging alone from the exceptional rarity of surviving copies. From its current scarcity (compared to the abundance of Ritchie/Carpenter prints that survive today) it seems reasonable to conclude that Blythe's design and the lithographer's adaptation (even though it made the portrait of Lincoln a bit more recognizable) elicited little notice or approval from picture-buying audiences of the Civil War era.[50]

The historian can draw several conclusions from this scant evidence. For one thing, it clearly helped a painter to secure popularity for an original image to have it issued by a major publisher in a large eastern city. Marchant's picture was adapted by the dean of American engravers, John Sartain. Carpenter's canvas was expertly recreated by Alexander H. Ritchie and issued by a major New York publisher who promoted it in his books. But Blythe's canvas was copied in lithograph—a hastier, less expensive, less prestigious medium. Although it was made available to purchasers for far less money than the Sartain or Ritchie tributes, the firm of M. Dupuy of Pittsburgh was hardly as robust an operation as its Philadelphia and New York competitors, and could not be expected to match its rivals' distribution and promotion ability.

That said, some of the blame for the Blythe picture's obscurity must rest squarely with the painter's artistic conception. Emancipation was controversial enough in the year it was promulgated and also in the year following, at which time it became a central and divisive issue of the presidential campaign. Americans who supported the proclamation in all likelihood preferred to celebrate their enthusiasm with straightforward, easy-to-understand pictorial tributes that touted emancipation and elevated the emancipator to the status of statesman. Blythe's canvas, thoughtful and original though it was, did neither. A print buyer contemplating its purchase for home display might have been thoroughly confused by the cacophony of discordant symbolic devices crowding the scene, and a bit offended by the sight of a tieless, unshod chief executive, hair askew, sitting amid perplexing disarray and painfully reminding viewers of his suffering and uncertainty. By attempting to reflect Lincoln's anguish, David Gilmour Blythe sacrificed commercial success to artistic integrity.

So did the Baltimore artist Adalbert Johann Volck, but not for want of dreaming of immediate popular approbation and influence. Volck was a Prussian-born dentist who stealthily pursued a wartime avocation as an etcher. He worked under a veil of secrecy imposed by the Union occupation of his prosouthern Maryland hometown. Although he created a portfolio of masterful anti-Lincoln, anti-Union, and anti-emancipation prints, he appears to have been forced to publish them secretly and in small editions, distributing copies only to a small band of fellow Confederate sympathizers. Not until the war ended and Volck's brilliant work was published for broad popular consumption did many Americans finally get to see it. The acidulous works, of course, seemed more benign once the war was over and the future of the Union secured. But the frequent republication of Volck's works since has left the mistaken impression that they were influential in their own time. In fact, censorship made it impossible for them to enjoy free distribution while the war raged. Nonetheless, Volck's work was so well executed that it certainly deserves consideration and appreciation within the body of Emancipation Proclamation iconography.[51] Moreover, his scene *Writing the Emancipation Proclamation* (Fig. 13) can in many ways be viewed as the anti-Lincoln analogue to Blythe's vision of the same scene—both wholly imagined, rich with symbolism, and all but unseen in their own time.

FIG. 13

Adalbert Johann Volck, [*Writing the Emancipation Proclamation*]. Etching in "V. Blada" [Volck], *Sketches from the Civil War in North America, Second Series*, Baltimore, ca. 1864, plate 24. (Collection of Harold Holzer)

Like Blythe's benevolent emancipator, Volck's evil Lincoln also uses the Constitution for "support." He does not hold it in his lap for easy consultation but keeps it on the floor, under the table, holding it shut with his big boot. There is no symbolic statue shedding her shackles here as Lincoln proclaims liberty with his pen. Volck's Lincoln writes at a table held upright by cloven feet, and draws ink from an inkwell held by the devil himself. There are pictures on these walls, too. Carpenter's scene includes a portrait of Andrew Jackson; Volck shows abolitionist John Brown dressed as a saint and the bloody slave insurrection at Santo Domingo. With these background decorations, the artist provocatively suggests that the proclamation will inspire dangerous uprisings by blacks against whites.

The window curtain in Volck's vision of the presidential office is not an American flag but a dark curtain held fast by a vulture-shaped tieback, exposing a flock of vultures circling expectantly outside, perhaps eager to feed on the imminent and deserved destruction of the Union. In one corner of the room is a decanter of liquor and some drinking glasses, implying that Lincoln must have been drunk to pursue an emancipation policy. Finally, in the opposite corner, sits a statue of the national symbol, Columbia, her face covered by a Scotch tam—a subtle reminder that two years earlier, Lincoln had infamously donned such a hat as a disguise to escape threats of assassination during his 1861 inau-

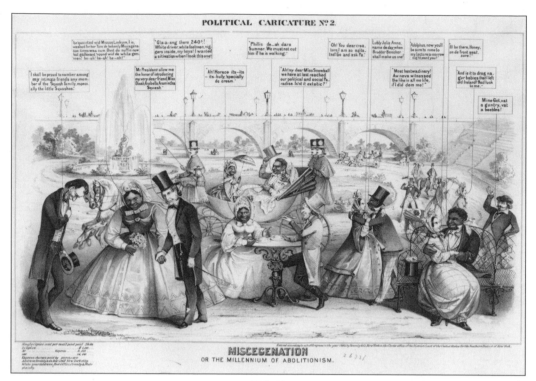

FIG. 14

Printmaker unknown, *Miscegenation or the Millennium of Abolitionism.* Lithograph, published in New York by
Bromly and Co., 1864. (Library of Congress)

gural journey to Washington. Now the symbol returns to haunt him and here serves two purposes:
to renew the charge of cowardice against the president and to cover the eyes of the patriotic symbol
that must be shielded from Lincoln's dictatorial proclamation.[52]

Ironically, given free access to the marketplace in 1864, it is possible that Volck's rabid anti-Lincoln etching would have achieved far more popularity than Blythe's flattering, if discombobulated,
tribute. Volck's work, symbolism notwithstanding, boasts something Blythe's work lacked—emphatic
simplicity. His Lincoln looks unkempt and sinister, a perfect caricature for the large audience of
Americans hostile to the Republican president and his policies.

Indeed, evidence abounds that like-minded pictorial statements, albeit less accomplished than
Volck's, were circulated in the North by other publishers during the 1864 presidential campaign.
New York printmakers closely aligned with the Democratic Party issued cartoons bearing such racist titles as *The Abolition Catastrophe* and *The Miscegenation Ball,* predicting dire societal upheavals
because of emancipation. In such prints, Copperheadism was described as a "badge of liberty," and
emancipation as an act of unimaginable madness. One cartoon, *Miscegenation or the Millennium of
Abolitionism* (Fig. 14), portrayed, in the words of an advertising sheet that promoted it, "society as it
is to be in the era of 'Equality and Fraternity.'" The cartoon depicted a fast-approaching, horrific day
in which liveried white drivers would chauffeur black passengers, in which mixed-race marriages

would become commonplace, and the president himself might scandalously bow in greeting to a woman of color.

The distasteful pictorial evidence of such unrepentant racism may help explain why many print-makers feared providing Lincoln's supporters with pro-proclamation prints in response. Emancipation had unleashed a combination of hope and nervous concern among most white Republicans. Such tepid support simply did not excite the passion—or the printmaking—evoked by furious white supremacists. For a time, Lincoln supporters continued to honor their hero with straightforward portraits. The time for broadly celebrating freedom in the visual arts had not quite arrived.[53]

Emancipation imagery—pro and con—did become somewhat more common during the 1864 race, which several scholars have called the most important presidential election in American history. Yet even though the constitutional eradication of slavery everywhere became a part of the Republican party platform endorsed by President Lincoln, the Emancipation Proclamation and the further prospect of universal liberty still did not excite as many tributes in the graphic arts as it did criticism. The modern observer can detect a kind of stubborn timidity on the issue among northern printmakers. On the other side of the political spectrum, meanwhile, the racist New York Weekly Day-Book was emboldened to boast of the twenty-five-cent-per-copy anti-emancipation print, Miscegenation: "It ought to be circulated far and wide as a campaign document."[54]

More often than not, pro-Lincoln 1864 campaign prints stressed a return to peace and prosperity, rather than the grandest achievement of the administration: the unshackling of a black labor source which, some whites feared, might yet compete with them for jobs once the war ended. In the end, however, the anti-Lincoln, anti-emancipation caricatures of 1864 made little difference to the outcome. The president won reelection by a healthy margin. What remains remarkable from the point of view of American iconography is that Lincoln triumphed without the help of a large body of pictorial celebrations of his most important act, the Emancipation Proclamation.

Rare indeed in this atmosphere was the decision by Lincoln supporters in Philadelphia to create and display one of the largest (if least permanent) visual tributes to emancipation ever conceived. A week before election day, Lincoln received a "rough wood-engraving" illustrating their plans to illuminate the façade of the four-story Republican headquarters on Chestnut Street with "transparencies executed in the highest style of art commemorating emancipation in Maryland and your glorious proclamation and official acts."[55]

Planners clearly intended the display—to be accompanied by music and "Fire-works"—to "make votes" for the president on November 8 in defiance of "certain timorous men" who believed "this commemoration will take voters away from you." The pictorial message was designed to be bold, dazzling, and gigantic in size, featuring, one newspaper reported, "well executed portraits of Abraham Lincoln" and other war heroes, accompanied by a 200-gun salute fired by U.S. Colored troops from nearby Camp William Penn. As the organizer boasted to the president,[56] "Symbolic devices of Army and navy, Portraits of you, Johnson, Grant, Sherman, Sheridan, Farragut and others will adorn the house, 'God save the Republic,' will be in a Gas jet, salutes will be fired, extracts from the writings of Washington, Jefferson, Henry, Jackson, O'Connell, Pope and the Bible are parts of the designs[.] The centre piece is the Liberty arch, Port Hudson [a Civil War battle] is one of the panels. The negro does figure among our emblems [sic] so does the flag and the eagle."[57]

FIG. 15

Celebration of the abolition of Negro slavery in Maryland, at Philadelphia, Penn., Nov. 1—from a sketch by our Phila-delphia artist. Wood engraving, published in *Frank Leslie's Illustrated Newspaper,* November 19, 1864. (Courtesy of the Lincoln Museum, Fort Wayne, IN, Ref. #4468)

The tide inhibiting the unbridled political commemoration of emancipation was finally turning. The Philadelphia illumination, surely the largest emancipation image ever created, would endure beyond the temporary display on Chestnut Street on November 1, 1864. Eighteen days later, the national weekly *Frank Leslie's Illustrated Newspaper* carried a full-page woodcut of the event on its cover (Fig. 15). Shortly thereafter, local printers Ringwalt and Brown issued a hand-colored lithograph of the same scene from a slightly different perspective (Fig. 16).[58]

Still, the Philadelphia experience proved an exception. Not until five months later, when Lincoln died heroically at the hands of an assassin, did most artists feel liberated from the real or imagined

FIG. 16

Ringwalt and Brown, *View of Transparency in front of headquarters of Supervisory committee for recruiting colored regiments, Chestnut Street, Philadelphia, in commemoration of Emancipation in Maryland, November 1, 1864.* Lithograph, Philadelphia, ca. 1864. (The Library Company of Philadelphia)

commercial restraints that inhibited such celebratory portraiture on a wide scale. Only when Lincoln was martyred did emancipation become a safe, indeed lucrative, subject for the graphic arts. While he lived, Lincoln himself may have sensed what the future held for his document in iconography and public memory. The president's own personal experiences with ambitious White House artists-in-residence had surely convinced him that heroic portraiture would somehow, someday recognize the document and its author and treat both with the laudatory attention they deserved.

The gifts Lincoln received late in his life—of the Carlton *Midnight Hour* painting, the calligraphy, and the Thomas B. Bryan lithograph, among others—represented, he likely knew, just the beginning

FIG. 17

Waeschle, *Emancipation of the Slaves, Proclaimed on the 22d of September 1862, by Abraham Lincoln, President of the United States of North America*. Lithograph, Chicago, ca. 1864–65. (Library of Congress)

of a burgeoning pictorial archive. But even he might have been surprised by the array of mass-produced emancipation portraiture that flooded the market once his murder sanctified the edict and seemed to place it beyond controversy, into the realm of glory where Lincoln from the first believed it belonged.

In life, Lincoln signed the Emancipation Proclamation in private, with only a few witnesses at his side. Thus he provided artists with no "emancipation moment"—no photo opportunity, no press conference, no ceremony—to mark the precise instant at which he changed America by signing the document. Historian David Brion Davis has pointed to such rituals as crucial for emphasizing the "moral obligations of the emancipated slaves as well as their dependence on the culture of the libera-

FIG. 18

Currier and Ives, *Freedom to the Slaves. Proclaimed January 1ˢᵗ. 1863, by Abraham Lincoln, President of the United States. "Proclaim liberty throughout All the land unto All the inhabitants thereof"—Lev. XXV, 10.* Lithograph, New York, ca. 1865. (Collection of Harold Holzer)

tors." Lincoln—who once urged that spontaneously kneeling freedman show their gratitude only to God, not to him—may have been grateful that few such scenes appeared in his lifetime. They would surely have embarrassed him. After his death, however, "emancipation-moment" art evolved quickly and widely.[59]

To either the giant printmakers Currier and Ives of New York, or the virtually unknown Philadelphia firm of J. Waeschle, belongs the "credit" for first imagining the ritualized unshackling that Lincoln failed to provide. One of these firms—it is unclear which—touched off what soon became an industry in emancipation graphics and, later, in public statuary.

Copyright laws were seldom strictly enforced in the Civil War era, and as a result, the period print buyer, as well as the modern collector and historian, frequently finds evidence that lithographers and engravers routinely stole ideas from each other, and issued the results as originals. Because printmakers did not always register their compositions with the federal authorities, it is sometimes impossible to know for sure which of two similar, undated prints arrived on the market first, and which served as the model for a thinly disguised copy.[60]

Where emancipation was concerned, Waeschle and Currier and Ives issued virtually identical prints showing Lincoln, his right arm pointed heavenward, allowing his left hand to be kissed by a freshly liberated, kneeling slave, broken shackles lying at his feet, his tattered wife and family looking on. Waeschle's print was called *Emancipation of the Slaves* (Fig. 17). Currier and Ives's bore the title *Freedom to the Slaves* (Fig. 18). It is impossible that either print appeared before 1864—once again, in time for the crucial election campaign—because in each the portrait of the president was modeled after a photograph made that year.[61]

The most persuasive clue about which publisher first thought of the design can be found in their respective subtitles. Currier and Ives called their print *Freedom to the Slaves. Proclaimed January 1st 1863 by Abraham Lincoln, President of the United States.* "*Proclaim liberty throughout All the Land unto All the inhabitants thereof.*" —*Lev. XXV, 10*. Waeschle's picture, on the other hand, celebrated not the final 1863 proclamation but the preliminary version issued one hundred days earlier. It was called *Emancipation of the Slaves. Proclaimed on the 22d September 1862 by Abraham Lincoln, President of the United States of North America.*

It is not unreasonable to conclude from this small hint that, in this singular case, the fabulously successful and always news-conscious New York lithography firm may have "borrowed" one of its most important emancipation images from an obscure Chicago rival. What remains indisputable is that both pictures perfectly fit what David Brion Davis describes as the typical "emancipation moment" image, "depicting joyous, half-clad blacks holding up broken manacles and kneeling in gratitude to well-dressed whites." What might be added is that such images were principally crafted to make emancipation seem less dangerous to whites—less a threat to the social order than a benevolent act aimed at ending injustice.

True, as Davis has said, such art was in part "designed to emphasize the indebtedness and moral obligations of the emancipated slaves as well as their dependence on the culture and expectations of their liberators." But it is also true that such imagery, however politically incorrect it may appear to twenty-first-century eyes, helped make Lincoln's revolution palpable to the skittish white population of the 1860s. It is unreasonable to take sides on the long-term effect of such images without acknowledging their sanguinary impact, in their own time, on the predominately white audiences for whom they were published.[62]

Until well after the Emancipation Proclamation and Thirteenth Amendment officially ended American slavery, almost no artistic depictions of what Francis B. Carpenter described as the "second Declaration of Independence" were principally designed for its chief beneficiaries, African Americans.[63]

This deficit is not altogether surprising. With few exceptions, newly freed blacks were not wealthy enough to afford to purchase art for their homes. Their principal goal was basic survival, not interior decoration. Confirming this point in 1870, Frederick Douglass wrote: "Heretofore, colored Americans have thought little of adorning their parlors with pictures . . . Pictures come not with slavery and oppression and destitution, but with liberty, fair play, leisure, and refinement." But sounding a

FIG. 19

J. W. Watte, after a drawing by H. W. Herrick, *Reading the Emancipation Proclamation*. Published by Lucius
Stebbins, Hartford, 1864. (Library of Congress)

hopeful note, Douglass hastened to add: "These conditions are now possible to colored American
citizens, and I think the walls of their houses will soon begin to bear evidence of their altered relations to the people about them."[64]

By the time he made these observations, Douglass was celebrating the appearance of a handsome
L. Prang and Company chromolithograph of Hiram Revels, the first African American ever elected to
the U.S. Senate. "We colored men so often see ourselves described and painted as monkeys," he rue-
fully noted, "that we think it a great piece of good fortune to find an exception to this general rule."
In fact, one notable exception had appeared much earlier, during the crucial election campaign of
1864, when a few emancipation graphics first appeared.[65]

That year, S. A. Peters and Co. of Hartford, Connecticut, issued J. W. Watte's engraved adaptation
of H. W. Herrick's drawing *Reading the Proclamation of Emancipation in the Slaves' Cabin* (Fig. 19),
identified in subsequent editions as *Reading the Emancipation Proclamation, or The Midnight Hour*.

The poignant scene, sold originally at $2.50 each, portrayed a Union soldier reading aloud the words of Lincoln's order to an excited slave family and their guests, who gather by torchlight in a primitive cabin somewhere in the Confederacy. The picture, copyrighted by Hartford book publisher Lucius Stebbins, was accompanied by a small promotional pamphlet, *Emancipation Proclamation of January 1st, 1864 [sic]*.

Its artist, Henry W. Herrick (1824–after 1904), was a New Hampshire-born painter and engraver who worked for a time for book and bank-note printers in New York City before returning to spend his final working years as an artist and historian in his native state. Little else is known about him, and the identity of engraver Watte and the other collaborators in this worthy project remains shrouded in mystery.[66] But the product they created was certainly exceptional. According to a "Description of the Engraving," published in the pamphlet, the scene was meant to show emancipation from a unique perspective:

> Old man at the right with folded hands, Grand-father; old lady at the left with cane in hand, Grand-mother; man leaning on ladder, the father; woman with child in her arms, the mother; lad swings his hat, oldest son; little girl, oldest daughter; infant in the arms of its mother. Young woman with two children, the house servant of her master, not belonging to the cabin but happened to be in on the occasion. Party reading, Union Soldier.
>
> The internal view of the cabin is true to nature. The stone chimney, garrett [sic], ladder, side of bacon, rough cradle, piece of sugar cane and cotton balls, etc., all combine to give a correct idea of the slaves home.[67]

Its publisher promoted the print enthusiastically. When Lucius Stebbins issued a book called *Life and Death in Rebel Prisons*, for example, he made sure that it included a full-page notice describing the "new national engraving." The advertisement left little doubt that even for a print as daring as this one, its creators expected the principal audience to be not newly liberated slaves but philanthropic white abolitionists. Frederick Douglass's appeal to African Americans to decorate their homes with pictures was still six years in the future. As Stebbins wrote in 1864:

> This is a beautiful illustration of a great event in the world's history—the emancipation of slavery in the United States will ever be so considered by all civilized nations and for all time to come.
>
> The sight of this engraving will always produce happy reflections in the minds of every Christian and philanthropist, and should adorn the dwelling of every family in our country.
>
> It is the most appropriate illustration that can be made, as it represents the only way in which the glorious news could reach the downtrodden and oppressed slaves, viz.: through the faithful soldier, without whom the Proclamation would ever have remained a dead letter.
>
> The design is entirely original, by a bank note artist, and is truly elegant. The engraving is by one of the best workmen in the country, and is superbly executed.[68]

Whatever its popular reception, the Stebbins engraving proved to be the only print to show a "first reading of the Emancipation Proclamation" from the point of view of those whom the order was de-

FIG. 20

Thomas Eakins, *Negro Boy Dancing*. Watercolor on wove paper, 1878.
(The Metropolitan Museum of Art, Fletcher Fund, 1925, 25.97.1)

signed to free. Whether or not the finished result appealed, as Frederick Douglass would have liked, to black as well as white audiences, remains a matter of conjecture. Sales records for this print, as for all prints of the era, are long lost, and the historian is left to judge from imperfect and incomplete evidence—like the number of copies observed in modern institutional and private collections over a period of years. In fact, relatively few copies of *Reading the Emancipation Proclamation* have survived, indicating that, like most of the ground-breaking and atypical emancipation art of the period, Stebbins's laudable engraving proved rather like the proclamation itself—not immediately popular with everyone.

Yet evidence exists to suggest that Lincoln—and his portrait—did indeed become enormously popular with African Americans. Writing from Galveston, Texas, in 1867, a Reconstruction-era schoolteacher named Sarah M. Barnes who had gone south to educate freedmen, testified: "I have often noticed in their cabins pictures of Abraham Lincoln, sometimes when there was wanting the bare necessities of life, his face has appeared looking down from the black murky ceilings. I asked at one house, why this was so, and was answered, 'He freed us, and I like him, so I have it there.'"[69]

Other African Americans shared this view. Historian Benjamin Quarles has noted that, "to the mass of Negroes, Lincoln had passed from history to legend even before Booth's bullet. The flesh-and-blood Lincoln paled before this legendary figure—a figure who came alive in the hopes and aspirations of colored Americans." Quarles concluded of Lincoln's reputation among African Americans: "They loved him first and have loved him longest." That affection was reflected in art.[70]

The celebrated American artist Thomas Eakins (1844–1916) offered intriguing evidence of his own, albeit from the perspective of a white painter who during his lifetime suffered from what he bitterly described as "misunderstanding, persecution, and neglect." In his 1878 watercolor *Negro Boy Dancing* (Fig. 20), he showed three African-American males—an elderly man, a young man, and a boy, respectively making, enjoying, and responding to music. It is a simple scene, set in a bare room. A top hat and cane sitting on a chair suggest that this is a professional troupe, rehearsing or simply expressing their tireless love of music by "jamming" during their off hours. The only decoration in the room is a small portrait on the wall: a reproduction of the famous Mathew Brady photograph of Lincoln and his son Tad.[71]

Art historian Albert Boime has praised Eakins's *Negro Boy Dancing* for its "individualized treatment of the people he portrayed." More recently, Alan C. Braddock countered that the picture reveals Eakins to be less a "sympathetic progressive" than a "detached voyeur" with an "ambivalent approach to racial and ethnic issues." Acknowledging the significant inclusion of the Lincoln-and-Tad image, Braddock perceptively recognized that it might have been meant "to mirror and promote the apparent father-son dynamic" reflected by the family of dancers. He went on to suggest, however, that the Lincoln image "produces mixed signals about black education in the aftermath of emancipation." White children may rise in life, Braddock asserted, but blacks like Eakins's dancers remain locked in a "holding pattern" dictated by racial inequality, "doomed to a life of representing stereotypical blackness." However we respond to this gloomy interpretation, for purposes of this study what remains remarkable is that, painting fifteen years after emancipation, Lincoln seemed to Eakins an enduring touchstone representing freedom and opportunity—whether or not its full promise had been fulfilled.[72]

One piece of unforgettable, unimpeachable visual evidence has survived to support the Quarles theory that African Americans at one time venerated Lincoln as an emancipator: a remarkable photograph (Fig. 21) taken on a Richmond, Virginia, street on "Emancipation Day"—presumably January 1—1888. It portrays a day of celebration: the twenty-fifth anniversary of the proclamation. The scene shows a group of African Americans gathered in front of a shop decorated for the occasion. This family is a generation removed from the slave family listening breathlessly to the words of the Emancipation Proclamation in the cabin depicted by H. W. Herrick for the 1864 Lucius Stebbins lithograph. Here, instead, is a grandfather in his ankle-length white apron; a mature man in a handsome derby, perhaps his son; and three young males—two little boys and one teenager playfully holding what appears to be a wad of cotton over the face of one of the smallest of the boys. A little girl at left moves during the camera exposure and only her tiny feet remain in focus. Huddled in the doorway is a woman cradling an infant in her arms.

What sets this image apart from the Stebbins scene is first, of course, that the 1888 family is now engaged in trade, not involuntary servitude. The slave cabin has been discarded for a small shop, perhaps with a residence on the second floor whose balcony the viewer can glimpse in the photograph. What astonishes the modern viewer is the sight of a banner-sized portrait, strung from the rafters of the porch. It distinctly shows Abraham Lincoln.[73]

FIG. 21

Photographer unknown, Emancipation Day Celebration in Richmond, Virginia, January 1, 1888.
(Valentine Richmond History Center)

So did a number of Great Emancipator prints, thoughtful and insensitive alike, whose prolifera-
tion suggested a growing audience for such graphic tributes in the months following Lincoln's assassination. As noted, nineteenth-century art publishers, even those whose product was political in
nature, worked independent of organized political parties and politically motivated commissions.
They portrayed their subjects whenever they sensed a potentially lucrative market. The Emancipation
Proclamation—its controversial, and socially threatening nature softened in the afterglow of Lincoln's
murder and martyrdom—became such a subject because the market evidently demanded it.

After 1865, for example, printmakers rushed out a variety of calligraphic tributes to emancipation
(Fig. 22) and, once A. H. Ritchie's engraving of the Carpenter painting arrived on the market, thinly
disguised piracies of Lincoln and his cabinet as well. Even Lincoln's widow recognized the image-
altering significance of the Ritchie print. Notwithstanding her intense and prolonged mourning, she
took time to thank its publishers for a copy of the picture, adding, as if by way of endorsement: "I
have always regarded the original painting, as very perfect, and the engraving, appears to me quite
equal to it." She never wavered in her belief that it included the most "accurate" representation of
her "lamented husband."[74]

Generic postassassination tributes frequently eulogized Lincoln not only as a national martyr
but also as an unforgettable emancipator. Lithographer C. Nahl's extravagant *In Memoriam* (Fig. 23),
for example, the only important contemporary Lincoln image ever published on the West Coast,

FIG. 22

W. H. Pratt, [*Abraham Lincoln*]. Calligraphic lithograph, published by A. Hageboeck, Davenport, Iowa, 1865.
(The Lincoln Museum, Fort Wayne, IN, Ref. #3314)

showed the plump figure of Columbia weeping at Lincoln's grave—behind which a half-naked black man sheds tears of his own. In the foreground lies the slain dragon of rebellion, and beside it a scroll marked "Emancipation," accompanied by the inevitable broken shackles. The viewer is left with little doubt about what weapon killed the disunion monster: Lincoln's proclamation.[75]

Many such mourning prints showed Lincoln, his portrait festooned with flags, holding some sort of document marked "Proclamation" or "Emancipation." Broken shackles abounded in such prints, as did saddened women carrying laurel wreaths, and goddesses of liberty holding capped liberty poles—the enduring symbol of slave manumission. E. J. Post's 1865 lithograph *The Father [and] the Preserver of Our Country* (Fig. 24) used these figures in depicting the first and sixteenth presidents

FIG. 23

C. Nahl, *To Abraham Lincoln the Best Beloved of the Nation. In Memoriam.* Printed by L. Nagel, published with
Puck, the Pacific Pictorial. Lithograph, San Francisco, 1865. (Courtesy of Harold Holzer)

side-by-side, adding the tiny figure of a liberated slave raising his arms in tribute, with the broken
shackles and Emancipation scroll lying nearby.[76]

Engraver John Chester Buttre reiterated this notion of veneration and—implicitly—obligation,
in his 1866 print, *Abraham Lincoln Entering Richmond, April 3d, 1865* (Fig. 25). The picture showed
Lincoln being greeted with wild enthusiasm by the African-American residents of the conquered
Confederate capital, a welcome to which several eyewitnesses testified. Interestingly, here was one
occasion in which a freed slave might accurately have been portrayed kneeling—for one elderly laborer, crying, "There is the great Messiah," actually did fall to his knees at the sight of the president,
only to see Lincoln, in turn, lift his hat and reply: "Don't kneel to me. That is not right. You must

FIG. 24

E. J. Post, *The Father [and] the Preserver of our Country*. Lithograph, New York, 1865. (Courtesy of the Lincoln Museum, Fort Wayne, IN, Ref. #3451)

kneel to God only, and thank Him for the liberty you will hereafter enjoy." Thomas Nast produced a similar scene of jubilant welcome.[77]

Philadelphia printmaker John L. Magee's *Emancipation* (Fig. 26) went significantly further. Quoting the words of the proclamation—"And by virtue of the power and for the purpose aforesaid, I do order and declare that all persons held as SLAVES within designated States and parts of States are and henceforward SHALL BE FREE"—the print showed Lincoln grandly displaying his document before *two* groups of kneeling beneficiaries. What sets the print apart is that only half of the group is comprised of liberated slaves. Joining them in gratitude are poor Southern whites, seen on their knees as well. The whites, the picture suggests, are just as likely to benefit from emancipation through "education to all classes," the words on a banner seen flying over a public school in the background.

The lively small engraving *Proclamation of Emancipation* (Fig. 27) by Richardson of New York similarly portrays a group of kneeling black people falling into a posture of supplication not merely at the sight of the late president emerging from a niche at left, but a vision of the hand of God hovering above, holding the Bible. The message here is that emancipation was heaven-sent, with Lincoln acting as emancipator but also virtually as God's blessed agent.

FIG. 25

J[ohn]. C[hester]. Buttre, after a drawing by L. Hollis. *Abraham Lincoln Entering Richmond, April 3d, 1865.*
Engraving, published by B. B. Russell and Co., Boston, 1866. (Collection of Harold Holzer)

FIG. 26

J[ohn]. L. Magee, *Emancipation.* Lithograph, Philadelphia, 1865.
(Stern Collection, Library of Congress)

PROCLAMATION OF EMANCIPATION.

FIG. 27

Richardson, *Proclamation of Emancipation*. Lithograph, New York, ca. 1865. (Collection of Harold Holzer)

In a similarly reverential tone, A. B. Daniel's 1896 print *Emancipation Proclamation* (Fig. 28) reprinted the words of the document above scenes contrasting the previous and present lives of African Americans: slaves picking cotton at left, and a black senator speaking in the halls of Congress at right. Surmounting all was a standing portrait of Lincoln receiving his inspiration from a female angel whom the artist has portrayed, most unusually, as a woman of color. The verse printed below this image leaves little doubt about the meaning or marketing appeal of the picture. It was designed specifically for African-American print buyers, the heirs to Frederick Douglass's 1870 recommendation that people of color decorate their homes with pictures. As the caption proclaimed:

> This angel was sent from the Lord above,
> With her flapping wings, just as a dove.
> She came in the morning, with the dew,
> Bearing greatest blessings our race ever knew.
> Looking down on us, our toils she views,
> Singing and shouting the joyful news:
> Freedom! oh, Freedom! oh, sweet welcome!
> This joyful news was spoken by Lincoln.

FIG. 28

A. B. Daniel, *Emancipation Proclamation of President Abraham Lincoln, Freeing the Slaves of the United States.*
Lithograph, 1896. (Collection of Harold Holzer)

Reverence him, though our skins are dark,

Reverence him in our churches and parks;

Let us teach our children to do the same,

And teach them never to forget his name.

He was our Moses, to us and our race,

And our children should never forget his face.

Let them look on it with much delight,

He was our Moses and for us did right:

God was with him, as we all can see.

Praise him; reverence Lincoln! we are forever free![78]

FIG. 29

Erie Litho. Co., poster for Parson & Pool's *Uncle Tom's Cabin*. Lithograph, Erie, Pennsylvania, date unknown.
(Courtesy of the Lincoln Museum, Fort Wayne, IN, Ref. #3833)

Just as the poem urged, children—white as well as black—did not forget Lincoln's face. They might be reminded of his liberating work by a retrograde poster for a stage adaptation of *Uncle Tom's Cabin* (featuring Lincoln's portrait together with that of a kneeling slave; see Fig. 29) or by the enlightened post–World War I illustration *Welcome Home* (depicting a black veteran returning to a family parlor decorated with a flag-festooned portrait of Lincoln; see Fig. 30). As both types of images suggest, Americans uncritically embraced the image of the Great Emancipator in the graphic arts well into the twentieth century. Only since the 1970s, in fact, have some historians urged modern readers to reexamine the proclamation and its celebrated author.[79] In the meantime—although the definitive scholarly study has yet to be undertaken—late-twentieth-century American painters, black as well as white, continued to address, and occasionally challenge, Lincoln's emancipator image in artistically inventive and historically provocative ways.[80]

FIG. 30
Printmaker unknown, *Welcome Home*. Poster, ca. 1916.
(Courtesy of the Lincoln Museum, Fort Wayne, IN, Ref. #3843)

As recently as 1937, however, a WPA-sponsored effort to collect slave narratives revealed that a substantial 43 percent of those surveyed—ancient, living survivors of American slavery—volunteered, a full seventy-four years after emancipation, that Lincoln remained in their hearts their savior and liberator. Such numbers would undoubtedly be far smaller today, but no amount of revisionism can possibly dispute the ubiquity and influence of Lincoln's emancipator image over an extraordinary length of time. In the words of a World War I–era cartoon showing a young white boy peering at a framed portrait of the sixteenth president, "No American Home is Complete without a Picture of Abraham Lincoln." Such was the case virtually as long as the fashion endured for political portraits in private parlors. For decades, America's independent printmaking industry provided such tributes, due to which Lincoln's face was indeed looked on by blacks and whites alike—in the words of A. B. Daniel's print—"with much delight."[81]

FIG. 31

Printmaker unknown, *Monument to Abraham Lincoln.* Hand-colored lithograph, ca. 1865.
(Courtesy of the Lincoln Museum, Fort Wayne, IN, Ref. #2293)

In 1865, an anonymous printmaker issued a quaint, hand-colored lithograph entitled *Monument to Abraham Lincoln* (Fig. 31). The print imagined a huge statue of Lincoln set high on a lavishly carved pedestal in a grove of trees. Admirers young and old (all of them white, in this case) gather to take inspiration from the imposing marble figure. A young girl offering a flower contemplates the words carved on the pedestal, "In Memory of Abraham Lincoln," followed by a succession of important dates and achievements in his life. Standing out in boldest relief is a single word: "Emancipation."

The print predated by at least four years the dedication of the first important emancipation-themed public sculpture, Henry Kirke Browne's *Abraham Lincoln Declaring Emancipation* (Prospect Park, Brooklyn, 1869), and by more than a decade the most famous and enduringly controversial, Thomas Ball's *Emancipation Group* (Lincoln Park, Washington, 1876). It is instructive to note that even a printmaker—whose stock in trade, after all, consisted of portraits for indoor, not outdoor, settings—was willing to acknowledge that perhaps the most powerful of all possible visual tributes to a national hero came in the form of public statuary.

Prints might testify to an individual owner's private admiration in the sacred setting of the family home. But statues reflected—and influenced—mass national memory in public spheres in which neighbors and visitors shared recollection and aspiration. Often citizens joined together, through small contributions, to commission the works of art themselves. And the array of emancipation statues that appeared throughout the North in the late nineteenth century signaled, and profoundly advanced, Lincoln's full emergence as a mythical liberator.

Henry Kirke Brown (1814–86) was hired by Brooklyn's War Fund Committee, which raised $13,000 for its statue project through individual donations of no more than a dollar. While the principal speaker at its dedication stressed Lincoln's commitment to "regulated liberty," the large bronze itself clearly identified Lincoln as an emancipator. Brown showed him holding a scroll in one hand, and with the other pointing to the inscribed words from the proclamation: "shall be then, thenceforward, and forever free." For most sculptors, depictions of Lincoln as divinely inspired author best suited their patrons and their public. Brown's model for yet another emancipation tribute to Lincoln, for example—a plaster showing a grateful slave kneeling at Lincoln's feet—probably struck potential customers as too much of a cliché to earn a commission. A Randolph Rogers plaster showing Lincoln personally lifting a slave woman from her knees met with similar indifference. The fashion for the Waeschle–Currier and Ives "emancipation moment" Moses image eventually passed.[82]

Heroic sculptural tributes to Lincoln the Emancipator soon graced other large cities as well. Randolph Rogers's heroic bronze was unveiled in Philadelphia in 1871. Larkin Mead's bronze Emancipator was erected over the Lincoln tomb in Springfield in 1874. The first of Alonzo Pelzer's emancipation statues was unveiled in Lincoln, New Jersey, in 1898, and an imposing emancipation statue by George E. Bissell was erected in Edinburgh, Scotland, in 1893, and a replica in Clermont, Iowa, ten years later. Interestingly, Bissell's original concept featured, like the others, the figure of Lincoln clutching an emancipation scroll, as well as a black man standing at the bottom of the granite pedestal, clutching the furled American flag with one hand and raising his hand to Lincoln in salute with the other. When the statue was duplicated for Iowa, Bissell omitted the liberated slave.[83]

Like the others, Bissell's work was specifically designed—in the words of a Lincolnian inscription chiseled on the base of the Edinburgh original—to honor Lincoln's resolve "to preserve the jewel of liberty in the framework of freedom." It was an unabashed tribute to emancipation. A writer named Wallace Bruce contributed a poem for the dedication exercises that reiterated this theme. "Our Lincoln," he recited, remained "the noblest flower / Of freedom in its widening course . . . "[84]

In Philadelphia, 50,000 onlookers crowded Fairmount Park on September 22, 1871—the ninth anniversary of the preliminary Emancipation Proclamation—for the ceremonies dedicating the nearly ten-foot-high statue by Randolph Rogers (1825–92). Declared one of the principal speakers that day, "May the whole nation ever recall with gratitude the services of Abraham Lincoln, and still renew his noble resolve 'that government of the people, by the people, for the people, shall not perish from the earth.'" By all accounts, it was a deeply emotional occasion, with few in the large audience disappointed when the canvas shroud was dramatically lifted from the statue.[85]

Such public portraits—and such public ceremonies—were capable of stirring profound response on a wide scale. Day after day in their prominent settings, heroic statues like the works of Rogers,

FIG. 32

Photographer unknown, view of Thomas Ball's statue, *Emancipation Group*, Lincoln Park, Washington, D.C.
Stereoptican photograph, Washington, ca. 1890s. (Collection of Harold Holzer)

Brown, and Bissell testified convincingly to heartfelt community spirit, as manifested by generous
financial subscription and eager involvement in dedication ceremonies. "The moment was thrilling,"
went one typical recollection of a ceremony unveiling an "Emancipator" statue. "Vast numbers of
people manifested their emotion."[86]

It is fair to say that no Lincoln-as-emancipator sculpture ever generated the emotional excite-
ment—or aroused as much comment or controversy since—as Thomas Ball's *Emancipation Group*,
or *Freedmen's Memorial to Abraham Lincoln* (Fig. 32), unveiled in Washington on the eleventh anniversary of Lincoln's assassination, April 14, 1876. It was, and remains, the quintessential image of
noble liberator and eternally grateful slave, and it has evoked passionate response almost from the
moment it was unveiled.

The Massachusetts-born Ball (1819–1911) actually created the design for the figures before he ever received a commission to make a public statue. He was not invited to create the group; he imagined it. Ironically, although some modern art historians maintain that Ball's muscular slave helped transform the image of the African American through physical idealization, the white artist modeled the figure for his original plaster model after his own body, stripping and setting up mirrors in his studio to aid him as he sculpted.[87]

Earlier, just after Lincoln's assassination, a Virginia-born former slave named Charlotte Scott— "one of those made free by President Lincoln's proclamation," noted a contemporary—spontaneously offered five dollars of her own hard-earned money in Ohio "to make a monument" for Lincoln. Inspired by her generosity, the Western Sanitary Commission sought further contributions from freedmen throughout the nation. More than $16,000 quickly poured in, but fundraising stalled amid the painfully slow progress of Reconstruction.

Eventually, perhaps embarrassed by its failure to protect civil and voting rights for blacks in the former Confederacy, Congress took up the crusade, appropriating $3,000 to build a pedestal for the Ball statue in 1874. When the Freedman's Memorial Society organized a committee to select a design for a Lincoln statue in the nation's capital, one of its members, Rev. William G. Elliott of St. Louis, who had seen Ball's original model years earlier in his Florence studio, asked the sculptor to submit photographs of the piece. Delighted with what they saw, Elliott and the committee offered Ball $17,000 to cast it in bronze. The sculptor made one significant change in his original design. He replaced the self-portrait of the kneeling slave with a finely muscled figure, modeled after a photograph of Rev. Elliot's servant, a former Missouri slave named Archer Alexander. Now the slave was depicted as participating in his own liberation by straining heroically against the chains that bound him.[88]

The pedestal built for the statue bore a bronze plaque featuring the closing words of the otherwise desultory final proclamation: "And upon this act, sincerely believed to be an act of justice, warranted by the Constitution upon military necessity, I invoke the considerate judgment of mankind and the gracious favor of almighty God." More evocatively, the front of the pedestal featured a plaque boldly inscribed with what amounted to a full genesis of the statue's creation.

FREEDOM'S MEMORIAL

IN GRATEFUL MEMORY OF

ABRAHAM LINCOLN

THIS MONUMENT WAS ERECTED

BY THE WESTERN SANITARY COMMISSION

OF SAINT LOUIS, MO.

WITH FUNDS CONTRIBUTED BY

EMANCIPATED CITIZENS OF THE UNITED STATES

DECLARED FREE BY HIS PROCLAMATION

JANUARY 1, A.D. 1863.

THE FIRST CONTRIBUTION WAS MADE

BY CHARLOTTE SCOTT, A FREED WOMAN OF VIRGINIA

AND CONSECRATED

BY HER SUGGESTION AND REQUEST

ON THE DAY SHE HEARD OF PRESIDENT LINCOLN'S

DEATH

TO BUILD A MONUMENT TO HIS MEMORY.

Dedication day, April 14, 1876, was declared a holiday by Congress, and thousands of people, many African American, gathered in Washington to attend the unveiling ceremonies. The principal orator for the occasion was Frederick Douglass, who had known Lincoln personally and had worked with him in the darkest days of his 1864 reelection campaign to make certain that as many slaves as possible were freed before what loomed as the president's inevitable defeat. "It is the first time," Douglass noted in his address, "that, in this form and manner, we have sought to do honor to an American great man." He called on the assembled dignitaries to take note that "we, the colored people, newly emancipated and rejoicing in our blood-brought freedom, near the close of the first century in the life of this Republic, have now and here unveiled, set apart, and dedicated a monument of enduring granite and bronze, in every line, feature, and figure of which the men of this generation may read, and those of aftercoming generations may read, something of the exalted character of and great works of Abraham Lincoln, the first martyr President of the United States."[89]

Yet Douglass also sounded a critical note. Although he acknowledged Lincoln's "wise and beneficent rule," he also pointed out that "the Union was more to him than our freedom under our future," adding that Lincoln "was preeminently the white man's President, entirely devoted to the welfare of white men." Although the Ball statue had been financed almost entirely by African Americans, it was to white America that Douglass declared: "To you it especially belongs to sound his praises, to preserve and perpetuate his memory, to multiply his statues, to hang his pictures high upon your walls, and commend his example, for to you he was a great and glorious friend and benefactor. Instead of supplanting you at his altar, we would exhort you to build high his monuments; let them be of the most costly material, of the most cunning workmanship; let their forms be symmetrical, beautiful, and perfect; let their bases be upon solid rocks, and their summits lean against the unchanging blue, overhanging sky, and let them endure forever."[90]

It is entirely possible that Douglass's frequently quoted assessment may have reflected more distaste for Ball's composition than a revised opinion of his old friend Lincoln, about whom he later said: "I was impressed with his entire freedom from popular prejudice against the colored race." Art historian Freeman H. M. Murray probably offered a valuable clue to Douglass's complicated message on that 1876 dedication day when he noted thirty years later that the Ball emancipation group insensitively "showed the Negro on his knees when a more manly attitude would have been indicative of freedom."[91]

Yet when President Ulysses S. Grant rose to tug at the cord that unveiled the statue, "a silence of breathless expectation fell on that dense mass when the supreme moment came." Then, as the statue appeared unveiled, the crowd erupted "with shouts and music and cannon." Even Douglass conceded that "no such demonstration" from African Americans "would have been tolerated here twenty years ago." As he noted, "Few facts could better illustrate the vast and wonderful change which has taken place in our condition as a people than the fact of our assembling here for the purpose we have today."[92]

At the climax of his long, powerful address—which Senator George S. Boutwell immediately called "the best . . . since the days of Mr. Webster"—Douglass concluded his fascinating, complex struggle with his own response to the Ball monument by offering "congratulations." Back in 1862, Lincoln had urged emancipation on a skeptical white nation by insisting: "In *giving* freedom to the *slave* we *assure* freedom to the *free*." Now, no doubt in conscious reference to this sentiment, Douglass echoed those words, ultimately pronouncing the statue worthy.

> In doing honor to the memory of our friend and liberator, we have been doing highest honor to ourselves and those who came after us; we have been fastening ourselves to a name and fame imperishable and immortal; we have also been defending ourselves from a blighting scandal. When now it shall be said that the colored man is soulless, that he has no appreciation of benefits or benefactors; when the foul reproach of ingratitude is hurled at us, and it is attempted to scourge us beyond the range of human brotherhood, we may calmly point to the monument we have this day erected to the memory of Abraham Lincoln.[93]

Why was Thomas Ball able to sell his "kneeling slave" group to his African-American patrons around the same time that Henry Kirke Brown and Randolph Rogers failed to attract patrons for their similarly conceived sculptures? One reason was Ball's audacity. His original kneeling figure wore a symbolic liberty cap, emphasizing the myth-worthy significance of Lincoln's act. Second, his work was simply superior: better crafted, better balanced, and better conceived. And, third, Ball marketed his concept brilliantly, using other visual media to introduce his idea to the general public long before the Western Sanitary Commission named him to enlarge it for public display in Washington.

As early as 1867, for example, Ball authorized A. A. Childs of Boston to publish a stereo photograph of his original model (Fig. 33). Later, his final heroic bronze was reproduced in a number of photographs copied for wall display and preservation in family photo albums. Currier and Ives issued a lithograph *The Lincoln Statue. In Lincoln Square, Washington D.C., Unveiled April 14th, 1876,*" with the publishers noting in their caption: "The first contribution of $5. To the Statue Fund, was made the morning after the assassination of President Lincoln, by Charlotte Scott, a colored woman, of Marietta, Ohio, and the cost of the monument $17000. Was paid by subscriptions of the colored people." Ball, ironically, was not mentioned.[94]

Later the statue inspired posters, medallions, and postcards (Fig. 34), resonating in these forms as one of the signature images of the 1909 centennial celebration of Abraham Lincoln's birth. Through these successively smaller reproductions, Ball's work uniquely evolved in civic consciousness from a majestic figure designed to evoke historical memory on a massive scale in a public setting, into an intimate keepsake created specifically for individual collectors to cherish in their private homes. The combination was powerful.

No admirer of Ball's work, art historian Kirk Savage recently labeled the *Freedmen's Memorial to Lincoln* a discordant "hybrid of allegory and realism," representing "a failure to imagine emancipation at its most fundamental level, in the language of the human body and its interaction with other bodies." Although Savage views the work from a late-twentieth-century, white perspective, he may well be right. But even Savage concedes that Ball's was also that "rare public sculpture creating a potent image that enters the culture at large." Indeed, it is probably fair to say that the final statue

Entered according to Act of Congress in the year 1867, by A. A. Childs & Co., in the Clerk's Office of the District Court of the District of Massachusetts.

FIG. 33

A. A. Childs and Co., [*Thomas Ball's Emancipation Group*]. Stereoptican photograph, Boston, 1867.
(Collection of Harold Holzer)

was photographed more often than any other Lincoln sculpture of the nineteenth century (See Fig. 35). For better or for worse, and despite all its deficiencies, insensitivity, and patronizing treatment of the slave, Thomas Ball's frequently reproduced sculpture helped to permanently forge the image of Lincoln as benevolent liberator of a race.[95]

Frederick Douglass came extraordinarily close to the basic truth about the statue—and Lincoln's overall Great Emancipator image—when he told his audience on its dedication day that Ball's work offered a strong rebuttal to the "foul reproach of ingratitude" that had been leveled against former slaves. In a sense, though perhaps innocently, Ball's work emphasized the gratitude of African Americans. Whether Ball's slave is kneeling or rising—this particular debate has never been settled—he nonetheless crouches or slowly ascends due to Lincoln's benevolence.

Did the work, as some critics now suggest, possess the power to inhibit the development of full African-American participation in American society? Did it increase a sense of indebtedness among blacks and philanthropic paternalism among whites? If any of these responses was indeed provoked by the statue, it is entirely understandable that the work has fallen out of favor. But modern analysts tend to forget that Ball's statue was originally inspired and, in part, financed by the African-American community. In its own day, it evoked considerable praise and reproduction in other media. In the end, it was but one of countless variations on a single, enduring theme: Lincoln as emancipator, unvarnished by nuance and untarnished by politically correct revisionism.

In works in many media—whether designed to ameliorate the genuinely revolutionary impact of the emancipation for predominately white audiences, to illustrate Lincoln's emergence as a martyr to liberty for his most enlightened admirers, to support or oppose his campaign for reelection, or to

FIG. 34

C. Chapman, *Abraham Lincoln Presenting the Proclamation of Freedom to a Slave [including Thomas Ball's Emancipation Group]*. Postcard, printed by the Fine Art Publishing Co., 1908. (Collection of Harold Holzer)

memorialize freedom for African Americans—the sixteenth president's most famous proclamation lived an extraordinarily long and varied life in art and iconography. No dose of revisionist analysis can erase the photographs, engravings, lithographs, postcards, and sculpture that celebrated Abraham Lincoln as a liberator.

To impose modern sensibilities on art created to respond to demonstrable political and emotional needs would be as foolhardy as dismissing any of history's inventions that were subsequently improved or refined. To use another, purely technological example, was black-and-white television less revolutionary a medium for American society because it has been supplanted by HDTV and DVDs? In any discussion of historical memory, true memory can never be replaced by the post-facto imposition of modern attitudes. And in the realm of genuine public memory, Abraham Lincoln's Great

FIG. 35

J. F. Jarvis, [*View of Thomas Ball's Emancipation Statue*]. Stereoptican View, Washington, D.C., ca. 1876.
(Collection of Harold Holzer)

Emancipator image, whether or not it makes twenty-first-century Americans uncomfortable, thrived with white and black audiences alike.

Three years after Thomas Ball's statue took its place in Lincoln Park in Washington, a bronze duplicate was unveiled in Boston. At ceremonies at Faneuil Hall, a young black man named Andrew Chamberlain stood to recite a poem written especially for the occasion by John Greenleaf Whittier. Its opening verse neatly summarized the perpetual appeal of Lincoln to both black and white admirers who continued to celebrate the "second Declaration of Independence" in art and memory. Urged the poem:

> Amidst thy sacred effigies
> Of old renown give place,
> O city Freedom-loved! to his
> Whose hand unchained a race.

Boston, like so many other Northern cities, eagerly gave pride of place to the "sacred effigy" of Lincoln. The day Ball's statue was unveiled, the city's mayor maintained that, "No monument of granite or bronze is needed to perpetuate his memory, and hold his place in the affections of his countrymen." He went on to predict of Abraham Lincoln: "His fame will suffer nothing from the corrosion of time, but increase with the advancing years."[96] That prognostication proved true for generations. Even now, as historians black and white debate anew the meanings and limitations of the Emancipation Proclamation, no observer can doubt that art and artists in all media played a pivotal role in successfully securing and, for the most part preserving, Lincoln's reputation "from the corrosion of time."

APPENDIX

The First and Second Confiscation Acts

THE FIRST CONFISCATION ACT, AUGUST 6, 1861
U.S. Statutes at Large, XII, 319

Be it enacted by the Senate and House of Representatives of the United States of America in Congress assembled, That if, during the present or any future insurrection against the Government of the United States, after the President of the United States shall have declared by proclamation, that the laws of the United States are opposed, and the execution thereof obstructed, by combinations too powerful to be suppressed by the ordinary course of judicial proceedings, or by the power vested in marshals by law, any person or persons, his, her or their agent, attorney or employee, shall purchase or acquire, sell or give, any property of whatsoever kind or description, with intent to use or employ the same, or suffer the same to be used or employed, in aiding, abetting or promoting such insurrection or resistance to the laws, or any person or persons engaged therein; or if any person or persons, being the owner or owners of any such property, shall knowingly use or employ, or consent to the use or employment of the same as aforesaid, all such property is hereby declared to be lawful subject of prize and capture wherever found; and it shall be the duty of the President of the United States to cause the same to be seized, confiscated and condemned.

SEC. 2. *And be it further enacted,* That such prizes and capture shall be condemned in the District or Circuit Court of the United States having jurisdiction of the amount, or in admiralty in any district in which the same may be seized, or into which they may be taken and proceedings first instituted.

SEC. 3. *And be it further enacted,* That the Attorney General, or any District Attorney of the United States in which said property may be at the time be, may institute the proceedings of condemnation, and in such case they shall be wholly for the benefit of the United States; or any person may file an information with such attorney, in which case the proceedings shall be for the use of such informer and the United States in equal parts.

SEC. 4. *And be it further enacted,* That whenever any person claiming to be entitled to the service or labor of any other person, under the laws of any State, shall employ such person in aiding or promoting any insurrection, or in resisting the laws of the United States, or shall permit him to be so employed, he shall forfeit all right to such service or labor, and the person whose labor or service is thus claimed shall be thenceforth discharged therefrom, any law to the contrary notwithstanding.

THE SECOND CONFISCATION ACT, JULY 17, 1862
U.S. Statutes at Large, XII, 589–592

An Act to suppress Insurrection, to punish Treason and Rebellion, to seize and confiscate the Property of Rebels, and for other Purposes.

Be it enacted by the Senate and House of Representatives of the United States of America in Congress assembled, That every person who shall hereafter commit the crime of treason against the United States, and shall be adjudged guilty thereof, shall suffer death, and all his slaves, if any, shall be declared and made free; or, at the discretion of the court, he shall be imprisoned for not less than five years and fined not less than ten thousand dollars, and all his slaves, if any, shall be declared and made free; said fine shall be levied and collected on any or all of the property, real and personal, excluding slaves, of which the said person so convicted was the owner at the time of committing the said crime, any sale or conveyance to the contrary notwithstanding.

2. *And be it further enacted,* That if any person shall hereafter incite, set on foot, assist, or engage in any rebellion or insurrection against the authority of the United States, or the laws thereof, or shall give aid or comfort thereto, or shall engage in, or give aid and comfort to, any such existing rebellion or insurrection, and be convicted thereof, such person shall be punished by imprisonment for a period not exceeding ten years, or by a fine not exceeding ten thousand dollars, and by the liberation of all his slaves, if any he have; or by both of said punishments, at the discretion of the court.

3. *And be it further enacted,* That every person guilty of either of the offences described in this act shall be forever incapable and disqualified to hold any office under the United States.

4. *And be it further enacted,* That this act shall not be construed in any way to affect or alter the prosecution, conviction, or punishment of any person or persons guilty of treason against the United States before the passage of this act, unless such person is convicted under this act.

5. *And be it further enacted,* That, to insure the speedy termination of the present rebellion, it shall be the duty of the President of the United States to cause the seizure of all the estate and property, money, stocks, credits, and effects of the persons hereinafter named in this section, and to apply and use the same and the proceeds thereof for the support of the army of the United States, that is to say:

First. Of any person hereafter acting as an officer of the army or navy of the rebels in arms against the government of the Untied States.

Secondly. Of any person hereafter acting as President, Vice-President, member of Congress, judge of any court, cabinet officer, foreign minister, commissioner or consul of the so-called confederate states of America.

Thirdly. Of any person acting as governor of a state, member of a convention or legislature, or judge of any court of any of the so-called confederate states of America.

Fourthly. Of any person who, having held an office of honor, trust, or profit in the United States, shall hereafter hold an office in the so-called confederate states of America.

Fifthly. Of any person hereafter holding any office or agency under the government of the so-called confederate states of America, or under any of the several states of the said confederacy, or the laws thereof, whether such office or agency be national, state, or municipal in its name or character: *Provided,* That the persons, thirdly, fourthly, and fifthly above described shall have accepted their appointment or election since the date of the pretended ordinance of secession of the state, or shall have taken an oath of allegiance to, or to support the constitution of the so-called confederate states.

Sixthly. Of any person who, owning property in any loyal State or Territory of the United States, or in the District of Columbia, shall hereafter assist and give aid and comfort to such rebellion; and all sales, transfers, or conveyances of any such property shall be null and void; and it shall be a sufficient bar to any suit brought by such person for the possession or the use of such property, or any of it, to allege and prove that he is one of the persons described in this section.

6. *And be it further enacted,* That if any person within any State or Territory of the United States, other than those named as aforesaid, after the passage of this act, being engaged in armed rebellion against the government of the United States, or aiding or abetting such rebellion, shall not, within sixty days after public warning and proclamation duly given and made by the President of the United States, cease to aid, countenance, and abet

such rebellion, and return to his allegiance to the United States, all the estate and property, moneys, stocks, and credits of such person shall be liable to seizure as aforesaid, and it shall be the duty of the President to seize and use them as aforesaid or the proceeds thereof. And all sales, transfers, or conveyances, of any such property after the expiration of the said sixty days from the date of such warning and proclamation shall be null and void; and it shall be a sufficient bar to any suit brought by such person for the possession or the use of such property, or any of it, to allege and prove that he is one of the persons described in this section.

7. *And be it further enacted,* That to secure the condemnation and sale of any of such property, after the same shall have been seized, so that it may be made available for the purpose aforesaid, proceedings in rem shall be instituted in the name of the United States in any district court thereof, or in any territorial court, or in the United States district court for the District of Columbia, within which the property above described, or any part thereof, may be found, or into which the same, if movable, may first be brought, which proceedings shall conform as nearly as may be to proceedings in admiralty or revenue cases, and if said property, whether real or personal, shall be found to have belonged to a person engaged in rebellion, or who has given aid or comfort thereto, the same shall be condemned as enemies' property and become the property of the United States, and may be disposed of as the court shall decree and the proceeds thereof paid into the treasury of the United States for the purpose aforesaid.

8. *And be it further enacted,* That the several courts aforesaid shall have power to make such orders, establish such forms of decree and sale, and direct such deeds and conveyances to be executed and delivered by the marshals thereof where real estate shall be the subject of sale, as shall fitly and efficiently effect the purposes of this act, and vest in the purchasers of such property good and valid titles thereto. And the said courts shall have power to allow such fees and charges of their officers as shall be reasonable and proper in the premises.

9. *And be it further enacted,* That all slaves of persons who shall hereafter be engaged in rebellion against the government of the United States, or who shall in any way give aid or comfort thereto, escaping from such persons and taking refuge within the lines of the army; and all slaves captured from such persons or deserted by them and coming under the control of the government of the United States; and all slaves of such person found on [*or*] being within any place occupied by rebel forces and afterwards occupied by the forces of the United States, shall be deemed captives of war, and shall be forever free of their servitude, and not again held as slaves.

10. *And be it further enacted,* That no slave escaping into any State, Territory, or the District of Columbia, from any other State, shall be delivered up, or in any way impeded or hindered of his liberty, except for crime, or some offence against the laws, unless the person claiming said fugitive shall first make oath that the person to whom the labor or service of such fugitive is alleged to be due is his lawful owner, and has not borne arms against the United States in the present rebellion, nor in any way given aid and comfort thereto; and no person engaged in the military or naval service of the United States shall, under any pretence whatever, assume to decide on the validity of the claim of any person to the service or labor of any other person, or surrender up any such person to the claimant, on pain of being dismissed from the service.

11. *And be it further enacted,* That the President of the United States is authorized to employ as many persons of African descent as he may deem necessary and proper for the suppression of this rebellion, and for this purpose he may organize and use them in such manner as he may judge best for the public welfare.

12. *And be it further enacted,* That the President of the United States is hereby authorized to make provision for the transportation, colonization, and settlement, in some tropical country beyond the limits of the United States, of such persons of the African race, made free by the provisions of this act, as may be willing to emigrate, having first obtained the consent of the government of said country to their protection and settlement within the same, with all the rights and privileges of freemen.

13. *And be it further enacted,* That the President is hereby authorized, at any time hereafter, by proclamation,

to extend to persons who may have participated in the existing rebellion in any State or part thereof, pardon and amnesty, with such exceptions and at such time and on such conditions as he may deem expedient for the public welfare.

14. *And be it further enacted,* That the courts of the United States shall have full power to institute proceedings, make orders and decrees, issue process, and do all other things necessary to carry this act into effect.

NOTES

INTRODUCTION

1. Frederick Douglass, "Emancipation Proclaimed," *Douglass Monthly,* October 1862, reprinted in *Frederick Douglass: Selected Speeches and Writings,* ed. Philip S. Foner and Yuval Taylor (Chicago: Lawrence Hill Books, 1995), 517–518.

2. *Richmond Enquirer,* quoted in *Abraham Lincoln: A Press Portrait,* ed. Herbert Mitgang (Chicago: Quadrangle Books, 1971), 314–315.

3. Francis B. Carpenter, *Six Months at the White House: The Story of a Picture* (New York: Hurd & Houghton, 1866), 12, 25; see John Hope Franklin, *The Emancipation Proclamation* (Garden City, NY: Doubleday, 1962). An earlier book by historian Charles Eberstadt focused only on the recorded reprints of the proclamation itself; see Eberstadt, *Lincoln's Emancipation Proclamation* (New York: privately printed, 1950).

4. Lerone Bennett Jr., *Forced into Glory: Abraham Lincoln's White Dream* (Chicago: Johnson Publishing, 2000), 9, 15.

5. Allen C. Guelzo, *Lincoln's Emancipation Proclamation: The End of Slavery in America* (New York: Simon & Schuster, 2004), 248–249; Michael Lind, *What Lincoln Believed: The Values and Convictions of America's Greatest President* (New York: Doubleday, 2005), 15, 38, 191–222.

IMAGINED PROMISES, BITTER REALITIES (EDNA GREENE MEDFORD)

1. B. F. Butler to His Excellency Thomas H. Hicks, April 23, 1861, *The War of the Rebellion: A Compilation of the Official Records of the Union and Confederate Armies,* 128 vols. (Washington: Government Printing Office, 1880–1901), ser. 2, 1:750. Hereafter this cite is referred to as *O. R.*

2. Benj. F. Butler to Lieut. Gen. Winfield Scott, May 24, 1861, *O. R.,* ser. 2, 1:752. The names of the three men are mentioned in *The Negro in Virginia,* compiled by workers of the Writers' Program of the Work Projects Administration in the State of Virginia (1940; reprint, Winston-Salem, NC: John F. Blair, Publisher, 1994), 210.

3. James McPherson, one of the chief proponents of the "Great Emancipator" view, argues that "careful leadership and timing" enabled Lincoln to win the war and secure the freedom of the slaves. See *Drawn with the Sword: Reflections on the American Civil War* (New York: Oxford University Press, 1996). In a recent variation on this view, see Allen Guelzo, *Lincoln's Emancipation Proclamation: The End of Slavery in America* (New York: Simon and Schuster, 2004). Guelzo suggests that the president moved consistently towards emancipation from the very beginning of his tenure. Prudence required him to seek a legal remedy that would stand up in federal court. The self-emancipation thesis is proposed by Barbara Jeanne Fields in "Who Freed the Slaves?" in Geoffrey C. Ward, with Ric Burns and Ken Burns, eds., *The Civil War: An Illustrated History* (New York: Alfred A. Knopf, 1990), 178–181; and Vincent Harding, *There is a River: The Black Struggle for Freedom in America* (New York: Vintage Books, 1981), 231–237. Ira Berlin's essay, "Who Freed the Slaves? Emancipation and Its Meaning," in *Union and Emancipation: Essays on Politics and Race in the Civil War Era,* ed. David W. Blight and Brooks D. Simpson (Kent, OH: Kent State University Press, 1997), 105–121, argues that no single person or group can take credit for emancipation; both Lincoln and the enslaved played vital roles, as did others. In a recent book that directly challenges Lincoln's motivations for issuing the proclamation, Lerone Bennett sees the president as a white supremacist whose proclamation was a "ploy . . . to keep as many slaves as possible in slavery until Lincoln could mobilize support for his conservative plan to free Blacks gradually and to ship them out of the country." See *Forced into Glory: Abraham Lincoln's White Dream* (Chicago: Johnson Publishing Company, 2000), 10.

4. It is a point Lincoln would make when in August 1862 he spoke to a delegation of black men whom he had invited to the White House with the object of encouraging colonization. Lincoln suggested that "on this broad continent, not a single man

of your race is made the equal of a single man of ours." See "Address on Colonization to a Delegation of Negroes," in *Collected Works of Abraham Lincoln,* 8 vols., ed. Roy P. Basler (New Brunswick, NJ: Rutgers University Press, 1953), 5:370–375. Hereafter this cite is referred to as *Collected Works.*

5. Although the Northwest Ordinance abolished slavery in the Northwest Territory (Ohio, Indiana, Illinois, Michigan, and Wisconsin) in 1787, loopholes in the law permitted the continuing enslavement of blacks in some areas, including Lincoln's own Illinois.

6. Frederick Douglass, "The Meaning of July Fourth for the Negro," speech at Rochester, New York, July 5, 1852, in *The Life and Writings of Frederick Douglass,* 4 vols., ed. Philip Foner (New York: International Publishers, 1950–55), 2:192.

7. Taney had argued that at the time of the Declaration of Independence, enslaved Africans were designated property and hence could not have been included in the definition of "the people." The prevailing view at that time was that African Americans were "so far inferior, that they had no rights which the white man was bound to respect." See Derrick A. Bell Jr., *Race, Racism and American Law* (Boston: Little, Brown and Co., 1973), 6.

8. Benjamin Quarles, *Lincoln and the Negro* (New York: Da Capo, 1991), 21–25.

9. See Benjamin Quarles, *Black Abolitionists* (New York: Oxford University Press, 1969), 47–50.

10. *Herndon's Life of Lincoln: The History and Personal Recollections of Abraham Lincoln as Originally Written by William H. Herndon and Jesse W. Weik* (New York: The World Publishing Co., 1942), 64.

11. "Protest in Illinois Legislature on Slavery" (March 3, 1837), *Collected Works,* 1:74–75. Lincoln and Stone also condemned the abolitionists as extremists whose "doctrines tend rather to increase than to abate slavery."

12. See David L. Lewis, *District of Columbia: A Bicentennial History* (New York: W. W. Norton and Co., 1976), 50–57. See also Stanley C. Harrold Jr., "The *Pearl* Affair: The Washington Riot of 1848," *Records of the Columbia Historical Society* (1980), 50:140–160; and Daniel Drayton, *Personal Memoirs of Daniel Drayton* (Boston: Bela Marsh, 1955).

13. "Speech in Reply to Douglas at Springfield, Illinois, July 17, 1858," in *Abraham Lincoln: His Speeches and Writings,* ed. Roy P. Basler (New York: Da Capo, 1990), 423.

14. "Address at Cooper Institute, New York, February 27, 1860," in Basler, *Abraham Lincoln: His Speeches and Writings,* 222. For an analysis of the Cooper Union speech, see Harold Holzer, *Lincoln at Cooper Union: The Speech That Made Abraham Lincoln President* (New York: Simon and Schuster, 2004).

15. For a discussion of Lincoln's rise to national prominence in the Republican Party, see David Herbert Donald, *Lincoln* (New York: Simon and Schuster, 1995), 235–256.

16. "First Inaugural Address," March 4, 1861, *Collected Works,* 4:250. In this address, Lincoln reminded the American people of the Republican platform under which he ran for office: "*Resolved:* That the maintenance inviolate of the rights of the States, and especially the right of each State to order and control its own domestic institutions according to its own judgment exclusively, is essential to that balance of power on which the perfection and endurance of our political fabric depend." For a discussion of the operation of the Fugitive Slave Act, see Stanley W. Campbell, *The Slave Catchers: The Enforcement of the Fugitive Slave Law, 1850–1860* (Chapel Hill: University of North Carolina Press, 1968).

17. Lieutenant A. J. Slemmer to Lt. Col. L. Thomas, Assistant Adjutant-General, March 18, 1861, *O. R.,* ser. 2, 1:750.

18. Report of Edward Conroy, Commanding U.S. Bark *Restless,* March 30, 1862, United States, Navy Department, *Official Records of the Union and Confederate Navies in the War of the Rebellion* (Washington, DC: Government Printing Office, 1894), ser. 1, 12:682. (Hereafter this cite is referred to as *Navy O. R.*) The opportunity to be had for escape when Union boats came near shore is revealed in the operations of the U.S. Steam Sloop *Seminole.* When the sloop anchored off the coast of Beaufort, South Carolina, its crew detected a lone fugitive, but shortly thereafter approximately 300 came out to greet the men. This occurred after the crowd had been visited and dispersed by a group of men earlier that day who had shot two contrabands. See John P. Gillis, Commanding U.S.S. *Seminole,* November 19, 1861, *Navy O. R.,* ser. 1, 12:353.

19. Enclosure, Statement of John T. Washington, May 7, 1861, *O. R.* ser. 1, 2:820.

20. Ibid.

21. John Pool to the Honorable Zebulon B. Vance, September 18, 1862, *O. R,* ser. 1, 18:745. See also Inclosure [*sic*], R. W. Mallard et al. to Brigadier-General Mercer, August 5, 1862, *O. R.,* ser. 4, 2:36.

22. Inclosure [*sic*], R. W. Mallard et al to Brigadier-General Mercer, August 5, 1862, *O. R.,* ser. 4, 2:38.

23. Ibid.

24. Ibid.

25. Colonel Harvey Brown to Lieutenant Colonel E. D. Townsend, June 22, 1861, *O. R.*, ser. 2, 1:755.

26. Geo. B. McClellan to the Union Men of Western Virginia, May 26, 1861, *O. R.*, ser. 2, 1:753.

27. Lieutenant Colonel Schuyler Hamilton to Brigadier General Irwin McDowell, Washington, July 16, 1861, *O. R.*, ser. 2, 1:760.

28. Ibid.; Assistant Adjutant-General E. D. Townsend to General Mansfield, and General Orders, No. 33, July 17, 1861, *O. R.*, ser. 2, 1:760.

29. See Edna Greene Medford, "Abraham Lincoln and Black Wartime Washington," in *Papers from the Thirteenth and Fourteenth Annual Lincoln Colloquia* (Springfield, Ill.: Lincoln Home National Historic Site, 2000), 120–125.

30. Reported in *New York Tribune*, May 20, 1862, 7.

31. Donald Yacovone, ed., *A Voice of Thunder: The Civil War Letters of George E. Stephens* (Urbana: University of Illinois Press, 1996), 146. Yacovone indicates that the Posey family was implicated in numerous instances of treachery during the war. In this instance, the culprit may have been Timothy Posey rather than Richard B. Posey, as Stephens suggests.

32. Ibid., 163. Stephens reported that Cox was "an ex-state representative, a returned rebel, the Captain of a Cavalry company organized for the rebel army, but disbanded by the Federal troops, and a Contraband trader."

33. Ibid. See also Ira Berlin, Barbara J. Fields, Steven F. Miller, Joseph P. Reidy, and Leslie S. Rowland, eds., *Free at Last: A Documentary History of Slavery, Freedom, and the Civil War* (New York: New Press, 1992), 11–12. There is some disagreement over the timing of the Scroggins incident. George Stephens's report to the *Weekly Anglo-African* is dated January 10, 1862, but he does not indicate when the incident actually occurred. Affidavits taken by Freedmen's Bureau agents after the war concerning the treatment of prisoners of war and Union citizens indicate that Cox confessed to one Henry Seward in December 1861 that he had murdered Scroggins in August of that year. In *Blood on the Moon: The Assassination of Abraham Lincoln* (Lexington: University of Kentucky Press, 2001), Edward Steers Jr. indicates that Cox was visited by Union troops twice, once in June 1861 and again in January 1862, when the Scroggins murder occurred.

34. Yacovone, *A Voice of Thunder*, 164.

35. Steers, *Blood on the Moon*, 150–160.

36. Quoted in James M. McPherson, *The Struggle for Equality: Abolitionists and the Negro in the Civil War and Reconstruction* (Princeton: Princeton University Press, 1964), 58.

37. Ibid., 61–63.

38. "Make Way for Liberty," *Weekly Anglo-African*, May 11, 1861, 1.

39. "The Fall of Sumter," *Douglass' Monthly*, May 1861.

40. "The Slaveholders' Rebellion (A Speech delivered on the 4th day of July, at Himrods Corners, Yates Co., N.Y.)," *Douglass' Monthly*, August 1862, 692.

41. McPherson, *The Struggle for Equality*, esp. chap. 3.

42. Ibid. See also George Winston Smith and Charles Judah, *Life in the North during the Civil War: A Source History* (Albuquerque: University of New Mexico Press, 1966).

43. For a discussion of attitudes on the goals of the war in the first few months of the conflict, and Lincoln's effort to build consensus, see Donald, *Lincoln*; and James M. McPherson, *Battle Cry of Freedom: The Civil War Era* (New York: Oxford University Press, 1988).

44. See James and Lois Horton, *In Hope of Liberty: Culture, Community, and Protest Among Northern Free Blacks, 1700–1860* (New York: Oxford University Press, 1997); and Leonard Curry, *The Free Black in Urban America, 1800–1850: The Shadow of the Dream* (Chicago: University of Chicago Press, 1981). See also Leon Litwack, *North of Slavery: The Negro in the Free States, 1790–1860* (Chicago: University of Chicago Press, 1961).

45. For a discussion of Frederick Douglass's encounters with segregation and discrimination in the North, see Douglass, *Autobiographies: The Life and Times of Fredrick Douglass* (New York: Library of America, 1994), 887–899.

46. In *The Confederate Negro: Virginia's Craftsmen and Military Laborers, 1861–1865* (Durham: Duke University Press, 1969), James Brewer discusses the role of African Americans as laborers within the Confederacy. See also Ervin Jordan, *Black Confederates and Afro-Yankees in Civil War Virginia* (Charlottesville: University Press of Virginia, 1995).

47. See Jordan, *Black Confederates and Afro-Yankees in Civil War Virginia*, for the range of black participation.

48. See McPherson, *Battle Cry of Freedom*, 356. For a discussion of Lincoln's concern over the act's effect on relations between the Union and the border states, see John Hope Franklin, *The Emancipation Proclamation* (Garden City, NY: Doubleday and Company, 1963), 18; and Benjamin Quarles, *Lincoln and the Negro* (1962; reprint, New York: Da Capo, 1990), 69–70.

49. "To the Senate and House of Representatives," July 17, 1862, *Collected Works*, 5:328–331.

50. Ibid., 5:331.

51. Ira Berlin et al., *Freedom: A Documentary History of Emancipation, 1861–1867*, ser. 1, vol.1, *The Destruction of Slavery* (New York: Cambridge University Press, 1985), 415.

52. "To John C. Frémont, " September 2, 1861, *Collected Works*, 4:506.

53. "Proclamation Revoking General Hunter's Order of Military Emancipation of May 9, 1862," May 19, 1862, *Collected Works*, 5:222.

54. Donald, *Lincoln*, 316–317.

55. "To Orville H. Browning," September 22, 1861, *Collected Works*, 4:531.

56. Ibid., 4:532.

57. "The Policy of the Administration," *Douglass' Monthly*, August 1862, 692–693.

58. "Gen. Hunter Overruled," *New York Tribune*, May 20, 1862.

59. "Proclamation Revoking General Hunter's Order . . . ," *Collected Works*, 5:223.

60. See Bennett, *Forced into Glory: Abraham Lincoln's White Dream*, 20–21.

61. "Annual Message to Congress," December 1, 1862, *Collected Works*, 5:531.

62. " Speech at Peoria . . . , " October 16, 1854, Basler, *Abraham Lincoln: His Speeches and Writings*, 291–292.

63. Ibid.

64. "Drafts of a Bill for Compensated Emancipation in Delaware," November 26, 1861, *Collected Works*, 5:29.

65. Ibid., 5:30.

66. "Message to Congress," March 6, 1862, *Collected Works*, 5:144–145.

67. For a discussion of emancipation in the District of Columbia, see Constance M. Green, *The Secret City: A History of Race Relations in the Nation's Capital* (Princeton: Princeton University Press, 1967), 57–59; and Margaret Leech, *Reveille in Washington: 1860–1865* (Westport, CT: Greenwood, 1941), 241–242.

68. "Message to Congress," April 16, 1862, *Collected Works*, 5:192.

69. "Appeal to Border State Representatives to Favor Compensated Emancipation," July 12, 1862, *Collected Works*, 5:318.

70. Ibid.

71. "Remarks to a Delegation of Progressive Friends," June 20, 1862, *Collected Works*, 5:278.

72. "What the People Expect of Mr. Lincoln," *Douglass' Monthly*, August 1862, 701.

73. "The Slaveholders Rebellion," in *Douglass' Monthly*, August 1862, 691.

74. Horace Greeley, "The Prayer of Twenty Millions," *New York Tribune*, August 20, 1862, 4.

75. "To Horace Greeley," August 22, 1862, *Collected Works*, 5:388–89.

76. "Preliminary Emancipation Proclamation," September 22, 1862, *Collected Works*, 5:433.

77. Ibid., 5:433–436.

78. McPherson, *Battle Cry of Freedom*, 560.

79. Ibid., 561–562. McPherson has indicated, however, that Democratic gains were not so overwhelming as to suggest that northerners were in solid opposition to the Emancipation Proclamation.

80. Donald, *Lincoln*, 379.

81. For an overview of the response to the Preliminary Emancipation Proclamation, see Guelzo, *Lincoln's Emancipation Proclamation*, 177–181; and Franklin, *The Emancipation Proclamation*, 58–93. See also McPherson, *The Struggle for Equality*, 117–122.

82. "Emancipation Proclaimed," in *Frederick Douglass: Selected Speeches and Writings*, ed. Philip S. Foner, abridged by Yuval Taylor (Chicago: Lawrence Hill Books, 1975), 517.

83. "A Call to Action," Rev. H. M. Turner, *Christian Recorder*, October 4, 1862.

84. Foner, *The Life and Writings of Frederick Douglass*, 3:440.

85. "January 1st, 1863," *Douglass' Monthly*, January 1, 1863, 770.

86. "Annual Message to Congress," December 1, 1862, *Collected Works*, 5:531.

87. Ibid.

88. Ibid.

89. "Address on Colonization to a Deputation of Negroes," August 14, 1862, *Collected Works*, 5:371–72.

90. Ibid., 372.

91. Ibid., 371.

92. Quoted in James M. McPherson, *The Negro's Civil War: How American Blacks Felt and Acted During the War for the Union* (New York: Ballantine Books, 1991), 95.

93. "Annual Message to Congress," December 1, 1862, *Collected Works*, 5:537.

94. Ibid., 536.

95. "Final Emancipation Proclamation," January 1, 1863, Basler, *Abraham Lincoln: His Speeches and Writings*, 691.

96. Plans for voluntary relocation had not gone well. The ill-conceived Chiriqui Project in Central America and I'lle a Vache in Haiti doubtless helped to convince Lincoln that colonization would not work.

97. For a discussion of the effect of the Emancipation Proclamation on foreign affairs, see Howard Jones, *Abraham Lincoln and a New Birth of Freedom: The Union and Slavery in the Diplomacy of the Civil War* (Lincoln: University of Nebraska Press, 1999). Allen Guelzo argues rather convincingly that Lincoln may have been more concerned that the proclamation would have a negative influence on the British and that England, fearful of a slave insurrection, would intervene because of it. See Guelzo, *Lincoln's Emancipation Proclamation*, 254.

98. "The Great Event," *Weekly Anglo-African*, January 3, 1863, 2.

99. Ibid.

100. In his February 1863 address at Cooper Institute, New York City, Frederick Douglass had contended: "When Virginia is a free state, Maryland cannot be a slave state . . . Slavery must stand or fall together. Strike it at either extreme—either on the head or at the heel, and it dies." See Foner, *The Life and Writings of Frederick Douglass*, 3:333

101. H. G. Wright, Major-General Commanding Headquarters Department of the Ohio to Major-General Halleck, General-in-Chief, Washington, D.C., December 30, 1862, *O. R*, ser. 1, 20:282.

102. Guelzo, *Lincoln's Emancipation Proclamation*, 212–213.

103. See Donald, *Lincoln*, 417–418.

104. For detailed reporting of these celebrations, see the *Weekly Anglo-African*.

105. "Rejoicings Over the Emancipation Proclamation," *Weekly Anglo-African*, January 17, 1863, 1.

106. See Edna Greene Medford, "Beckoning Them to the Dreamed of Promise of Freedom: African Americans and Lincoln's Proclamation of Emancipation," in *Abraham Lincoln, Gettysburg, and the Civil War*, ed. John Y. Simon, Harold Holzer, and William D. Pederson (Mason City, IA: Savas Publishing Co., 1999), 50.

107. Quoted in McPherson, *The Negro's Civil War*, 50–51.

108. "The Great Emancipation Demonstration," *Weekly Anglo-African*, January 10, 1863, 2.

109. *Douglass' Monthly*, February 1863.

110. "The Great Emancipation Demonstration," *Weekly Anglo-African*, January 10, 1863, 2.

111. "Final Report of the American Freedmen's Inquiry Commission to the Secretary of War," May 15, 1864, *O. R.*, ser. 3, 4:436.

112. Thomas Wentworth Higginson, *Army Life in a Black Regiment* (New York: Collier Books, 1969), 59–61.

113. "To Charles D. Robinson," August 17, 1864, *Collected Works*, 7:500.

114. "The Great Event," *Anglo-African*, January 3, 1863, 2.

115. Charles Wilder, Testimony Before the American Freedman's Inquiry Commission, 9 May 1863. In Berlin et al., *Freedom: A Documentary History of Emancipation, 1861–1867*, ser. 1, 1:89.

116. "Report of James Madison Frailey, Commander, U.S.S. *Quaker City*, February 2, 1864, *Navy O. R.*, ser. 1, 9:436.

117. Enclosure from John J. Almy, Commander, U.S.S. *South Carolina*, May 25, 1863, *Navy O. R.*, ser. 1, 14:217. Doubtless, some naval commanders were willing to rescue fugitives because they could provide information about Confederate activity.

118. Douglass, *Autobiographies*, 796.

119. Foner, *The Life and Writings of Fredrick Douglass*, 3:405.

120. "Address of Congress to the People of the Confederate States," *O. R.*, ser. 4, 3:132–133.

121. *A Compilation of the Messages and Papers of the Confederacy, Including the Diplomatic Correspondence, 1861–1865,* 2 vols. (Nashville: United States Publishing Co., 1906), 1: 290.

122. Ibid., 1:291–292.

123. "An Ordinance to provide for the removal of negroes and other property from portions of the state which may be invaded by the enemy," October 20, 1862, *O. R.*, ser. 4, 2:133–137.

124. Governor John J. Pettus to Gentlemen of the Senate and House of Representatives, November 3, 1863, *O. R.*, ser. 4, 2:922.

125. William T. Sherman, Major-General to General Lorenzo Thomas, April 12, 1864, *O. R.*, ser. 3, 4:225.

126. Charles Clark to Fellow Citizens, November 16, 1863, *O. R.*, ser. 4, 2:961.

127. P. R. Cleburne, Major-General et al. to Commanding General, January 2, 1864, *O. R.*, ser. 1, 52:587, 588.

128. Ibid., 52:590.

129. Ibid., 52:591.

130. Judah P. Benjamin to Fred A. Porcher, December 21, 1864, *O. R.*, ser. 4, 3:959.

131. John J. Pettus to Gentlemen of the Senate, November 3, 1863, *O. R.*, ser. 4, 2:922.

132. Major-General J. Bankhead Magruder to Brigadier-General W. R. Boggs, October 26, 1863, *O. R.*, ser. 1, 26:355.

133. For a discussion of the experiences of free blacks in the South, see Ira Berlin, *Slaves without Masters: The Free Negro in the Antebellum South* (New York: New Press, 1971), and Leonard Curry, *The Free Black in Urban America, 1800–1850: The Shadow of the Dream* (Chicago: University of Chicago Press, 1981).

134. William Smith to Gentlemen of the Senate, December 7, 1864, *O. R.*, ser. 4, 3:914.

135. N. A. M. Dudley, Acting Brigadier-General to Lieutenant Colonel Richard B. Irwin, August 12, 1863, *O. R.*, ser. 1, 26:668.

136. Major-General Lovell H. Rousseau to Brigadier-General W. D. Whipple, January 30, 1864, *O. R.*, ser. 1, 32:267.

137. For discussion of the destruction of slavery in the border states as a consequence of black enlistment, see Berlin et al., *Free at Last*, 333–424.

138. A. A. Rice, Provost-Marshal to Colonel J. P. Sanderson, March 31, 1864, 799; A. Kempinsky, Provost-Marshal to Colonel Marsh, February 7, 1864, *O. R.*, ser. 1, 34:268.

139. J. Holt, Judge Advocate-General to Secretary of War, November 22, 1864, *O. R.*, ser. 2, 7:1151.

140. Ibid. The second petition was signed by Major General Steele. Holt indicated that although Secretary of War Stanton and the president had upheld the sentence, Brown remained in Little Rock rather than being remanded to the Alton military prison.

141. Berlin et al., *Freedom*, 1:504–507.

142. Report of Charles S. Boggs, Captain, U.S.S. *Sacramento,* March 24, 1863, Navy *O. R.*, ser. 1, 8:625.

143. H. Walke, Captain U.S.S. Gunboat *Lafayette* to Commodore James S. Palmer, June 19, 1863, 239, *Navy O. R.*, ser. 1, 20:239.

144. Ira Berlin et al., *Freedom: A Documentary History of Emancipation, 1861–1867,* ser. 1, vol. 2, *The Wartime Genesis of Free Labor: The Upper South* (New York: Cambridge University Press, 1990); and ser. 1, vol. 3, *The Wartime Genesis of Slavery: The Lower South* (New York: Cambridge University Press, 1993).

145. R. Saxton, Brigadier-General of Volunteers to the Hon. Edwin M. Stanton, December 30, 1864, *O. R.*, ser. 3, 4:1029.

146. Quoted in James Mellon, ed., *Bullwhip Days: The Slaves Remember—An Oral History* (New York: Avon Books, 1988), 344.

147. An example is the case of Brig. Gen. William Dwight Jr., commander First Brigade in West Louisiana. Dwight's charge that "Negro women were ravished in the presence of white women and children" during the army's march to New Iberia, Louisiana, suggests that the crime was perpetrated more against the witnesses than the women who were defiled. See Reports of Brigadier-General William Dwight, Jr., April 27, 1863, *O. R.*, ser. 1, 15:374.

148. Quoted in McPherson, *The Negro's Civil War,* 302.

149. "Minutes of an interview between the colored ministers and church officers at Savannah with the Secretary of War and Major-General Sherman," January 12, 1865, *O. R.*, ser.1, 47:39.

150. Saxton to Stanton, December 30, 1864, *OR*, ser. 3, 4:1022.

151. F. B. Carpenter, *Six Months at the White House With Abraham Lincoln* (New York: Hurd and Houghton, 1867), 22.

152. Letter to James C. Conkling, August 26, 1863, Basler, *Abraham Lincoln: His Speeches and Writings*, 723.

153. "Formation of Colored Regiments," *Weekly Anglo-African*, September 28, 1861, 1.

154. "What are we Colored People Doing? Or Likely to Do?" *Anglo-African*, October 19, 1861.

155. "Michigan State Convention," *Anglo-African*, March 7, 1863, 1.

156. Ibid.

157. "Address for the Promotion of Colored Enlistments," delivered at a mass meeting in Philadelphia, July 6, 1863, Foner, *Frederick Douglass: Selected Speeches and Writings*, 536.

158. William J. Mays, Company B, Thirteenth Tennessee Cavalry, Mount City, April 18, 1864, *O. R.*, ser. 1, 32:525.

159. Quoted in *A Documentary History of the Negro People in the United States: From Colonial Times Through the Civil War*, ed. Herbert Aptheker (New York: Citadel Press, 1965), 483.

160. Ibid.

161. Frederick Douglass, *Autobiographies*, 786–787.

162. For a discussion of the unique problems black soldiers faced, see Benjamin Quarles, *The Negro in the Civil War* (1953; reprint, New York: Da Capo, 1989), 200–213. See also Ira Berlin et al., *Freedom: A Documentary History—The Black Military Experience* (New York: Cambridge University Press, 1982).

163. Quarles, *The Negro in the Civil War*, 208.

164. Aptheker, *A Documentary History of the Negro People*, 486–87. The Militia Act provided for payment for black troops, whatever the rank, in the amount of ten dollars per month, with three dollars deducted for clothing. White privates received thirteen dollars per month with an additional $3.50 for a clothing allowance.

165. "Another Law Against Common Sense," *Douglass' Monthly*, March 1863, 802.

166. McPherson, *The Negro's Civil War*, 71.

167. Ibid., 75–76.

168. Ibid., 256–265.

169. Report of Acting Master J. S. Eldridge, U.S.S. *Delaware*, May 7, 1864, *Navy O. R.*, ser. 1, 10:25; Enclosure from John Collins Jr., Acting Master, U.S.S. Schooner *George Mangham*, December 30, 1863, *Navy O. R.*, ser. 1, 15:158.

170. Quoted in Leon F. Litwack, *Been in the Storm So Long: The Aftermath of Slavery* (New York: Vintage, 1979), 187.

171. *The Negro in Virginia*, 224.

172. Speech of Thomas Morris Chester, *Anglo-African*, February 7, 1863.

173. Foner, *Frederick Douglass: Selected Speeches and Writings*, 427.

174. General Saxton to Stanton, December 30, 1864, *O. R.*, ser. 3, 4:1030.

175. Quoted in McPherson, *The Negro's Civil War*, 302.

176. For a discussion of Lincoln's role in passage of the Thirteenth Amendment, see Michael Vorenberg, *Final Freedom: The Civil War, the Abolition of Slavery, and the Thirteenth Amendment* (New York: Cambridge University Press, 2001), 113–115. Lincoln's leadership and strategy in facilitating the amendment's passage and adoption is addressed in Frank J. Williams, *Judging Lincoln* (Carbondale: Southern Illinois University Press, 2002), 128–145.

177. "Annual Message to Congress," December 6, 1864, *Speeches and Writings of Abraham Lincoln*, 785.

178. Quoted in *The Negro in Virginia*, 232.

179. Thomas Morris Chester, *Black Civil War Correspondent: His Dispatches from the Virginia Front*, ed. R. J. M. Blackett (Baton Route: Louisiana State University Press, 1989), 297. Chester is believed to be the only black correspondent to cover the war's progress for a major daily paper. He was present at Richmond when the Union army, led by black soldiers, entered the city (see Chester, 4).

180. Aptheker, *A Documentary History of the Negro People*, 490.

181. See Quarles, *Lincoln and the Negro*, 239–249.

182. Ibid., 3–4.

183. Quoted in Benjamin Quarles, *Frederick Douglass* (New York: Atheneum, 1968), 277.

184. "Our Work is Not Done," December 1863, Foner, *Frederick Douglass: Selected Speeches and Writings*, 547–548.

185. Ibid., 550.

186. Ibid., 547–553.

187. Aptheker, *A Documentary History of the Negro People,* 514.

188. Ibid., 516.

189. Ibid., 520.

190. "Freemen of North Carolina Striking for their Rights," *Anglo-African,* May 14, 1864, 1.

191. "To Michael Hahn," March 13, 1864, *Collected Works,* 7:243.

192. McPherson, *The Negro's Civil War,* 282–283.

193. "Last Public Address," April 11, 1865, Basler, *Abraham Lincoln: His Speeches and Writings,* 796–801.

194. *Celebration by the Colored People's Educational Monument Association in Memory of Abraham Lincoln, on the Fourth of July, 1865, in the Presidential Grounds, Washington, D.C.* Printed by Order of the Board of Directors, L. A. Bell, Recording Secretary (Washington, 1865).

195. Ibid. Letter from Frederick Douglass to Messrs. William Syphax and John Cook, July 1, 1865.

196. *Proceedings of the First Annual Meeting of the National Equal Rights League, Held in Cleveland, Ohio, October 19, 20, and 21, 1865* (Philadelphia, 1865).

197. Interview with President Andrew Johnson, Washington, D.C., February 8, 1866, reprinted in *Proceedings of the Black National and State Conventions, 1865–1900,* ed. Philip Foner and George E. Walker (Philadelphia: Temple University Press, 1986), 215.

198. For a discussion of the role of the black voter and office-holder during Reconstruction, see Thomas Holt, *Black Over White: Negro Political Leadership in South Carolina* (Urbana: University of Illinois Press, 1979).

199. Allen Guelzo suggests that political rights were of primary concern to the freed people. See Guelzo, *Lincoln's Emancipation Proclamation,* 274. One can conclude, however, that the privilege of casting a ballot did not outweigh the economic security that came with the former slave's ownership of the soil on which he labored.

200. "Letter to John A. McClernand," January 8, 1863, *Collected Works,* 6:48–49.

201. Letter to General N. P. Banks, August 5, 1863, Basler, *Abraham Lincoln: His Speeches and Writings,* 715.

202. "Nathaniel P. Banks," November 5, 1863, *Collected Works,* 7:1–2.

203. "Annual Message to Congress," December 8, 1863, *Collected Works,* 7:51.

204. Litwack, *Been in the Storm So Long,* 399–408.

205. Some African Americans in the South Carolina Sea Islands and in those areas designated by General Sherman's Special Field Order #15 received "possessory title" to certain lands but eventually lost them to the original owners when the latter were pardoned by President Andrew Johnson.

206. "The Colored People's National Monument to the Memory of Abraham Lincoln," *Christian Recorder* 2 (fall 1865).

207. Ibid.

208. "Oration in Memory of Abraham Lincoln, delivered at the unveiling of the Freedmen's Monument in Memory of Abraham Lincoln, in Lincoln Park, Washington, D.C.," April 14, 1876, in Foner, *Frederick Douglass: Selected Speeches and Writings,* 618–619.

209. Ibid., "Speech on the Occasion of the Twenty-Sixth Anniversary of Emancipation in the District of Columbia, Washington, D.C.," April 16, 1888, 715.

210. Ibid.

211. Given the changes wrought by the new industrial economy, Washington's advocacy of industrial arts (or vocational) education and the eschewing of labor unions was ill-conceived. To his credit, however, he encouraged the establishment of black-owned businesses and the acquisition of farm lands.

212. Booker T. Washington, "An Address on Abraham Lincoln Delivered Before the Republican Club of New York City," 12 February 1909, in *Selected Speeches of Booker T. Washington,* ed. E. David Washington (Garden City, NY: Doubleday, Doran, and Co., 1932), 195.

213. For a discussion of the downward spiral of African-American fortune in the late nineteenth and early twentieth centuries, see Rayford W. Logan, *The Betrayal of the Negro: From Rutherford B. Hayes to Woodrow Wilson* (1965; reprint, New York: Da Capo, 1997).

214. "A Lincoln Emancipation Conference," *Alexander's Magazine,* March–April 1909, 230.

215. Carter G. Woodson, *Negro Orators and their Orations* (New York: Russell and Russell, 1969), 567.

216. Ibid., 572.

217. For a discussion of the growing disaffection of African Americans with the Republican Party, see Nancy J. Weiss, *Farewell to the Party of Lincoln: Black Politics in the Age of FDR* (Princeton, NJ: Princeton University Press, 1983), 28.

218. Merrill Peterson, *Lincoln in American Memory* (New York: Oxford University Press, 1994). See, esp., 348–358.

219. See Franklin, *The Emancipation Proclamation,* 153–154.

220. Andrew Hacker, *Two Nations Black and White: Separate, Hostile, Unequal* (New York: Ballantine, 1995).

221. For a comprehensive discussion of American memory and its connection to race and post–Civil War efforts at national healing, see David Blight, *Race and Reunion: The Civil War in American Memory* (Cambridge: Belknap, 2001).

"DOING LESS" AND "DOING MORE" (FRANK J. WILLIAMS)

1. Gabor S. Boritt, *Lincoln and the Economics of the American Dream* (Urbana: University of Illinois Press, 1994), 285–286.

2. Roy P. Basler, ed., *The Collected Works of Abraham Lincoln,* 8 vols. (New Brunswick, NJ: Rutgers University Press, 1953–55), 4:240. (Hereafter this cite is referred to as *Collected Works.*) The president-elect was not being hyperbolic when he invited assassination, as he had heard earlier that there was a plot to do just that when his train changed tracks in Baltimore on the way to Washington.

3. Harry V. Jaffa, *A New Birth of Freedom: Abraham Lincoln and the Coming of the Civil War* (Linham, MD: Rowman and Littlefield, 2000), 109–110.

4. *Collected Works,* 2:245.

5. Ibid., 2:255.

6. Harold Holzer, ed., *The Lincoln-Douglas Debates: The First Complete Unexpurgated Text* (New York: Harper Collins, 1993), 63.

7. Ibid., 73.

8. Ibid., 359.

9. Ibid., 356–357.

10. *Collected Works,* 2:132, 3:233.

11. Ibid., 2:132.

12. Ibid., 5:534–535.

13. Tyler Dennett, ed., *Lincoln and the Civil War in the Diaries and Letters of John Hay* (New York: Dodd, Mead and Co., 1939), 203.

14. *Collected Works,* 5:537.

15. *Scott v. Sandford,* 60 U.S. 393 (1857).

16. *Collected Works,* 2:401, 405.

17. Ibid., 7:301–302.

18. Ibid., 7:281–282.

19. Ibid., 4:332, 338–339, 421–441; also see Frank J. Williams, "Abraham Lincoln and Civil Liberties: Then & Now—The Southern Rebellion and September 11," *New York University Annual Survey of American Law* (2004): 463–489.

20. Kermit L. Hall et al., eds., *The Oxford Companion to the Supreme Court of the United States* (1992), 428–429.

21. *Collected Works,* 4:430.

22. Silvana R. Siddali, *From Property to Person: Slavery and the Confiscation Acts, 1861–1862* (Baton Rouge: Louisiana State University Press, 2005), 91–92, 242–243.

23. Ibid., 113.

24. *Collected Works,* 5:330.

25. *Wallach v. Van Risweick,* 92 U.S. 202 (1876), 213.

26. *Collected Works,* 5:336–337.

27. "Reply to Emancipation Memorial Presented by Chicago Christians of All Denominations," September 1, 1862, in *Chicago Tribune*, September 23, 1862, *Collected Works*, 5:419–425.

28. This law, also known as the Militia Act of 1795 (*Statutes at Large*, February 28, 1795, c. 36, 1 Stat. 414), was intended for the collection of duties on imports. It provided that "whenever the Laws of the United States shall be opposed . . . the President may call the militia of such state." President Lincoln signed an amendment to the bill, the Militia Act of 1862, on July 17, 1862, which would authorize him "to receive into the service of the United States, for the purpose of constructing intrenchments, or performing camp service, or any other labor, or any military or naval service for which there may be found competent persons of African descent."

29. *Collected Works*, 5:338.

30. Ibid., 5:388–389.

31. For a discussion of Attorney General Edward Bates and the Confiscation Act, see Frank J. Williams, " 'Institutions Are Not Made, They Grow': Attorney General Bates and Attorney President Lincoln," *Lincoln Lore* (Spring 2004): 10–11.

32. Siddali, *From Property to Person*, 230.

33. William Whiting, *War Powers Under the Constitution of the United States* (Glonieta, NM: Rio Grande Press, 1971), 58.

34. Harold M. Hyman, *A More Perfect Union: The Impact of the Civil War and Reconstruction on the Constitution* (New York: Alfred A. Knopf, 1973), 178, 150.

35. *Miller v. United States*, 78 U.S. 268 (1870).

36. *Prize cases*, 67 U.S. 635 (1862), 306–307; *Miller v. United States*, 306–307.

37. *Collected Works*, 5:318–319.

38. Ibid., 5:388–389.

39. Don E. Fehrenbacher, "Only His Stepchildren," in *Lincoln in Text and Context: Collected Essays* (Stanford: Stanford University Press, 1987), 109.

40. Benjamin P. Thomas, *Abraham Lincoln* (New York: Alfred A. Knopf, 1952), 342.

41. E. B. Long with Barbara Long, *The Civil War: Day by Day: An Almanac 1861–1865* (New York: Da Capo, 1971), 268.

42. *Collected Works*, 5:433–436.

43. Henry Wheaton, *Elements of International Law*, 6th ed. (Boston: Little, Brown, 1855), 416–421.

44. *Collected Works*, 6:29.

45. James G. Randall, "Vindictives and Vindication," in *Mr. Lincoln*, ed. Richard N. Current (New York: Dodd, Meade, 1957), 317–340.

46. Hamlin to Lincoln, September 25, 1862, Abraham Lincoln Papers, Library of Congress.

47. *Collected Works*, 5:444.

48. William B. Hesseltine, *Lincoln and the War Governors* (New York: Alfred A. Knopf, 1948), 249.

49. *Collected Works*, 6:436–437.

50. Mark E. Neely Jr., *The Fate of Liberty: Abraham Lincoln and Civil Liberties* (New York: Oxford University Press, 1991), 52.

51. James A. Bayard to S. L. M. Barlow, September 30, 1862, Barlow MSS, Huntington Library, San Marino, California.

52. George B. McClellan, *McClellan's Own Story* (New York: Charles L. Webster and Co., 1889), 487–489.

53. *Collected Works*, 5:474.

54. Dennett, *Lincoln and the Civil War*, 218–219.

55. Allen Guelzo, *Lincoln's Emancipation Proclamation: The End of Slavery in America* (New York: Simon and Schuster, 2004), 167.

56. *Congressional Globe*, 37th Cong., 3d Session (1862), 15, 92.

57. *Collected Works*, 5:537.

58. For a recent full account of this battle, see Francis Augustín O'Reilly, *The Fredericksburg Campaign: Winter War on the Rappahannock* (Baton Rouge: Louisiana State University Press, 2003).

59. Theodore C. Pease and James G. Randall, eds., *The Diary of Orville Hickman Browning*, 2 vols. (Springfield: Illinois State Historical Library, 1925–1933), 1:600–601.

60. Allan Nevins, *The War for the Union: War Becomes Revolution, 1862–1862* (New York: Charles Scribner's Sons, 1960), 362.

61. *Collected Works,* 6:23–24.

62. Guelzo, *Lincoln's Emancipation Proclamation,* 201–202.

63. *Collected Works,* 6:28–32.

64. Horace White, *The Life of Lyman Trumbull* (Boston: Houghton Mifflin, 1913), 222.

65. As Allen Guelzo indicates in *Lincoln's Emancipation Proclamation* (352, n. 13), it is very difficult to determine the exact number of slaves freed by the proclamation. Herbert Aptheker, in 1958, estimated 500,000 slaved had escaped. According to Guelzo, Seward cited no source for his estimate of 200,000.

66. Randy Kennedy, " 'I Shall Never Forget the Weeping,' " in "Word for Word / Slave Journals," *New York Times,* June 20, 2004, Ideas and Trends section, 14.

67. James M. McPherson, *For Cause and Comrades: Why Men Fought In The Civil War* (Oxford: Oxford University Press, 1997), 118.

68. Jaffa, *A New Birth of Freedom,* 79.

69. Ibid.

70. James M. McPherson, *Abraham Lincoln and the Second Revolution* (Oxford: Oxford University Press, 1990), 34–37.

71. Garry Wills, *Lincoln at Gettysburg* (New York: Simon and Schuster, 1992), 120.

72. Ulysses S. Grant quoted by John Russell Young during Grant's trip around the world, *New York Herald,* May 27, 1878.

73. *Collected Works,* 7:500.

74. Ibid., 6:149–150.

75. *Collected Works,* 6:409.

76. On June 15, 1864, Congress finally enacted legislation granting equal pay to black soldiers. The law was made retroactive to January 1, 1864, for all colored soldiers and retroactive to the time of enlistment for those African Americans who had been free on April 19, 1861. Many black soldiers and their families suffered severe hardships because of the wage discrimination. Nevertheless, when the black troops finally received their full back pay, there was rejoicing and celebration. For a full account of the issue of equal pay, see James M. McPherson's, *The Struggle for Equality: Abolitionists and the Negro in the Civil War and Reconstruction* (Princeton: Princeton University Press, 1964), 212–220.

77. *Collected Works,* 6:357.

78. Ibid., 7:281–282.

79. Guelzo, *Lincoln's Emancipation Proclamation,* 214–215.

80. John Hope Franklin, *The Emancipation Proclamation* (Garden City: Doubleday & Company, Inc., 1962), vi.

81. Ibid., 153.

82. Moncure Conway, *Autobiography: Memories and Experiences* (Boston: Houghton Mifflin, 1904), 1:378–81.

83. Dudley T. Cornish, *The Sable Arm: Negro Troops in the Union Army, 1861–65* (New York: W. W. Norton, 1966), 99. The exact number of blacks serving in the Union army is difficult to determine. Allen C. Guelzo places the number at 180,000, of whom 110,000 were former slaves (*Lincoln's Emancipation Proclamation,* 352, n. 13).

84. Hesseltine, *Lincoln and the War Governors,* 313–315, 318.

85. *Collected Works,* 6:408.

86. Ibid., 409.

87. For a full treatment of the Thirteenth Amendment, see Michael Vorenberg, *Final Freedom: The Civil War, The Abolition of Slavery, and the Thirteenth Amendment* (New York: Cambridge University Press, 2001).

88. See Frank J. Williams, "The End of Slavery: Lincoln and the Thirteenth Amendment—What Did He Know and When Did He Know it?" in Williams, *Judging Lincoln* (Carbondale: Southern Illinois University Press, 2002).

89. Michael Vorenberg, " 'The Deformed Child': Slavery and the Election of 1864," *Civil War History* 47 (September 2001): 240–247.

90. David E. Long, *The Jewel of Liberty: Abraham Lincoln's Re-Election and The End of Slavery* (Mechanicsburg: Stackpole, 1994), Appendix B, 280.

91. *Hollingsworth v. Virginia,* 3 Dall. (3 U.S.) 378 (1798).

92. Bernard Schwartz, *Statutory History of the United States—Civil Rights* (New York: Chelsea House Publishers, 1970), 25–96.

93. Second Inaugural Address, *Collected Works,* 8:332.

94. *Collected Works,* 6:428–429.

95. McPherson, *The Struggle for Equality,* 100.

96. For a full modern treatment of the proclamation, see Guelzo, *Lincoln's Emancipation Proclamation.*

97. David Reinhand, "The Eloquence of a Wartime President," *Sunday Oregonian,* February 6, 2005.

98. *Collected Works,* 6:409.

99. Ibid., 7:19.

PICTURING FREEDOM (HAROLD HOLZER)

1. Roy P. Basler, ed., *The Collected Works of Abraham Lincoln,* 8 vols. (New Brunswick, NJ: Rutgers University Press, 1953–55), 8:333, 356. Hereafter this cite is referred to as *Collected Works.*

2. John D. Caldwell to Lincoln, March 16, 1865, Abraham Lincoln Papers, Library of Congress; Lincoln to Thurlow Weed, March 15, 1865, *Collected Works,* 8:356. By the time Caldwell wrote, Lincoln had probably given his manuscript copy of the inaugural to his assistant secretary, John M. Hay.

3. Lincoln's comments the day he signed the Emancipation Proclamation are in Francis B. Carpenter, *Six Months at the White House with President Lincoln: The Story of a Picture* (New York: Hurd and Houghton, 1866), 269.

4. It was a busy March 6 for Lincoln; Smith's visit that day was not his only experience with artists determined to capture the Lincoln image for posterity (and sales); he also posed on the balcony of the White House for Massachusetts photographer Henry Warren. See Charles Hamilton and Lloyd Ostendorf, *Lincoln in Photographs: An Album of Every Known Pose,* rev. ed. (Dayton, OH: Morningside Books, 1985), 214–215.

5. The advertising poster is in the Stern Collection, Rare Books Department, Library of Congress.

6. A cameraman from Brady's gallery later tried taking photographs of Lincoln at the table at which he signed the proclamation, but the resulting pictures, made in 1864, did not come out well; the lighting inside Lincoln's office proved too poor. Two years earlier, during a visit to the Army of the Potomac near Antietam, Lincoln did pose with Gen. George B. McClellan in what might be called the earliest "photo opportunity" in presidential history. See Hamilton and Ostendorf, *Lincoln in Photographs,* 107–113, 190–194.

7. *Collected Works,* 4:89.

8. "Perilous Voyage" appeared in *Frank Leslie's Budget of Fun,* October 15, 1860. See Gary L. Bunker, *From Rail-Splitter to Icon: Lincoln's Image in Illustrated Periodicals, 1860–1865* (Kent, OH: Kent State University Press, 2001), 52.

9. See, esp., Harold Holzer, Gabor S. Boritt, and Mark E. Neely Jr., *The Lincoln Image: Abraham Lincoln and the Popular Print* (New York: Charles Scribner's Sons, 1984), and *Changing the Lincoln Image* (Fort Wayne, IN: Louis A. Warren Lincoln Library and Museum, 1985). Perhaps nothing more convincingly attests to the commercial impetus for political prints than that the reigning firm, Currier and Ives of New York, was capable of producing flattering portraits of Lincoln as well as virulent caricature, each designed for a different segment of its large audience for pictures.

10. Herbert Mitgang, ed., *Lincoln as They Saw Him* (New York: Rinehart, 1956), 304; Charles Eberstadt, *Lincoln's Emancipation Proclamation* (New York: Duschnes Crawford, 1950), 23.

11. Eberstadt, *Lincoln's Emancipation Proclamation,* 24–34.

12. *Collected Works,* 5:444. This section on the surprising dearth of emancipation imagery in 1862 and 1863 appeared in "Prized in Every Liberty-Loving Household: The Image of the Great Emancipator in the Graphic Arts," in Harold Holzer, *Lincoln Seen and Heard* (Lawrence: University Press of Kansas, 2000), 9–12.

13. David W. Blight, "'For Something beyond the Battlefield': Frederick Douglass and the Struggle for the Memory of the Civil War," *Journal of American History* 75 (March 1989): 116, 117.

14. Carpenter, *Six Months at the White House,* 22.

15. Originals are in the Lincoln Museum, Fort Wayne, Indiana, and the print collection of the New York Public Library, respectively.

16. These factors were explored in Mark E. Neely Jr., Harold Holzer, and Gabor S. Boritt, *The Confederate Image: Prints of the Lost Cause* (Chapel Hill: University of North Carolina Press, 1987), esp. 3–10.

17. See Harold Holzer, "Lincoln in Confederate Cartoons: A 'Lean-Sided Yankee,' Seldom Seen," in Holzer, *Lincoln Seen and Heard,* 136–137.

18. Originals are in the Library of Congress, and the Frank and Virginia Williams Collection of Lincolniana, respectively,.

19. Andrew L. Thomas, "Portraiture, Politics, and Patronage: Edward Dalton Marchant's *Abraham Lincoln* (1863) and the Union League of Philadelphia," unpublished ms. The author is grateful to Mr. Thomas for sharing the text of his excellent paper.

20. Ibid.

21. John W. Forney to Abraham Lincoln, December 30, 1862, Abraham Lincoln Papers, Library of Congress.

22. *Collected Works,* 4:240.

23. "Lincoln's Growth as Portraits Tell It," *New York Times Magazine,* February 7, 1932; *Vineyard Gazette,* August 26, 1887.

24. Andrew L. Thomas, "Portraiture, Politics, and Patronage."

25. Thomas B. Bryan to Lincoln, January 7, 1864, Abraham Lincoln Papers, Library of Congress.

26. Lincoln to Bryan, January 18, 1864, *Collected Works,* 7:135. The Mendel print is discussed in Eberstadt, *Lincoln's Emancipation Proclamation,* 39–40.

27. A. Kidder to Lincoln, January 6, 1864, Abraham Lincoln Papers, Library of Congress. The engraved broadside *Emancipation* was one of several issued by Kidder and such co-publishers as Charles Shober of Chicago. See Eberstadt, *Lincoln's Emancipation Proclamation,* 35–37. Eberstadt Nos. 24–26 document the inclusion of the Lincoln facsimile autograph.

28. Lewis Dodge to Lincoln, August 1, 1864, with endorsement by Henry Tanner, Abraham Lincoln Papers, Library of Congress.

29. Carpenter, *Six Months at the White House,* 12–13.

30. Francis B. Carpenter to Owen Lovejoy, January 5, 1864, typed transcript in the Lincoln Museum, Fort Wayne, Indiana.

31. Carpenter, *Six Months at the White House,* 18–20.

32. The results of these sittings can be seen in Hamilton and Ostendorf, *Lincoln in Photographs,* 172–183, 186–195.

33. Carpenter, *Six Months at the White House,* 157–158.

34. These unfinished but expert portraits are now in the collection of the Union League Club of New York. Carpenter donated them in lieu of admission fees when he became a member.

35. Carpenter, *Six Months at the White House,* 25, 27–28.

36. Tyler Dennett, ed., *Lincoln and the Civil War in the Diaries and Letters of John Hay* (New York: Dodd, Mead, and Co., 1939), 197, 272.

37. Carpenter, *Six Months at the White House,* 353; Carpenter, "Anecdotes and Reminiscences," in Henry J. Raymond, *Life and Public Services of Abraham Lincoln* (New York: Derby and Miller, 1865), 763–764.

38. Testimonials published as end papers to Carpenter, *Six Months at the White House.*

39. Harold Holzer, Gabor S. Boritt, and Mark E. Neely Jr., "Francis Bicknell Carpenter (1830–1900): Painter of Abraham Lincoln and His Circle," *American Art Journal,* 16 (spring 1984): 77.

40. End papers to Carpenter, *Six Months at the White House.*

41. Ibid.

42. "Lincoln's Legacy to Mankind/A Great National Painting!" undated advertising broadside in the Lincoln Museum, Fort Wayne, Indiana. International Portrait Co. also offered artist's proofs at $25, india proofs for $15, and plain prints for $5 once the first thousand copies were sold at the bargain one-dollar price.

43. Ibid. *New York Independent,* February 2, 1871.

44. Quoted in Mark E. Neely Jr., *The Emancipation Proclamation* (Fort Wayne, IN: Lincoln National Life, n.d., n.p.).

45. William Lloyd Garrison to Lincoln, January 21, 1865, Abraham Lincoln Papers, Library of Congress.

46. Lincoln to Garrison, February 7, 1865, *Collected Works,* 8:265–66. Mary Lincoln evidently liked the painting a great deal; it seems likely that she took it with her when she left the White House after the assassination. It was returned in the 1970s. See William Kloss, *Art in the White House: A Nation's Pride* (Washington, DC: White House Historical Association, 1992), 152.

47. Dorothy Miller, *The Life and Work of David G. Blythe* (Pittsburgh: University of Pittsburgh Press, 1950), 1, 2, 5, 9, 14.

48. For the latter, see *American Paintings in the Museum of Fine Arts, Boston,* 2 vols. (Boston: Museum of Fine Arts, 1969) 1:39.

49. Ibid., 57–58, 88–89.

50. A rare copy is in the Lincoln Museum, Fort Wayne, Indiana.

51. The previously advanced notion that Blythe produced his pro-emancipation painting as a response to Volck is hardly possible; Volck's art could not easily have reached Blythe's Pittsburgh hometown during 1862. See Miller, *The Life and Work of David G. Blythe,* 87–88.

52. Harold Holzer, Mark E. Neely Jr., and Gabor S. Boritt, "Baltimore Artist Adalbert Volck Fought for the Southern Cause with His Pen," *America's Civil War* (May 1989): 29. Mark E. Neely pointed out the Scotch cap symbol, long overlooked by scholars, in *The Last Best Hope of Earth: Abraham Lincoln and the Promise of America* (Cambridge: Harvard University Press, 1993), opp. 118.

53. The cartoon is in the collection of the Library of Congress, as is the advertising broadside *Bromley & Co.'s Publications,* New York, 1864. The publishers were aligned with the Democratic newspaper, the *New York World.*

54. David E. Long, *The Jewel of Liberty: Abraham Lincoln's Re-Election and the End of Slavery* (Mechanicsburg, PA: Stackpole Books, 1994), 170.

55. Thomas Webster to Abraham Lincoln, October 27, 1864, October 30, 1864, Abraham Lincoln Papers, Library of Congress; transcriptions provided by the National Constitution Center, Philadelphia.

56. "Emancipation in Maryland," undated clipping from *Forney's Press,* National Constitution Center collection.

57. Thomas Webster to Abraham Lincoln, October 27, 1864, October 30, 1864.

58. *Frank Leslie's Illustrated Newspaper,* November 19, 1864; Blingwalt and Brown print courtesy the National Constitution Center.

59. See David Brion Davis, *The Emancipation Moment* (22nd annual Fortenbaugh Lecture, Gettysburg College, 1983), esp. 10–12. For an account of Lincoln's welcome by African Americans in Richmond, see David Donald, *Lincoln* (New York: Simon and Schuster, 1995), 576.

60. For example, Carpenter's emancipation print spawned several piracies, one of which, by Edward Herline of New York, jumbled the careful arrangement of liberals and conservatives surrounding Lincoln, and another, by Thomas Kelly, also of New York, added General Grant to the scene and identified it as a routine cabinet meeting. Kelly issued yet another edition of the print, transforming it into a portrait of Jefferson Davis and the Confederate cabinet! These originals are in the Lincoln Museum, Fort Wayne, Indiana. For a reproduction of the Kelly prints, see Holzer, Boritt, and Neely, *Changing the Lincoln Image,* 18.

61. The Waeschle portrait was modeled after a Wenderoth and Taylor photograph made sometime in 1864, the Currier and Ives on the Brady Studio's so-called "five-dollar-bill" photograph of February 9, 1864. See Hamilton and Ostendorf, *Lincoln in Photographs,* 395–396.

62. Davis, *The Emancipation Moment,* 12.

63. I have paraphrased Carpenter, who called the first reading of the proclamation "a scene second only in historical importance to that of the Declaration of Independence." See Carpenter, *Six Months at the White House,* 25.

64. Peter C. Marzio, *The Democratic Art: Chromolithography, 1840–1900—Pictures for a 19th-Century America* (Boston: David R. Godine, 1979), 104.

65. Ibid. For Prang's Revels chromo, see 308.

66. George C. Groce and David H. Wallace, *The New-York Historical Society's Dictionary of Artists in America* (New Haven: Yale University Press, 1957), 310–311.

67. Pamphlet quoted in R. Gerald McMurtry, "Indiana's Reaction to Lincoln's Proclamation of Emancipation," *Lincoln Lore,* no. 1494 (August 1962): 3. The original pamphlet is in the Lincoln Museum, Fort Wayne, Indiana.

68. L. Stebbins, "New National Engraving," in Robert H. Kellogg, *Life and Death in Rebel Prisons. . .* (Hartford: L. Stebbins, 1864). I am indebted to historian Michael Parrish for bringing this book to my attention.

69. Sarah M. Barnes to D. S. Bull, April 4, 1867. Transcript in Catalogue of Books, Maps, Manuscripts, Broadsides and Trade Catalogues, No. 292 (2003), Denning House Antiquarian Books, Salisbury Mills, New York. Once again, the generous Michael Parrish uncovered and shared this wonderful reminiscence. In quoting the owner of the Lincoln picture, Barnes made an unfortunate attempt to mimic black dialect, which I have restored to standard English.

70. Benjamin Quarles, *Lincoln and the Negro* (New York: Oxford University Press, 1962), ii–iii.

71. H. Barbara Weinberg, "Thomas Eakins and The Metropolitan Museum of Art," *Metropolitan Museum of Art Bulletin* 52 (winter 1994–95): 5, 22–23. The original watercolor entered the Met collection in 1925.

72. Alan C. Braddock, "Eakins, Race, and Ethnographic Ambivalence," *Winterthur Portfolio* 33 (1998): 135–136, 146–147.

73. The original is in the Valentine Museum, Richmond, Virginia.

74. Mary Lincoln to Derby and Miller, June 3, 1866, in Justin G. and Linda Levitt Turner, *Mary Todd Lincoln: Her Life and Letters* (New York: Alfred A. Knopf, 1972), 368, 279.

75. Original in the author's collection.

76. Such prints had the added impact of elevating Lincoln's reputation further by depicting Lincoln together with the revered Washington. For more on this subject, see Harold Holzer, *Lincoln and Washington Portrayed* (Jefferson, NC: McFarland Publications, 1993), esp. 222–236.

77. Harold Holzer, *When Lincoln and Son Came to Richmond* (Richmond: U.S. Historical Society, 2003), 2.

78. The original is in the Lincoln Museum, Fort Wayne, Indiana.

79. Notable among them is Lerone Bennett Jr., *Forced into Glory: Abraham Lincoln's White Dream* (Chicago: Johnson Publishing, 2000). This highly selective interpretation of Lincoln's attitudes on race and freedom claimed the "Emancipator" was "forced to an immortality he resisted with every fiber of his being" (23). The World War I–era images were illustrated and well analyzed in Gerald J. Prokopowicz, "Gone with the Wind: Myths and Memories of the Old South," *Lincoln Lore,* no. 1869 (summer 2002).

80. See, e.g., William H. Johnson's *Let Me Free,* Palmer Hayden's *The Janitor Who Paints,* and Thomas Hart Benton's mural for Lincoln University, all illustrated in Harold Holzer and Gabor Boritt, "Lincoln in 'Modern' Art," in Gabor Boritt, ed., *The Lincoln Enigma* (New York: Oxford University Press, 2001), following p. 152. Jean-Michel Basquiat's *The Obnoxious Liberals* (1982), featuring a top-hatted Lincoln whose suit is emblazoned with the words "Not for Sale," appeared in the 2005 Brooklyn Museum of Art Basquiat retrospective.

81. The survey was reported in Barry Schwartz, *Abraham Lincoln and the Forge of National Memory* (Chicago: University of Chicago Press, 2000), 83. In his insightful study, Schwartz maintains that Lincoln's reputation among African Americans has declined precipitously and can never be resurrected. The original cartoon, which Schwartz reproduces on p. 250, is in the collection of the Abraham Lincoln Museum at Lincoln Memorial University, Harrogate, Tennessee.

82. Donald Charles Durman, *He Belongs to the Ages: The Statues of Abraham Lincoln* (Ann Arbor, Michigan: Edwards Brothers, 1951), 33; Kirk Savage, *Standing Soldiers, Kneeling Slaves: Race, War, and Monument in Nineteenth-Century America* (Princeton: Princeton University Press, 1997), 73–76.

83. Ibid., 38–43, 65–67, 77–84.

84. F. Lauriston Bullard, *Lincoln in Marble and Bronze* (New Brunswick, NJ: Rutgers University Press, 1952), 98.

85. Ibid., 48–49.

86. Ibid., 49.

87. Ibid., 66; Michael Hatt, "Making a Man of Him: Masculinity and the Black Body in Mid-Nineteenth-Century American Sculpture," *Oxford Art Journal* 15 (1992): 21–35; Durman, *He Belongs to the Ages,* 45.

88. Bullard, *Lincoln in Marble and Bronze,* 68–69; Durman, *He Belongs to the Ages,* 45.

89. Philip Foner, ed., *Frederick Douglass: Selected Speeches and Writings* (Chicago: Lawrence Hill Books, 1999), 618.

90. Ibid., 618–620.

91. Douglass quoted in Allen Thorndike Rice, ed., *Reminiscences of Abraham Lincoln by Distinguished Men of His Time* (New York: North American Publishing, 1886), 193; Freeman H. M. Murray, *Emancipation and the Freed in American Sculpture* (Washington, privately printed, 1916), 199.

92. Bullard, *Lincoln in Marble and Bronze*, 69; Foner, *Frederick Douglass: Selected Speeches and Writings*, 616.

93. Boutwell's April 15, 1876, letter to Douglass in the Frederick Douglass Papers, Frederick Douglass Memorial Home, Washington. *Collected Works*, 5:537; Foner, *Frederick Douglass: Selected Speeches and Writings*, 624.

94. Original in the Jack Smith Collection, now in the Indiana Historical Society.

95. Savage, *Standing Soldiers, Kneeling Slaves*, 115, 120.

96. Durman, *He Belongs to the Ages*, 46, 50.

INDEX